D1260718

JOHN WYCLIF
AS LEGAL REFORMER

STUDIES IN THE HISTORY
OF
CHRISTIAN THOUGHT

EDITED BY

HEIKO A. OBERMAN, Tübingen

IN COOPERATION WITH

HENRY CHADWICK, Oxford
EDWARD A. DOWEY, Princeton, N.J.
JAROSLAV PELIKAN, New Haven, Conn.
BRIAN TIERNEY, Ithaca, N.Y.
E. DAVID WILLIS, San Anselmo, California

VOLUME X

WILLIAM FARR

JOHN WYCLIF
AS LEGAL REFORMER

LEIDEN
E. J. BRILL
1974

JOHN WYCLIF
AS LEGAL REFORMER

BY

WILLIAM FARR

LEIDEN
E. J. BRILL
1974

ISBN 90 04 04027 7

Copyright 1974 by E. J. Brill, Leiden, Netherlands

PRINTED IN THE NETHERLANDS

FOR MY GRANDMOTHER,
FATHER AND MOTHER

TABLE OF CONTENTS

PREFACE

My intention was to write a preface. Instead, I wish to acknowledge several debts incurred in acquiring the historian's craft—some of these are professional, some are not; all are personal.

This work began as a doctoral dissertation under the direction of Professor Howard Kaminisky at the University of Washington. I wish to thank him here for being a "doctor-father" whose precision in defining issues, whose exacting standards and whose general readiness to help a tardy Latinist, gave direction, discipline and motive. I would also like to thank Professor S. Harrison Thomson, another Wyclif scholar under whom I had the privilege of studying, for communicating the immediacy and meaningfulness of historical scholarship. And certainly I am indebted to Professor H. A. Oberman, editor of the monographic series, *Studies in the History of Christian Thought*, for his encouragement and guidance in this, my first, publishing enterprise. A grant from the University of Montana Research Fund helped smooth the way.

Finally, I would like to thank my wife, Marianne.

Missoula, Montana   WILLIAM FARR

INTRODUCTION

By the time he died on 31 December 1384, John Wyclif had long since ceased being anything other than a man dedicated to the reformation of the current church. Most criticism of the church and its clergy in the fourteenth century stemmed from a nagging sense of moral decay coupled with degrees of religious concern that permeated all orders of society. Wyclif's did not. Instead of seeing the challenge of secularization and moral deterioration in terms of individual inadequacy, Wyclif looked primarily at institutions, as the titles of his more important works indicate. The object of his criticism was not so much individual human beings and their drive to approach likeness with God, as it was with institutions, both human and divine. [1] The most important of these institutions was the Roman Church. Wyclif's reformation then was primarily an institutional one. Its purpose was to return the present church to the purity of its origins, to the condition instituted by Christ and his disciples. That was the model: a model where all members, all believers were of one mind and soul; where individuals held no property as individuals but in common, sharing with others, dividing as to need, living alike without rich, without poor, without hierarchy, without coercion—all preaching the resurrection of Christ through His precept and example. [2] Found in the Bible, it was a model which presented a constant reminder of what the church should be.

---

[1] Although only the outstanding works, the following titles should indicate the primary direction of Wyclif's interest as well as the fundamental nature of his reform: Johannes Wyclif, *Tractatus de Ecclesia* (henceforth *DE*), ed. Johann Loserth (London, 1886); Johannes Wyclif, *Tractatus de Officio Regis* (henceforth *DOR*), eds. A. W. Pollard and C. Sayle (London, 1887); Johannes Wyclif, *Tractatus de Potestate Pape* (henceforth *DPP*), ed. Johann Loserth (London, 1907); Johannes Wyclif, *Tractatus de Civili Dominio* (henceforth *DCD*), eds. Reginald Lane Poole and Johann Loserth (4 vols.; London, 1885-1904). For man's "renovatio ad imaginem Dei" see Gerhart B. Ladner, *The Idea of Reform* (New York, 1967), pp. 2-34.

[2] For the biblical descriptions of the Primitive Church found in the New Testament see especially Acts and the books of the two evangelists, Matthew and Luke. Here is found the text for the ever-presentiality of the Holy Spirit (Acts II, 1-4), the foundation for the belief that because the early followers of Christ had one heart and soul they also hold all things in common (Acts IV, 32, and Acts II, 44-46). *DCD*, III, 78-81, relates in detail why the evangelical church ought to be the model of all true religion. See also *ibid.*, p. 206, and Johannes Wyclif, *Opera Minora* (henceforth *OM*), ed. Johann Loserth (London, 1913), p. 24.

The Bible had always been a provocative tool. Capable of generating ideas and emotions, it ranged from pleas of charity and compassion to a political apology for kingship. [3] In short, it possessed an almost unlimited capacity to inspire and inspiration could easily lead to advocacy. By the fourteenth century, this same Bible could provoke and goad an increasingly literate group of men into a critical appraisal of the contemporary church, on the basis of what they found of Christ's Church as set down in the books of the New Testament. But their sense of what had been, as well as what should be, did not accord with what critics saw of the institutional church in the fourteenth century with its authority, hierarchy and expanding fiscal and legal systems. Enmeshed, involved and at peace with this world, this church was not that primitive, free fellowship of men inspired; it was not that Church of Christ, the Man-God, but that of Rome. It was a Roman church; directed, guided, ruled by authoritative, vice-regal popes, who both actively and passively sometimes with design, more often without, increased the strength of papal authority, extended the grasp of its jurisdiction, inflated the fullness of its power. [4]

Contrasting the Primitive Church and the Roman Church was not unique with Wyclif. Far from distinguishing him, Wyclif's appeal to a historic, apostolic ideal, to the methodology of comparison with its resulting criticism, its opposition to papal power, clearly delineated an attitude that was characteristic of the period. Dante, Marsilius of Padua and William of Ockham all used the visible and apparent contradictions between the two churches to focus criticism; and growing more critical, they grew more historical. [5]

The idea of the church as a congregation of the faithful, an in-

---

[3] Walter Ullmann's inaugural lecture at Cambridge, *The Relevance of Medieval Ecclesiastical History* (Cambridge, 1966), pp. 13-19, gives a stimulating discussion of "governmental ideology" in the Bible as well as numerous examples of the Bible's generative force.

[4] For the growth and extension of papal power in general see Johannes Haller, *Das Papsttum, Idee und Wirklichkeit* (Esslingen am Neckar, 1962) and Walter Ullmann, *The Growth of Papal Government in the Middle Ages* (London, 1944). Provocative as it is, much of Ullmann's work is either limited or refuted by F. Kempf, "Die päpstliche Gewalt in der mittelalterlichen Welt," *Miscellanea Historiae Pontificiae*, XXI (Rome, 1959). Actual administrative, if not jurisdictional, growth is dealt with by Geoffrey Barraclough, *Papal Provisions* (Oxford, 1935).

[5] See Gordon Leff, "The Apostolic Ideal in Later Medieval Ecclesiology," *Journal of Theological Studies*, N.S. XVIII (1967), 67, where the appropriate citations from the *Defensor Pacis* of Marsilius of Padua are given. In addition see Gordon Leff, *Heresy in the Later Middle Ages* (2 vols.; New York, 1967), I, 81-82, for various examples of the common appeal to the apostolic ideal.

visible, mystical union of believers and followers, is detailed in the Bible. This idea of the church was not only exhorted but vividly illustrated in word and deed. Moreover, the Bible's reality was as much historical as ideological. Those who viewed the church as such a mystical union of believers rejected entirely the ecclesiastical traditions codified by legions of jurisdiction-minded canonists and relied instead upon the Bible. For these the Bible alone became the touchstone of authority and the source of all human knowledge. Historically located in time and place, Christ and His Church now came to possess an existence far more inspirational than any conceptual construct. The admonishment "and come follow me" was not restricted, but applied to individual and institution alike. For Wyclif the "imitatio" and prototype remained Christ and His apostolic church, paradigms that proved to be catalysts for reform if not revolution. [6]

No one begins as a reformer, however, without first being a critic and Wyclif's criticism was incited and honed by fact and circumstance. He inherited a tradition of English pulpit literature that lavished criticism and censure upon the clerical orders; [7] he developed a highly exaggerated moral sense and he suffered and chafed over promotional disappointments, legitimate or otherwise. [8] While these undoubtedly played a part in Wyclif's transformation from critic to reformer—whether passively or actively remains uncertain—their role was mainly contributory; more significant was a philosophical conversion to realism that was only strengthened in the nominalist fire of Oxford criticism and his own penchant for integrating the Church more thoroughly into the reality of historical England.

---

[6] *DE*, pp. 365-366. Quoted by Howard Kaminsky, "Wyclifism as Ideology of Revolution," *Church History*, XXXII (1963), 63.

[7] G. R. Owst, *Preaching in Medieval England* (Cambridge, 1926) especially Chapter VI and the same author's subsequent work, *Literature and Pulpit in Medieval England* (Cambridge, 1933), Chapters V, VI and VII which deal with the preaching of satire and complaint. The majority of the often very illustrative examples quoted are of ecclesiastics railing against one another and this most frequently in front of the laity.

[8] K. B. McFarlane, *John Wycliffe and the Beginnings of English Non-conformity* (New York, 1952), p. 63.

PART I

REFORMATION DEFINED

CHAPTER ONE

THE REALISTIC MIRROR:
WYCLIF'S PHILOSOPHICAL FOUNDATION

The first substantiated evidence of John Wyclif's existence indicates that he was already at Oxford, a Bachelor of Arts and a Mertonian. [1] Wyclif's birthdate and place of birth remain uncertain. Having become a graduate in 1356, he migrated from Merton across to Balliol college where he completed the next step in his scholastic "cursus honorum" by becoming the third Master of Balliol in 1360. Before continuing his studies beyond the Master of Arts, Wyclif interrupted his promising career to take the living of Fillingham in Lincolnshire. He did not stay long; and when he returned to Oxford in 1362 he did so as a bona-fide and registered non-resident pluralist licensed for theological studies. Ten years later he received his doctorate and with few exceptions—his diplomatic mission to Bruges in 1374 and the pulpit attacks against William of Wickham on John of Gaunt's behalf in London—Wyclif remained at Oxford until forced out in 1381 when his eucharistic doctrine was censured by an Oxford commission and his appeal to parliament had failed. His teaching proscribed, Wyclif retired to Lutterworth; while there he saw his works condemned by the so-called Earthquake Council at Blackfriars in May 1382 and later banned at Oxford. Unmolested, however, at Lutterworth, he spent his last three years in feverish activity, pouring forth a variety of intense, vitriolic and repetitive attacks on the contemporary church in a last ditch effort to bring about the reform he so zealously desired.

---

[1] Although antiquated in certain areas the standard biography of Wyclif is still H. B. Workman's *John Wyclif: A Study of the English Medieval Church* (2 vols.; Oxford, 1926). The most recent treatment is that of K. B. McFarlane, *John Wycliffe*, whose major contribution, like that of Robson's *Wyclif and the Oxford Schools*, is a fuller, more precise elucidation of Wyclif's Oxford years. For the most part I have followed these accounts and A. B. Emden, *A Bibliographical Register of the University of Oxford to A. D. 1500* (3 vols.; Oxford, 1957-59) rather closely; where I have deviated, such places are indicated. The older scholarly bibliography is voluminous, at times erroneous, but still, when used with caution, rewarding. Among these see especially Reginald Lane Poole, *Wycliffe and the Movements for Reform* (London, 1902); Gotthard Lechler, *John Wycliffe and his English Precursors*, trans. Lorimer (London, 1884), and a small, very uneven work by Charles Webb LeBas, *Life of Wiclif* (London, 1832). See also Rudolf Buddensieg, *Johann Wiclif und seine Zeit* (Halle, 1885).

Indications of Wyclif's personal life, his manners, even his appearance are meager; official records of the colleges, papal petitions and episcopal letters are spare; yet this dearth of information should not deceive. Wyclif's leanness in terms of institutional records was belied by the full-bodied stature of his influence among his contemporaries. Even opponents, totally committed to eradicating his confessed heretical opinions on doctrinal issues, could admire and fear the punch of his logic, the dynamism of his metaphysic: "in philosophy he was thought second to none, incomparible in scholastic disciplines ... the most eminent doctor of theology in those days." [2] Clearly Wyclif's considerable abilities and "perfect living" were recognized and esteemed; [3] nor should the sometimes extreme flattery paid by his disputatious colleagues be written off as tongue-in-cheek pandering to Wyclif's admitted egotism. [4]

In a climate of apparent intellectual decline, when confusion and discord were the hallmarks of metaphysics and theology at Oxford, Wyclif conservatively, almost anachronistically, reached back beyond his immediate predecessors to a pre-nominalist interest in the interpenetration of philosophy and theology. He would not truckle to the "modernists" penchant for disassociating human from divine knowledge. [5] His reaction, conservative as it was, was directed against the then dominant "via moderna." His reaction also emphasized a systematic approach that relied upon Augustine so extensively that Wyclif's later followers could refer to him as "John, the son of Augustine." [6]

---

[2] Both Buddensieg, *Johann Wiclif*, p. 101 and Workman, *John Wyclif*, I 4, quote the *Chronicon Henrici Knighton vel Cnitthon, Monachi Leycest rensis*, ed. Joseph Rawson Lumby (2 vols.; London, 1895), II, 151, whose author was a contemporary of Wyclif and a decided opponent, to indicate the reputation of Wyclif: "In philosophia nulli reputabatur secundus, inscholasticis disciplinis incomparabilis ... doctor in theologia eminentissimus in illis diebus. Hic maxime nitebatur aliorum ingenia subtiliate scientiae et profunditate igenii sui transcendere." Also see Robson, *Wyclif and the Oxford Schools*, p. 162, for other examples of the deep respect Wyclif enjoyed from his colleagues.

[3] Archbishop Arundel in questioning the Lollard, William Thorpe, replied to Thorpe's assertion that Wyclif was "an innocent in his living" by saying: "Wyclif, your author was a great clerk, and many men held him a perfect liver." A. W. Pollard, *Fifteenth-century Prose and Verse* (1903), pp. 118-120 as quoted in Workman, *John Wyclif*, I, 5.

[4] McFarlane, *John Wyclif*, p. 40.

[5] Robson, *Wyclif and the Oxford Schools*, p. 11. See also M. D. Knowles, "The Censured Opinions of Uthred of Boldon," *Proceedings of the British Academy*, XXXVII (1951), 307-308.

[6] This notation is given by Thomas Netter of Walden: *Thomae Waldensis Doctrinale antiquitatum fidei catholicae ecclesiae*, ed. B. Blanciotti (Venice, 1757),

Criticized "for confounding God and Man in a single metaphysical system, for excessive determinism and for depreciating unduly the play of divine and human will," Wyclif's Augustinian system nonetheless effectively combated much of the uncertainty and confusion engendered by the "via moderna." [7] Augustinianism, accepted and approved by use and age, provided a somewhat beleaguered and conservative minority a weapon of defense and a modicum of shelter against terminist attack. Two generations of intellectual decline joined by the prevalence of terminism with its interest in problems of necessity and contingency and finally the lack of a clearly defined school in metaphysics and theology, all made for great fluidity and opportunity. [8] It encouraged an approach at Oxford in the 1360's that was at once ecletic and personal. Traditional doctrine was left behind, novelty was championed and eccentricity tolerated. [9]

Wyclif matured under these conditions and they go a long way in assessing the position of influence that Wyclif held at Oxford in the fourteen years between 1358 and 1372. Wyclif, in maturing, became Oxford's foremost logician and the ornament of its schoolmen; learned, impressive and above all else productive. [10] For Wyclif Oxford was almost literally a beginning and an end—philosophy was another.

Philosophy interested Wyclif first and it remained throughout his long career an abiding interest, if not the force that motivated his

---

I, 186 (Book I, ch. 34), as cited in Robson, *Wyclif and the Oxford Schools*, p. 25. This quotation is also to be found in Workman, *John Wyclif*, I, 119.

[7] Robson, *Wyclif and the Oxford Schools*, p. 19; see also M. Wilks, "The Early Oxford Wyclif: Papalist or Nominalist?" *Studies in Church History*, V (1969), 69-98. Wilks views Wyclif not as an "extreme Augustinian realist," but rather as a "Christian Aristotelian, utilizing the Thomism principle of the mean to achieve a via media, employing the Aristotelian technique of equivocation to harmonize traditional Christian teachings with the secular humanism of the classical past." This is a radical departure from current scholarship and while Wilks' argument is provocative, it is hardly convincing. Not only does Thomas Aquinas appear infrequently in the thought of Wyclif, but seemingly Wilks has committed the same error he ascribes to Leff and Gewirth, namely, that of identifying a philosophical commitment with papal or antipapalist tendencies. Robson, *Wyclif and the Oxford Schools*, p. 19.

[8] Knowles, "Censured Opinions," pp. 307-311.

[9] *Ibid.*, p. 330.

[10] Even the *Eulogium Historiarum sive Temporis: Chronicon ab Orbe Condito usque ad Annum Domini MCCLXVI, a Monacho quodam Malmesburiensi Exartum. Accedunt Continuationes duae quarum una ad Annum MCCCCXIII*, ed. Frank Scott Haydon (3 vols.; London, 1863), III, 345, could call Wyclif the flower of Oxford.

thought even in the most tangential areas. [11] The philosopher became the theologian, but only nominally; in fact, philosophy so conditioned his approach to problems, theological or otherwise, that he was never really able to leap over the wall of his own training. This was not unusual; what was unusual, was the degree of his confinement.

The characteristic theological principle of the early thirteenth century had been that human reason was generally compatible with faith, that reason and revelation were not in opposition but complemented one another. [12] In time Aristotelian logic and metaphysics began to force theology into scientific channels governed by laws ascertainable on the basis of Aristotle's categories. Thus, under the impulse of Aristotelian thought, theology was given a metaphysical foundation and in the process a philosophical theology emerged taking the form of the great all-comprising system. [13] The "Summa" was the mold and St. Thomas of Aquinas and others poured into it a stream of ratiocinated theology.

In the course of the thirteenth century these various systems coalesced into particular schools of thought. Yet the first decades of this same century also saw an intense reaction to this tradition as thinkers of every persuasion began to question the synthesis-minded investigations of Aquinas and Albert the Great. Questioning and analysis soon became scepticism and doubt. The emphasis now was not upon all-penetrating reason, but on the absolute freedom and sovereignty of God, on reducing the concept of causality to a simple scheme of

---

[11] See S. Harrison Thomson, "The Philosophical Basis of Wyclif's Theology," *Journal of Religion*, XI (1931), 96f.

[12] The following paragraphs are a brief, almost schematic, sketch which is largely dependent, naturally enough, upon the already large and yet rapidly expanding secondary literature. While by no means complete, these works are more than adequate considering the introductory nature of this summary. See M. D. Knowles, *The Evolution of Medieval Thought* (New York, 1964); Gordon Leff, *Medieval Thought: From St. Augustine to Ockham* (Baltimore, 1958) especially ch. VII; Gordon Leff, *Paris and Oxford Universities in the Thirteenth and Fourteenth Centuries* (New York, 1968); F. C. Copleston, *Medieval Philosophy* (New York, 1961), and the appropriate chapters in Etienne Gilson, *History of Christian Philosophy in the Middle Ages* (New York, 1955). See also the well-honed article of Gordon Leff, "The Changing Pattern of Thought in the Earlier Fourteenth Century," *John Rylands Library Bulletin*, XXXXIII (1961), 354-372, as well as M. D. Knowles, "A Characteristic of the Mental Climate of the Fourteenth Century," in *Melanges offerts d' Etienne Gilson. Etudes de Philosophie Medievale*, hors Serie (Toronto/Paris, 1959), pp. 315-325.

[13] Leff, *Medieval Thought*, p. 170, and Knowles, "Characteristic of the Mental Climate," p. 321.

chronology, of questioning the connection between God and man. [14] Perhaps most significant, scepticism tended to effect a hiatus between theology and philosophy; people felt a need to differentiate between that which pertained to the sphere of faith and that which reason was responsible for. Each sphere was divorced and liberated from the other; rational demonstration and understanding now became independent from faith and revelation with each form of cognition shrinking back into an earlier domain of interest. [15]

Recognizing these novel limitations both philosophers and theologians sought comprehensively to explore their new, independent areas and in so doing they further enlarged the breach. Philosophy spun off analytical galaxies of doubt while theology, no longer in a position to employ reason as its hand-maiden, became ever more authoritarian, relying on revealed truth and dogma to do what reason had formerly done. Discussion of what had been common problems were marked "by such formulas as 'non asserendo sed disputando' and the distinction between speaking 'a ratione' and 'a fide'." [16] It was impossible to know God, one simply believed and instead of attempting to prove the existence of God in a demonstrable fashion, one was reduced to accepting the evidence of religious authority. Rational certainty became, in short, the certainty of belief.

Crucial to this reactive "via moderna" was the reappearance of the age-old problem of universals. The problem of the universal was to what degree can significance and reality be attributed to species and genera like "man" and "animal." What was the nature and status of these general terms "man" and "animal" in this world of actual, individual, men and animals? Were these general terms only words, perhaps mental concepts, or were they rather actual entities existing outside of and independent of the mind? If the latter was true, what was the relationship between such a term and the individual? This was the problem and it reoccurred periodically from Boethius, quoting Porphyry's classic question, to William of Ockham: "do universals exist or are they but deductions for the convenience of the mind?" [17] If the problem was almost constant, the answers were not. Differing solutions had a history of dividing thinkers; now Nominalists and Realists, as their names indicate, split over this problem.

---

[14] Knowles, "Characteristic of the Mental Climate," p. 321ff.
[15] Leff, "Changing Pattern," p. 355.
[16] *Ibid.*, p. 367.
[17] Thomson, "Philosophical Basis," p. 93.

For the Nominalist only individuals existed, or as the Franciscan Aureole, later Archbishop of Aix-en-Provence, expressed it: "Everything is singular and nothing else." [18] The individual was the sole reality. Universals, categories, whether genera or species, were purely intra-mental signs for the classes of individual things; they were concepts having no existence outside the mind, corresponding to nothing in this world. What this meant, of course, was at once the sovereignty of individual existences and the "rejection of all universals and general categories as the constituents of being: natures, essences, genera, species lost their independent standing." [19]

Realism had always been an alternative solution to the problem of universals. Long representing the established tradition, all realists recognized to some degree the independent, extra-mental status and existant being in genera and species. Universals were real. To be sure there were gradations among realists, from the extremists, who posited the priority of universals over individuals, with individuation being a nuance of a common essence, to moderate realists, who saw the presence of universals in individuals while retaining a notion of the individual's identity. Whatever the grade, realists found reality and being in the universality of categories rather than in the diversity of individuals.

Initially, there was little that was unique with Wyclif or indicated the radical nature of his later development. There were, indeed, a few asides that gave cause for thought in retrospect, but generally his work simply canvassed the conventional scholastic fields of logic, grammar and metaphysics, subjects that could hardly be expected to elicit penetrating and highly original thought. What these studies did do, was to build for Wyclif a solid reputation as a schoolman and construct a sound foundation for his metaphysical development. Wyclif then committed himself to realism and this philosophic orientation remained forever after fundamental to much of his thinking whether philosophical, theological or reformatory. [20]

This total commitment, however, had not always been so, for Wyclif, early in his training, seems to have adherred to such nominalist tenets as positing the priority of the individual over the general. [21]

---

[18] Leff, *Medieval Thought*, p. 273.

[19] Leff, *Paris and Oxford*, p. 244.

[20] Thomson, "Philosophical Basis," p. 96.

[21] Robson, *Wyclif and the Oxford Schools*, p. 145: "There are a number of hints in the Summa that he had once been less than a full-blooded realist, that he

In both the "de actibus anime" and the "de universalibus" there are occasions of doubt; he refused to believe that the power of God could be annihilative and confessed that "when I was younger, I used to ignorantly confuse universals." [22] This was only natural as the then prevalent philosophical school at Oxford was nominalism; it was on the ascendency, was new, "modern" and most attractive to bright, young, aspiring students like Wyclif. [23] But the engagement was short-lived. Before too long Wyclif experienced what amounted to an intellectual conversion to realism, a conversion prepared for through searching, thoughtful, time-consuming theological studies of the Bible and the Fathers. Augustine helped too. [24] Laboriously prepared for, when the conversion did come, it did so rapidly, suddenly, in an intuitive flash. It was just that, a conversion:

> I took a long time to understand this theory of ideas from Scripture. When I discovered it unexpectedly, having been enlightened by God, I gave joyful thanks to him, with his servant Augustine and others, whom God eternally ordains to help me to this as his ministers. [25]

God himself, through revelation, had saved Wyclif from following

---

had, for example, regarded the singular as prior to the universal." Also *ibid.*, pp. 139, 188, and Gustav Adolf Benrath, *Wyclifs Bibelkommentar* (Berlin, 1966), p. 311ff. where the author cites the "adnihilatio" thesis used by Wyclif in Johannes Wyclif, *Miscellanea Philosophica*, ed. M. H. Dziewicki (2 vols.; London, 1902-1905), I, 49, 127.

22 "Et sic quando fui iunior involvebam ignoranter universalie sicut forte faciunt multi hodie qui pertinaciter universalia detestantur." *De universalibus*, MS Univ. Prag., VIII, G. 23, fol. 53a. as cited by Thomson, "Philosophical Basis," p. 89. This passage is also quoted by Robson, *Wyclif and the Oxford Schools*, p. 145.

23 Knowles, "Censured Opinions," p. 308: "In the fifth and sixth decades of the fourteenth century, therefore, a number of influences were at work at Oxford. The most pervasive of all was Ockhamism, Protean in its many manifestations, now appearing as Terminism, now as secularism, now as extreme voluntarism and semi-Pelagianism, now as fideism." For the prevailing hold of terminism at Oxford see also Leff, *Paris and Oxford*, p. 306.

24 The most recent Wyclif scholarship totally accepts and, in varying degrees, emphasizes Wyclif's conversion to realism. The best treatment of this particular aspect of Wyclif's development is Beryl Smalley, "The Bible and Eternity: John Wyclif's Dilemma," *Journal of the Warburg and Courtauld Institutes*, XXVII (1964), 78-81. See also Benrath, *Bibelkommentar*, p. 311ff. where Benrath terms the conversion "... das wichtigste Faktum in Wyclifs theologischem Studiengang...." I have bent before this assessment, not out of simple deference to the majority, but because their argument appears to be more sound than that of Wilks.

25 *DDD*, p. 63, as cited by Smalley, "Bible and Eternity," p. 80: "Et diu fui antequam ex scripturis intellexi istam sententiam de ydeis; quam cum illustratus a Deo perfunctorie repperissem cum gaudio gratias egi Deo, cum suo famulo Augustino et aliis quos Deus eternaliter ordinat ad hoc ministerialiter me iuvare."

the erroneous paths of those who were caught up in signs and the "superficial snares of words." [26]

Self-confident as Wyclif was, he seldom became autobiographical or personal; when he did, as in this case, his words rang true. Still caution is necessary. The conservative Augustinian theologian Thomas Bradwardine also experienced a philosophical conversion. A chance reading of his account of his own conversion in the *Causa Dei*, quoted by Workman, created a slight specter of convention. [27] Bradwardine wrote: "I was at one time far from the true knowledge of God and held captive in opposing error." Then following a description of his Pelagian tendencies and his adherence to the Manichaean School, he continued:

> But afterwards, and before I had become a student of theology, the truth before mentioned struck upon me like a beam of grace. It seemed to me as if I beheld in the distance, under a transparent image of truth, the grace of God as it is prevenient both in time and nature to all good works—that is to say, the gracious will of God, which precedently wills that he who merits salvation shall be saved and precedently works this merit in him.

There are similarities in these two conversions. Both Bradwardine and Wyclif begin with a confession, but then conversions are by their nature confessions. Yet considering Wyclif's use of Bradwardine as an oft cited authority, considering the esteem with which he held "Doctor Profundus," [28] as Wyclif calls him and his general influence over Wyclif, the parallels of their respective conversions are striking and go beyond an Augustinian penchant to confess. Both conversions were intellectual and of a theological nature even though Bradwardine and Wyclif were still students of philosophy in the Arts faculty; both were sudden, divine revelations and both were in opposition to the then prevailing philosophical schools. [29]

Whether convention or not, in retrospect, Wyclif saw his salvation as a philosopher and as a Christian in his inspired conversion to

---

[26] *Ibid.*, p. 65: "Sed benedictur Deus qui nos liberavit ab inviscationibus superficialibus verborum as penetrative dirigendum mentis intuitum ad signata."

[27] Workman, *John Wyclif*, I, 120-121.

[28] *DD*, p. 115.

[29] While hardly compelling, such comparisons as these are thought-provoking in assessing influence, direct or indirect, and the intensity and style of Wyclif's own conversion. For Bradwardine and his thought, see Gordon Leff, *Bradwardine and the Pelagians. A Study of His "De Causa Dei" and Its Opponents* (Cambridge, 1957) and Heiko Oberman, *Archbishop Thomas Bradwardine, A Fourteenth Century Augustinian* (Utrecht, 1958).

realism. [30] Facilitated by scriptural study, encouraged by Augustine and revealed by God, realism became his fundamental doctrine, the starting point for any discussion. Once the commitment to realism had been made, Wyclif freed himself entirely from any terminist influence—it could be damning—and succumbed to the righteous enthusiasm of the convert. Now wholly preoccupied with an extreme form of realism, he devoted considerable energy attempting to inflate its philosophical tenets into major tracts like those found in the *Summa de Ente* whose titles include "de universalibus," "de ydeis," and "de materia et forma." [31] Titles indicate direction and Wyclif's was toward a metaphysical system whose key was realism: "a knowledge of universals is the pre-eminent step on the ladder of wisdom, by which we search out hidden truth; and this, I believe, is the reason why God does not permit the school of universals utterly to fail." [32] The nominalists are now sophists, former colleagues, enemies, and this transformation in Wyclif's mind takes place because of their intransigent refusal to accept, as Wyclif has, the reality of universals. Realism is not only the key to knowledge but, in the *Ente Predicamentali*, it becomes a test of orthodoxy itself. Here Wyclif equates the denial of self-subsistent archetypes with heresy, citing the authority of Augustine, who emphatically asserted that "qui negat ydeas infidelis

---

[30] Benrath, *Bibelkommentar*, pp. 47-49, 312-313 and 338-346. In editing and analyzing Wyclif's commentary Benrath refers to his edition of Wyclif's Second Prologue to the Song of Solomon (pp. 339-346) where Wyclif considers various prerequisites for the study of the Bible and theology. Of these the prime requisite for understanding the Scriptures and a correct theological knowledge is a thorough mastery of the realistic "dialectica vel ars silogizandi." The reason is clear. "Sie enhüllt die ewigen, für sich bestehenden Fähigkeiten und die das Streben des Geistes bestimmenden, selbst aber unverrückbaren, vor allem Irrtum bewahrenden Wahrheiten. Sie erläutert die universalen Substanzen und erweitert die präsentischen Aussagen auf die Vergangenheit und die Zukunft, wie es der Ewigkeit des Seienden angemessen ist." See also B. Smalley, "Wyclif's Postilla on the Old Testament and his Principium" in *Oxford Studies Presented to D. Callus O.P.* (Oxford, 1964), pp. 254-296.

[31] See Chapter V of Robson, *Wyclif and the Oxford Schools*, pp. 115-140, concerning the dating, content and construction of the *Summa de Ente*. For the most part all included treatises have not yet been edited; an exception is Book I, Tract I, *De Ente in communi* edited by S. Harrison Thomson: Johannis Wyclif, *Summa de Ente, Libri Primi, Tractatus Primus et Secundus* (henceforth *Summa de Ente*), ed. S. Harrison Thomson (Oxford, 1930).

[32] As quoted by Robson, *Wyclif and the Oxford Schools*, pp. 153-154, who cites *De Universalibus*, ch. 2, MS, Gonville and Caius, pp. 337-565, Fo. 24r[b]: "Ideo noticia universalium est gradus precipuus scale sapientie ad indagandum veritates absconditas; et hec credo est racio quare deus non permittit scolam de universalibus in toto deficere." See also Benrath, *Bibelkommentar*, pp. 312-313.

est." [33] This same theme—that a correct knowledge of universals is the measure of religious truth—is also found in the early work "de universalibus," where Wyclif weighs the merit of the Joachites and Peter Lombard on this basis, condemning the former for their ignorance, championing the Lombard for his realism. [34]

The metaphysical system set down in these fundamental tracts was neo-platonist in inspiration, Augustinian in focus and thoroughly in agreement with the authority of the bishop of Lincoln, Robert Grosseteste. [35] It was a system that gave universal concepts a reality of their own, that made them self-subsistent and located them in the mind of God where they achieved being. [36]

Wyclif saw, however, varying levels or grades of being from the lowest, the material being of individuals in this world, up through potential being and finally supreme or intelligible being which inhered eternally in God. This highest level or intelligible being "constituted a creatures supreme being and was external in the sense that God eternally intended its existence to be realized at a specific time." [37] By positing in a neo-platonic fashion these various gradations of being, Wyclif created a hierarchical chain of being from the universal down to its individuation in the material world, from the multiplicity of archetypes in God's mind to the multiplicity of individuals in this world. [38] In giving the archetype reality in God's mind, Wyclif extended God's being to include that of the archetypes; they became interdependent. [39] For in sharing God's being, these universals also shared in the deity's attributes of eternity, necessity and indestructi-

---

[33] Augustine's dictum is quoted by Wyclif in Johannes Wyclif, *De Ente Predicamentali* (henceforth *DEP*), ed. R. Beer (London, 1884), p. 277, and cited by Thomson, "Philosophical Basis," p. 96.

[34] Robson, *Wyclif and the Oxford Schools*, p. 153, and B. Smalley, "The Bible and Eternity," pp. 73-89.

[35] See Johannes Wyclif, *Trialogus cum Supplemento Trialogi* (henceforth *Trialogus*), ed. Gotthard Lechler (Oxford, 1869), pp. 65, 69, and Robson, *Wyclif and the Oxford Schools*, p. 148; p. 152: "The metaphysical system, developed in *De Universalibus*, can therefore be called thoroughly platonist, yielding nothing either to terminalism or to conceptualism.

[36] Robson, *Wyclif and the Oxford Schools*, pp. 148-152, and Leff, *Heresy*, II, 502-505.

[37] Leff, *Heresy*, II, 502.

[38] In Wyclif's *DEP*, p. 276, he indicates, as we would expect, his preference for Plato over Aristotle and the reason is simply that Plato proceeds from the unchanging, and eternal to the fluctuating, while Aristotle confusedly begins with the mutable and temporal.

[39] Robson, *Wyclif and the Oxford Schools*, p. 147.

bility. And these common attributes shared by God and the archetypes, spilled down the ladder of being until they reached the created world of individuals. This rather peculiar process depended upon the assumption that individually created existence is merely an individuation of the eternal exemplar inhering in God, a temporal manifestation of pure, intelligible being. The essences present as intelligible being also occurred, if only accidentally, in particulars so that even particular realizations retained something of the eternal and universal. [40]

A product of this inter-linked chain of being, as contemporaries were quick to point out, was a flirtatious approach to pantheism. [41] Although Wyclif defended himself against this charge, and was perhaps technically correct, he did in fact conjoin the created to the uncreated, the singular to the universal by positing that being was common to both; by so conjoining the two Wyclif allowed the created individual to partake of the eternity and necessity of God's own being. [42]

This descending scale of being forced a radically altered conception of time; the universal exemplars were to Wyclif's mind, a part of God's being and, located in God's mind, they participated in His divine attributes. If the universal exemplars were a part of God's being, then Wyclif reasoned, they existed outside time; in other words, they were eternal and indestructible.

Scholastic tradition had long asserted the ever-presentiality of God's knowledge. What it had not done was to extend this divine attribute to beings that God knew; Wyclif did: "All that is present to God, is; all that was or will be is present to God; therefore all that was or will be, is." [43] Clearly Wyclif felt that whatever God was cognizant of, whatever had been or was to be, whatever the mood, past or future, all is present eternally to God as intelligible being; present because it existed and was known extra-temporally.

---

[40] Robson, *Wyclif and the Oxford Schools*, p. 155ff.

[41] Thomson, "Philosophical Basis," p. 101, and Leff, *Heresy*, II, 503.

[42] Thomson, "Philosophical Basis," p. 99: "But, says Wyclif, the creature is joined (convenit cum Deo) to God in pure being only, not in existence (the attribute of a created thing) but in intelligible being which is God. Or again, it may be granted that being is common to both God and the creature, the difference being in the way in which they possess it...."

[43] "Omne quod est deo presens est; omne quod fuit vel erit est deo presens; igitur omne quod fuit vel erit, est." This passage is quoted by Leff, *Heresy*, II, 506, and is found in the *Fasciculi Zizaniorum Johannis Wyclif cum Tritico* (henceforth *FZ*), ascribed to Thomas Netter of Walden, ed. W. W. Shirley (London, 1858), p. 475.

The individual realization of the archetype at the bottom of the ladder of being, although retaining something of the distinctive features of divinity, was nonetheless created temporally; it comes into being. [44] As such the imperfect being of the particular was subject to time, having been created in time, and this subjectivity transformed the individual. It now had to operate in time and time, as the old saw goes, changes everything; it mutates, alters, corrupts. Particulars then, because of their creation, experience change even to the point of being destroyed; but this in no way affects the immutability or existence of the archetypes. They, as known by God and God's knowledge, remain eternal. [45] Under these circumstances Wyclif found it impossible to employ the same conception of time to measure the operation of both the universal and its particular. His requirement then was for two different time schemes and these he created through the scholastic devise of drawing distinctions. [46]

Wyclif first distinguished between eternal or extra-temporal time and "particular or successive time as apprehended by men." [47] The former he termed "duratio" and the latter he called "tempus." As the extended chain of being conjoins intelligible being and its particular manifestation, so were these two time schemes conjoined. In neither case was there an absolute division. Instead Wyclif saw the actualization of the individual "as its conversion from existence in duration to existence in successive moments of consecutive and calculable length." [48] Creation individuated and in distinguishing the general from the particular, it marked out those substances that exist "duratively" and those that existed temporally. [49] The nexus of creation allowed conjoinment of both intelligible being and its particular, or duration and time, but in the latter case there was no possibility for the two conceptions of time to commingle; existence in the one was immutable, indestructible, sempiternal; existence in the other was mutable, corruptible, temporal. [50] Duration and time could be contiguous but they could never merge in a blurring of the two time

---

[44] Leff, *Heresy*, II, 507ff.

[45] Robson, *Wyclif and the Oxford Schools*, p. 157.

[46] *Ibid.*, pp. 156-217, summarized in detail Wyclif's conception of time with respect to its development, peculiarities and significance. In the following section I have relied heavily on Professor Robson's treatment.

[47] *Ibid.*, p. 157.

[48] *Ibid.*, p. 156.

[49] *Ibid.*, p. 161, and Leff, *Heresy*, II, 507.

[50] *Ibid.*, p. 157.

schemes. The two had to remain separate in order that temporal change, whether creation, decline, or destruction, could in no way affect durative being. There were conjunctions in the neo-platonic stream of being but the flow was always downwards and in no way reversible.

Time alone was the agency or medium of actualizing existence; by individuating being, time enabled the creation of the great chain of being which descended from Godhead to individual.[51] In giving singularity, in distinguishing the individual existant, time allowed intelligible being, however weakly or imperfectly, to manifest itself in the distinct existence of the singular.

Time, however, did more than merely bridge the gap between intelligible being and its particular realization. By employing his dual conception of time, by distinguishing between "duration" and "time," Wyclif created a conceptual framework within which he could dispose of the obvious contradiction. On the one hand, it gave Wyclif access to immutable, eternal being, which he identified with truth, and on the other it allowed him the certitude he so ardently desired, for now, through this conception of time, eternal truths became intelligible and rationally demonstrable.

Clearly Wyclif's philosophical development revolved around the metaphysical pole of being. His realism became extreme, his authorities anachronistic, his conception of truth and time dependent, if not contingent, upon the intelligible being inhering in the Godhead. The conversion he had experienced through the agency of Augustine, Grosseteste and ultimately divine illumination, was really one of first principles, whose acceptance led him into speculative bondage. Leaving the Arts and incepting in theology, Wyclif applied his realistic convictions to the problems of theology, be they questions of necessity, free will or man's relationship to God. Convinced of the correctness of his intellectual tool, Wyclif allowed his realism to shape his theological development.

This process was no where more apparent than in his ascerbic, antagonistic dispute with the East Anglican Carmelite monk, John Kenningham, shortly after Wyclif had incepted in the theological faculty at Oxford.[52] The area of contention was Wyclif's assumption that

---

[51] *Ibid.*, p. 161, and Leff, *Heresy*, II, 507.

[52] Wyclif's dispute with Kenningham, long available in the *FZ*, pp. 4-103, 453-80, has been dealt with in almost all the standard biographies. The philosophical implications, however, are covered most thoroughly by Robson, *Wyclif and the Oxford*

intelligible being was both necessary and eternal and, equally, that contingent truth was likewise beyond the limitations of time. The foundation of this position was, of course, Wyclif's ultrarealism coupled with his rather unique conception of the duality of time. Kenningham cautiously and competently objected to these ideas held by Wyclif whom he referred to as "reverendus magister meus et dominus." [53] While apparently centering on the reality of being, the actual issue was Wyclif's application of realism to theology and biblical exegesis and, in the course of the debate, Wyclif was again and again forced to define and sharpen that which had been indefinite if not obtuse. In the process his philosophical peculiarities became theological ones. Moreover, Wyclif would recognize no limitation in applying his realism. It was, he thought, a methodology capable of solving all problems and consequently his realism became something more than simply a speculative tool for comprehending metaphysical and logical reality—it became a necessary element for all theological understanding as well.

Wyclif reached this point by positing an interesting equivocation. Utilizing his philosophical concept of being, Wyclif equated the word of Scripture with God himself which meant, essentially, that the Bible was now "an emanation of the Supreme Being 'transposed into writing.'" [54] Therefore, in Wyclif's mind, the Bible was divinely revealed, literally true and everpresent; and it possessed these attributes just because, as the Word of God, it was the revelation of the eternal Word; it was the material, actualized form of the divine archetype. Created in time, individuated in space, the Scriptures derived from, and partook in, the intelligible being of the divine exemplar in the same fashion as all other existents at the bottom of Wyclif's philosophical ladder of being. [55] This made, of course, the Scriptures not only literally true, but a mirror of all the eternal truths. It was into this mirror that Christianity had to look to see the celestial things, the eternal truths, the knowledge of Christ. [56] This could only be

---

Schools, pp. 162-170; Leff, *Heresy*, II, 503-507; Smalley, "Bible and Eternity," pp. 84-87, and Benrath, *Bibelkommentar*, p. 313ff.

[53] *FZ*, p. 43.

[54] Robson, *Wyclif and the Oxford Schools*, p. 146, and Smalley, "Bible and Eternity," p. 86.

[55] *Ibid.*, pp. 163-164.

[56] Benrath, *Bibelkommentar*, 315-326. See also p. 38, commenting on Psalms 17:12, Wyclif says: "Scriptura antem est quasi aubes quia a terrenis elevate, per quas speculantes videmus celestia."

accomplished he argued, already in the *Tractatus de Benedicta Incarnacione*, through "a knowledge of the true philosophy and especially a true view of time"; these, he went on to say, "were essential to a right understanding of Scripture." [57] Wyclif also argued the corollary: if contradictions existed, if errors appeared, this was the result of human misunderstanding or error and not that of God's revelation nor of any inherent imperfection reflected in the Bible.

Both Adolf Benrath and Beryl Smalley have investigated Wyclif's comparison of the Bible to a mirror, discovering that, if not original with Wyclif, this metaphor was certainly peculiar to him. [58] By 1372-1373 and his inaugural address, following his inception into the theological faculty, he had altered his informal prerequisites of "a knowledge of the true philosophy and especially a true view of time" into formal, axiomatic truths. His *Principium*, as all principii must, praised the Scriptures in flowering terms; yet in doing so Wyclif did not fall back upon convention to laud, but rather in his own unique fashion invented the metaphorical device of the mirror. [59] Mirroring the eternal things, the beings and truths of existence contained in the infinite mind of God, the Bible, understood realistically, became a vehicle to correctness. In conjunction, the two became necessary for all correct understanding, whether philosophical, biblical or historical. Using the metaphor of the mirror, Wyclif graphically, economically, syncretized his biblical exegesis, his theological development and teaching, even his God and Scripture, within the confining framework of his realistic conception of being. Sliding up and down his scale of being, working beyond the fallacies found in time, John Wyclif could now apprehend the truth contained in the Bible and it freed him to formulate a positive alternative to the contemporary conception of the Church.

---

[57] Smalley, "Bible and Eternity," p. 81, quoting Wyclif.

[58] *Ibid.*, pp. 81-84, and Benrath, *Bibelkommentar*, pp. 311-336.

[59] *Ibid.* See also Wyclif's text in Benrath, *Bibelkommentar*, p. 345. "Ipse [The Scriptures] enim sunt speculum, in quo veritates eterne relucent, via per quam viator ad terminum salutis perducitru [326V] et consolatorium in quo languentis animus vigoratur."

CHAPTER TWO

WYCLIF'S EMERGING ECCLESIOLOGY

What Wyclif discovered of the Primitive Church under the aegis of his philosophical mirror was an ideal of the church—an ecclesiology —that in no way accorded with the conception of the contemporary Roman church as expounded by its hierarchy or theorized by its canonists. The laws and opinions of the hierarchy and its theorists concerning the preeminence of the Roman church and its jurisdictional primacy, Wyclif wrote, were to be shunned as the fruit of ignorance.

> There are many laws and opinions of the saints about the pre-eminence of the Roman Church. But to understand these decrees of the holy doctors of theology, it is necessary to put aside the glosses of John de Deo, John Andree, John Monachus, and those like them, who are ignorant of logic, metaphysics, and the theological meaning of the saints. [1]

No single idea was more important or fundamental to Wyclif's entire body of thought than his rejection of that Roman church. Under the pressure of his metaphysical realism, utilizing the identity of scriptural and realistic logic, Wyclif broke into an older Christian tradition. In doing so, he discovered the refreshing church-idea of the Gospel, persuaded that it alone manifested and mirrored the church's true, archetypal reality. This true church was of Christ and of His institution. Thus, in the fullness of the New Testament, this church *became* Christ; nor could He be separated from His church. [2]

The unifying force or bond between Christ and His church was the

---

[1] *DPP*, p. 250, quoted by Howard Kaminsky, "Wyclifism," p. 60: "Multe sunt et leges et sanctorum sentencie de pre-eminencis Romane ecclesie. Sed ad inteligendum ista decreta sanctorum doctorum theologie oportet postponere glossas Johannis de Deo, Johannis Andree, Johannis Monachi et eis similium, qui logice, metaphisice, theologice sanctorum sentencie sunt ignari." See also *OM*, p. 136, as quoted by Kaminsky, p. 60, where Wyclif calls the word jurisdiction a poisonous term introduced by the craft of the devil. Elsewhere, *DPP*, p. 115, Wyclif remarks that "the names of jurisdiction and authority were introduced irreligiously after the endowment of the church."

[2] *Trialogus*, pp. 231ff.; *DE*, p. 4. Citing Augustine's commentary on Tychonius, *De doctrina christiana*, III, chapter XXXII, Wyclif quotes with obvious approval, "...quod corpus Christi et caput eius Christus sunt una persona...."

notion of the church as the mystical body of Christ and its ever-present companion, the church conceived as the bride of Christ. Both ideas lured and soothed John Wyclif; both were biblical in their foundation and theocentric in their orientation; both enjoyed such a tradition as to make their identity a commonplace as well as a point of departure. The church was the immaculate bride of Christ; He had taken her, had given her spiritual life, and had made her His mystical body through the words of eternal predestination. [3] Describing the church as Christ's mystical body, Wyclif referred to one of the regular scriptural references so often employed by the traditionalists for support.

> For just as the body is one and has many members, and all the members of the body, though many, are one body, so it is with Christ. For by one spirit we were all baptized into one body ... and all were made to drink of one spirit. For the body does not consist of one member but many .... Now you are the body of Christ and individually members of it. [4]

Having been instituted by the perfect Christ, this body, His body, was likewise flawless.

Wyclif was often so attuned to the standard interpretation that he found it unnecessary to cite the traditional reference. In this case the appropriate biblical reference for the immaculate church was Ephesians 5:23-27. Wyclif was aware of it; unlike others, he chose not to use it.

---

[3] *Trialogus*, p. 324: "Vere dicitur ecclesia corpus Christi mysticum quod verbis predestinationis aeternis est cum Christo sponso ecclesiae copulatum"; *De Veritate Sacrae Scripturae* (henceforth *VSS*), ed. Rudolf Buddensieg (London, 1905-1907), III, 68: "...corpus Christi, quod est sancta ecclesia." See also *DE*, pp. 2-3: "Illa autem est 'sponsa' Christi, de qua est processus Cantici canticorum; de qua loquitur scriptura Isaie LXI, 10: 'Tamquam sponsam decoravit me corona'. Hec eciam est 'mulier fortis', de qua Proverb, XXXI, 10, et 'corpus Christi' misticum, de quo I Cor. 12."

For an excellent discussion of the Church as the bride of Christ in Wyclif see Martin Schmidt, "John Wyclifs Kirchenbegriff. Der Christus humilis Augustins bei Wyclif," in *Gedenkschrift für D. Werner Elert*, ed. Friedrich Hubner (Berlin, 1955), pp. 72-109. See especially pp. 73-75, where Schmidt considers the impact of predestination on the biblical notion of Christ's marriage with the church.

[4] *Ibid.*, p. 3, where Wyclif cites the standard reference, I Corinthians, 12:12-14 and 27. The church is designated as Christ's bride in numerous places; see *DCD*, I, 358; *DE*, p. 17, as well as the citations above in footnote 3. Another reference Wyclif could have used to augment his argument that the church is only in the body of Christ would be Romans 12:5: "...so we, though many, are one body in Christ, and individually members one of another." The church is totally dependent on Christ.

> For the husband is the head of the wife as Christ is the head of
> the church, his body, and is himself its Savior .... Husbands, love
> your wives, as Christ loved the church and gave himself up for her,
> that he might sanctify her, having cleansed her by the washing of
> water with the word, that the church might be presented before him
> in splendor, without spot or blemish. 5

This was Christ's church. It was a cleansed and perfected church and
the faithful were assured, in the words of the New Testament, that
the gates of hell would not, could not, prevail against this divine
institution. Yet these words of promise bore a crushing enigma: How
could the attributes of divinity, holiness, and unblemished perfectibi-
lity be predicated of a particular, terrestrial, human organization?

Early in the development of the Catholic church, indeed as early as
Pope Leo I, the theory of the Petrine commission had been set forth
in the Latin West as a response to this riddle. 6 This doctrinal solution
identified Christ's holy, immaculate church with the existing, visible
and very human institution of the Roman church under its bishop,
the successor of St. Peter. According to this doctrine, Christ had given
Peter alone the power of the keys to heaven—and with this commission of power, Peter, as the vicar of Christ, was to bind and to loose.
What Peter bound or loosed on earth was equally bound and loosed
in heaven (Matthew 16:13-20).

As the prince of the apostles, the vicar of Christ, and the bishop
of Rome, Peter was to govern the whole of Christ's earthly church.
This was Peter's charge and the foundation of his authority. What
applied to Peter applied equally to his successors in that office, the
popes, for they too, in the manner of Peter, were princes and vicars.
They too received an *ex officio* position and a function that in no way
depended upon their own personal merits. 7 Receiving the merits of
Peter through the grace of apostolic succession, they assumed and
continued Peter's primacy over Christ's earthly institution. This pri-

---

5 Ephesians, 5:23-27; cf. Kaminsky, *A History of the Hussite Revolution* (Berkeley
and Los Angeles, 1967), p. 25.

6 For Pope Leo I's contribution and the following treatment of the Petrine
commission in general, see Walter Ullmann, *The Growth of Papal Government in
the Middle Ages* (London, 1955), pp. 2-28, who demonstrates how, on the basis of
the ambiguous biblical text of Matthew XVI: 18-19, the Petrine text, Leo I gave
monarchical government a permanent place in the developing ecclesiology of the
church. See also Ullmann's *Principles of Government and Politics in the Middle Ages*
(London, 1961), pp. 32-56, and Brian Tierney, *Foundations of the Conciliar Theory*
(Cambridge, 1955), pp. 25-35, referred to in Kaminsky, *Hussite Revolution*, p. 26.

7 Ullmann, *Principles of Government*, pp. 38-39.

macy rested on Peter's commission and his authority to expose the law—that is, to teach right interpretation and correct application of Christ's law. Considering the mediatory role of the church in the redemptive process, interpretation and application were the figurative keys to heaven, upon whose strength the jurisdictional basis of church government developed.

By the end of the eleventh century, this general but indefinite jurisdictional foundation had evolved into a thoroughly articulated concept which identified the biblical church, the body and immaculate bride of Christ with the Roman church, that human, juridical institution. In effect such an equation adjudged the two churches coterminous, allowing the church or *ecclesia* to be at once a clerical corporation and the mystical body of Christ, to be both visible and invisible. [8] This equivocation provided the legal underpinning for the full-blown doctrine of papal sovereignty with its whole apparatus of government. All the rights, privileges, and prerogatives of the New Testament Church were now transferred to papal government.

This equivocal treatment did not go unchallenged. As the reality of papal sovereignty grew at the expense of the other estates in the organizational church, it drew criticism from a number of quarters including St. Bernard and some of the most important decretists. Repeatedly they directed their criticism at the incongruity of applying the predicates of perfection found in Christ's church to the institutional, juridical, and historical Roman church under the direction of the papacy—at the absurdity of equating the human with the divine. [9]

In light of this criticism, schoolmen, used a favorite scholastic devise, to avoid the simple equivocation for a more complex one. They did so by drawing distinctions between the church as the community of the faithful—an invisible abstraction—and the church, both human and visible, as an institution. There was immense practical value in such a distinction: in a thoroughly comprehensible fashion, it provided the Roman church with a solution to the problem of

---

[8] Gerhart B. Ladner, "Aspects of Medieval Thought on Church and State," *Review of Politics*, IX (1947), 410ff., as quoted by Kaminsky, *Hussite Revolution*, p. 26, "...the terms Ecclesia and Ecclesia Romana ... appear to coalesce into one concept comprising the Church both as an institution, that is, as an essentially clerical corporation, and as the community of all the faithful, the Body of Christ."

[9] The extent of this criticism is pointed out and discussed in considerable detail by Kaminsky, *Hussite Revolution*, p. 27, and Tierney, pp. 39-41, 50-58. Tierney, pp. 35-41, also deals with the problems the decretalists had in dealing with the indefectibility of Christ's church.

predication that Christ's church raised. Now the Roman church, *qua*
congregation of the faithful, could partake of and be associated with
those predicates of Christ's perfection, while the Roman church, *qua*
clerical corporation, could remain so human, so visible, and so obviously wanting. Henceforth with the aid of this scholastic distinction,
the Roman church could straddle both concepts of the church. It
could conform to the definition of the church as an invisible, abstract,
and perfect manifestation of Christ, or act as a fallible, concrete, and
visible clerical organization depending upon the issue at question. [10]
The tandem elements of equivocation and distinction enhanced one
another, each functioning as a justification of papal sovereignty if not
papal monarchy. John Wyclif totally rejected this justification and
with it papalism itself.

Wyclif developed his own ecclesiology. As early as 1372, in his
Principium or inaugural lecture given upon receiving his doctorate of
theology, Wyclif indicated he had begun to question the identification
of the Roman church with Christ's and the view that one had but to
seek the presence of the papacy to find the church of divine promise. [11]
Even at this early date, Wyclif indicated growing dissatisfaction with
the prevalent papal ecclesiology. [12] And most of what can only be
inferred here is spelled out a decade later in detail and supported
by historical circumstance.

During the intervening years, the Great Schism had broken out,
resulting in the creation of two popes, two obediences—each emphasizing the divinity and identity of his church with that of Christ's.
Each damned the other and Wyclif said they were both right. [13]
In such a situation the unity of the visible church was shattered and
yet this predicate could not be sacrificed because unity was one of the

---

[10] The basic argument in the preceding paragraphs has been presented by Kaminsky,
"Wyclifism," pp. 59-60, and later expanded in his monograph, *Hussite Revolution*,
pp. 25-27. This argument is supplemented by Tierney, especially pp. 41-42. For an
assessment of Kaminsky's article in light of recent literature see Amedeo Molnar,
"Recent Literature on Wyclif's Theology," *Communio Viatorum*, VII (1964), 186-
192, especially 186-188.

[11] B. Smalley, "Wyclif's Postilla," pp. 254-296, demonstrates that the second prologue to the Song of Solomon is in fact Wyclif's *Principium* and offers a discussion
of the nature of the "principia" in general while assessing Wyclif's contribution in
this interesting category.

[12] Benrath, *Bibelkommentar*, p. 44ff.

[13] Johannes Wyclif, *Sermones* (henceforth *SS*) ed. Johann Loserth (4 vols.;
London, 1886-1889), IV, 157. See also *DOR*, p. 226; and Johannis Wyclif, *Dialogus
Sive Speculum Ecclesie Militantis* (henceforth *Dialogus*), ed. A. W. Pollard (London,
1886), p. 22.

essential attributes of perfection assured by Christ. If the church was not rent, then how was the individual Christian to determine which of the two antagonistic bodies was the *true church* against which the gates of hell would not prevail? It was a crushing decision because to choose wrongly was to choose Christ's opponent and antithesis, the Antichrist as well as the damnation he would bring. [14]

The conclusion Wyclif drew from this intolerable quandary was brutal in its simplicity and directness. Christ had ordained just such a schism in the earthly church to demonstrate to the faithful that it did not belong to the "substance of faith to believe explicitly that either one of them was pope." [15] In short, Wyclif saw the schism, disillusioning and troubling as it might be for the majority of Christians, as a silver-lined cloud whose deleterious effects were restricted primarily to the papacy. [16] He blurted out his satisfaction purposefully and almost gleefully. "O that happy schism that teaches fully so many, beautiful, catholic truths." [17] Wyclif's point was clear:

---

[14] *SS*, III, 275-276. At another point, *OM*, p. 252, Wyclif claims that neither pope is Christ's vicar—each is Antichrist.

[15] *DPP*, p. 248, as quoted by Kaminsky, *Hussite Revolution*, p. 28: "...nec est de substancia fidei explicite credere alterum eorum esse papam." Later, *ibid.*, pp. 258-259, Wyclif returns to this theme and relates how some people maintain that no one can be saved unless they believe as an article of faith that the pope is the cause of all spiritual profit. Wyclif's reply is immediate: "Si enim iste sit tam necessarius articulus fidei, cum apostoli et omnes christiani ante dotacionem non crediderunt istum articulum, videtur quod absit quod eorum quilibet sit dampnandus." Johann Loserth, in his interesting article, "Johann von Wiclif und Robert Grosseteste," *Sitzungsberichte der Kaiserlichen Akademie der Wissenschaften*, philosophisch-historische Klasse, 186 (1921), Wien, p. 58, touches upon the above problem concerning the sovereignty of the papacy.

[16] *DDP*, p. 149. Applying Matthew 24: 23-25, "Then if any one says to you, 'Lo, here is the Christ!' or 'There he is!' do not believe it. For false Christs and false prophets will arise and show great signs.... Lo, I have told you," to the schismatic popes Wyclif baldly states: "Istam propheciam Chrisi omnis catholicus tenetur credere. Et videtur michi ipsam posse exponi de istis dicentibus hodie se esse papas ... et certum est quod ista divisio est ad instruccionem ecclesie."

[17] *DPP*, p. 353: "Ideo multas pulcras veritates catholicas plane docet ista felix dissensio." Kaminsky, *Hussite Revolution*, p. 28, found a very similar passage earlier in *DPP*, p. 248: "Benedictus Deus veritatis, qui ordinavit istam dissensionem, ut veritas huius fidei elucescat." Many other selections show Wyclif welcoming the schism. See Johannes Wyclif, *Polemical Works* (henceforth *PW*), ed. Rudolf Buddensieg (2 vols.; London, 1883), I, 243: "Et si allegetur papa, illud precipiens, benedictus deus, qui non permittit tantam culpam in anticristo ulterius prevalere, sed divisit caput serpentis movens unam partem ad aliam conterendam," and *PW*, II, 604, where the Lord "caput anticristi diverserat et excitat unam partem aliam debellare." Also *Trialogus*, p. 424; *Opus Evangelicum* (henceforth *OE*), ed. Johann Loserth (2 vols.; London, 1895-1896), I, 75.

Neither of the schismatic popes mattered because the true church, Christ's Church, could not be identified with the papal institution. [18] The essential purity of the church could only be salvaged in that earlier, biblical ideal of the church as the bride and body of Christ. [19]

Wyclif's rejection of the Roman conception of the church did not stem from the schism. The schism he saw as divine instruction, clarifying a muddled situation, but it had not been the precipitating cause of his rejection—that had taken place before. [20] Nor did Wyclif's rejection mean that he uncritically accepted the developing conciliar notions of the church as a "congregatio fidelium." [21] Quite the contrary: Wyclif labored as much and as diligently against this position as he did against its alternative, papalism. Instead, when faced with the question of the nature and composition of Christ's cleansed and flawless church, Wyclif decided that there was no conceivable way to identify it with a visible institution. [22] The church necessarily would be invisible and would be of Christ's own choosing.

Wyclif's commitment to this conception of the church is nowhere more explicitly stated—his ideas nowhere more clearly delineated— than in the first few pages of his tract, *De Ecclesia.* There he concludes that the church is best known and understood as a "congregatio omnium predestinatorum," a congregation of all the possessors of grace, which most properly is the church, the bride of Christ, and mystical body of Christ.

This definition of the church as the congregation of all the pre- destined gave the church the degree of constancy Wyclif so ardently

[18] *SS*, III, 161. Disregard the two popes "...quia nesciunt si sint de Christi ecclesia...."

[19] See *DE*, p. 115, where Wyclif, after determining that the Holy Roman Church is not the multitude of Christians who keep whole the true faith, denies the leader- ship of the papacy over the universal church as well as its identification with Christ's Church. In identification the church would lose all the distinctions and attributes that scripture predicates to it; p. 84 relates how the papal conception of the church can be only wrinkled and spotted and therefore not Christ's eternal church.

[20] See Johann Loserth, "Studien zur Kirchenpolitik Englands in 14. Jahrhundert. II Teil. Die Genesis von Wiclifs Summa Theologiae und seine Lehre vom wahren und falschen Papsttum," *Sitzungsberichte der Kaiserlichen Akademie der Wissen- schaften*, philosophisch-historische Klasse, 156 Wien, p. 50: "Man darf nicht glauben, dass Wiclif seinen Kirchenbegriff erst infolge der Eindrucke gebildet hat, die der Ausbruch des grossen Schismas auf ihn gemacht hatte. Wir finden seine Lehren hierüber mit aller Deutlichkeit schon im ersten Bände seines Werkes *De Dominia Civili*, dessen Abfassung doch noch in die Zeit vor dem Ausbruch des grossen Schismas fällt...."

[21] Tierney, *Foundations of Conciliar Theory*, p. 222ff.

[22] *Supra*, fn. 20.

desired. It was a definition which relied upon the omniscience and omnipotence of God. Christ would be determinative; He would be His own instrument, elect His own bride and would, in the holiness of His divinity, structure His own church. In this way Wyclif gave his conception of the church its predicates of divinity—eternal, immutable, and perfect—making the church an archetypal reality which could only be supernatural. [23]

Wyclif's development had always been a quest for certainty. Once he placed the constitutive element in Christ's hands, in His calling and election, then he could easily emphasize Augustinian traditions of predestination. [24] Absolute, divine, beyond the caprice of time and place—Christ, election, and even the church itself were now all eternal paradigms whose reality for Wyclif was at once supernatural and normative. [25]

Wyclif's church then is an eternal congregation of the predestinate (past, present, and future) who are united in everlasting marriage with Christ. It is necessary, Wyclif wrote, to accept as the metaphysical truth that "the catholic or apostolic church is a *universitas predestinatorum* of which some are dead, some living and some yet to be born." [26] Formulated early in the work on civil dominion, this idea of the church as a community often recurs.

---

[23] "Sed illa mater nostra post diem iudicii, quando erit sine macula vel ruga, non habebit prescitos sed solum predestinatos partes suas...," *ibid.*, p. 83. See also *ibid.*, p. 115, where these divine predicates are enumerated and applied to the church.

[24] Schmidt, "John Wyclif's Kirchenbegriff," pp. 74ff, 84ff.

[25] Answering the objection that the church cannot be one body because its parts are separate in space, Wyclif asserts that all the parts have a common point of union in the head, that distance does not interfere with this and that each part is in touch with every other. And from this it follows that "...sicut quelibet res est simpliciter eterna secundum esse suum intelligibile, sic est perpetua nedum in sua specie et principiis quiditatis, sed in suis causis individuis et in sua causacione, cum semper sit causacio cuiuslibet rei. Et conformiter est ubique, licet non secundum existenciam individui...," *ibid.*, p. 106. Later, *ibid.*, p. 412f, Wyclif proclaims it an error to hold that the church began at the death of Christ, that it comes into existence only through the Incarnation. Like any other being, the church has existed for all time; it is an archetype for its own individuals, for its own species. A lengthy discussion of Wyclif's attitude toward the position that the Church begins with Christ's death can be found in Schmidt, "John Wyclif's Kirchenbegriff," p. 85ff. where the author treats the historical growth of the church and the necessity conjoining it with the historical Christ and His bride. See also Benrath, *Bibelkommentar*, p. 264, on this topic and Leff, *Heresy*, II, 518.

[26] "Pro solucione huius materie necesse est supponere unam veritatem methaphysicam, necessariam ad explanacionem propositi et multorum sensuum Scripturarum, scilicet, quod ecclesia matholica sive apostolica sit universitas predestinatorum, quorum aliqui sunt mortui, aliqui vivi, et aliqui generandi...," *DCD*, I, 358.

Another and somewhat unusual ecclesiastical theme of Wyclif's is the distinction he draws between the church as a congregation and the church as a convocation. Based on his own denotation of the Greek word for church, "ecclesia," Wyclif demands that the church be interpreted as a convocation—a group called together—and never as a congregation or simple gathering. He does this because "a synagogue is interpreted as a congregation" and the fathers of the New Testament never termed the church a "synagoga Christianorum"; if we confuse the terms we obfuscate the differences between Judaism and Christianity. [27] These terms are important, for they indicate Wyclif's concern about the fundamental nature of Christ's Church: It is not a capricious gathering whose motive force is internal, but a passive assembly of the elected, who are summoned by an activating Christ.

These ideas of the church as a community and a convocation narrowed the conception and composition of the church to include the only band of people whom God has chosen for Himself. This is the true church. It is a conscious return to an earlier, biblical concept of the church as a community—a people, God's chosen people. Yet Wyclif's Christ chooses; whereas this act corresponds to God's earlier selection of His people in the Old Testament, there are important differences. Now individual Christians are summoned collectively to make up the "honorable people," [28] the "people of God." [29] Instead of traditionally seeing the church or community as a sociological unit Wyclif identifies

---

[27] "Sed notandum, pro modo loquendi in illa materia conformiter ad Scripturam, quod ecclesia secundum peritos linguarum est nomen Grecum et interpretatur 'convocacio'; sicut 'synagoga' interpretatur 'congregacio', quod nomen appropriatur cetui Iudeorum: nunquam enim appellant patres Novi Testamenti 'sinagogam' Christianorum, sicut econtra crebro in Veteri Testamento congregacio Iudeorum vocatur 'ecclesia', ... Racionem autem ponunt primi doctores triplicem: primo ad distinguendum Iudaismum a Christianismo; secundo ad notandum vitam spiritualem ecclesie Christi supra vitam corporalem et bestialem sinagoge...," *ibid.*, 287-88. This passage has also been quoted by Tatnall, *Church and State*, p. 96.

[28] Following the quotation from Psalms 147:20, "He has not dealt thus with any other Nation; they do not know his ordinances," Wyclif wrote: "Et ista gens signat mistice totam ecclesiam militantem. Ideo dicit predicta Sapiencia quod 'radicavit in populo honorificato,' hoc est, in dicta ecclesia, cum nedum fuit incarnaya in ipsa tamquam secundus Adam, tollens prevaricanciam primi Adam; sed multos produxit palmites quos in ipsa vite vel stipite radicavit. Et bene vocatur ista ecclesia 'populus honorificatus,' cum inicium summi honoris infinitum excedens omnem honorem mundanum sit honor predestinacionis...," *SS*, IV, 161. The appellation found in Ecclesiastes is transferred from the people of Israel to Wyclif's church.

[29] *VSS*, III, 57; *DCD*, I, 395: "sic populus christianus ... debet habere ad legem Christi...."

Christ's community as an invisible and mystical union of all those destined for salvation. The church is an eschatological unit standing in union with its animating force, Christ.

Since this church is the result of Christ's cleansing action and the object of the Matthean promise of invincibility, the individual Christian, if he is to be part of this church, must also be without spot or blemish. In this matter only the predestinate qualify and they are few and far between. [30]

This eternal church exists wherever the elect are and is a mystical union. As a mystical union it is neither a physical entity nor a "continuum with respect to time and place," for "the true members of Christ are scattered." [31] In fact, "it is the nature of the church that the predestinate are dispersed throughout heaven, purgatory and the world." [32] Unknown and dispersed, the only bonds between the members of Christ's Church are the bonds of eternal predestination. Although spiritual in nature, predestination suffices to unify the elect, from the beginning of the world to the day of judgment, as one person, which is the mother church. [33] Wyclif's church is independent of time and space, and conceived of only as the community of the elect; it stands in direct opposition to that papal ecclesiology which identified Christ's Church with its clerical institution. He denies its

---

[30] *Ibid.*, p. 5: "...et sic ecclesia est solum numerus predestinatorum."; p. 7: "Eo ipso quod est ecclesia universalis sive catholica, ipsa continet in se omnes predestinatos."; p. 15; *Trialogus*, p. 415, as quoted by Leff, *Heresy*, II, 515, fn. 1: "Ideo patet ex fide Christi scripture et multiplici testimonio sanctorum quod nullum est membrum sancte matris ecclesie nisi persona predestinata...."

[31] "Dicitur secundo quod propter elongacionem a vera ecclesia et ab irradiacione luminis capitalis frequenter putatur ecclesiam Christi esse continuam quo ad locum et tempus, dum tamen membra Christi et sponse per vaccuitates predestinacionis et operis rarenter sunt positi," *ibid.*, p. 99.

[32] Speaking of Christ's Church, Wyclif says: "... et illi predestinatorum in celo, in purgatorio et in nostra habitabili sint dispersi et illi more spicarum post messionem autumpni in multis congregacionibus hominum sint valde rari et nobis ignoti ..." Continuing, Wyclif maintains this Church is scattered as to place, time and disposition. "Est autem procul quoad locum, quoad tempus et quoad disposicionem; ... patet quod parvam et confusam noticiam habemus de ecclesia matre nostra ...," *SS*, IV, 148-149.

[33] To the objection that there is more than one way of membership in Wyclif's conception of Christ's Church, Wyclif responds: "Sed hic dicitur (ut supra) quod forma exemplaris eternaliter formans ab extra quodcunque membrum ecclesie est predestinacio Dei eterna. ... Et sic habet quilibet predestinatus fidem formatam caritate predestinacionis secundum quam constituitur ecclesia vel eius membrum." *DE*, p. 110. Further: "Sic redeundo ad propositum, patet quod gracia et caritas Jesu Christi que realiter est ipsemet Christus, est terminus communis copulans quodcunque membrum ecclesie cuilibet alteri," *ibid.*, p. 107.

ecclesiastical institutionalism and "realistically" develops a church that is essentially a universal beyond spatial or geographical consideration —an archetype whose reality is normative, whose essence is immaterial, and whose ideal is inspirational.

As the community of the predestinate, past, and future, Wyclif's church is a unit. Yet although it is united beyond time, this unity does not possess spatial bonds. In fact, the church is segregated as to place, and that place is dependent upon the condition of the predestinate. [34] On this basis the body of the church has three parts, namely, the Church Militant (Militans), the Church Sleeping (Dormiens), and the Church Triumphant (Triumphans). [35] Such a cleavage of the church probably rests on a christological conception of the church that allowed it to mirror the personal experience and destiny of a Christ, who fought on earth, reposed in his tomb, and finally arose in triumph. [36] These three forms comprehend the whole church of the predestinate; but while comprehending the entirety of the one church, they will not be unified in "a complete and glorified church" until after the final day of judgment. [37] Meanwhile the conditional wandering of the individual elect shall continue.

Over this invisible and metaphysical universal that Wyclif calls the church, reigns the reality of Christ, its head. Wyclif is emphatic: "Christ is the head of the whole church." [38] "The body of the church and Christ, its head are one person." [39] Wyclif spares no authority, however inimical, in his zeal to defend the leadership of Christ. If the witness is hostile—as in the case of Boniface VIII's bull,

---

[34] *SS*, IV, 148.

[35] "... notandum quod ecclesia catholica habet tres partes, scilicet triumphancium, dormiencium et militancium." *SS*, II, 353-354. This division is also set down in *DE*, pp. 7-8; p. 418: "Quoad tercium errorem patet ex testimonio sanctorum et ecclesia quod est unum corpus Christi misticum compositum ex ecclesia militante, dormiente et triumphante ..." See also *DCD*, I, 381.

[36] Schmidt, "John Wyclif's Kirchenbegriff," p. 78; see also Workman, II, 8, where Workman notes that Wyclif, *DE*, p. 125, speaks of the Church as being divided into the queens, concubines and virgins of Solomon, i.e., of Christ.

[37] "Tercio vero in ultimo adventu faciet agnus nupcias consummatas, coronondo et confirmando reginam integram que est una columba et universalis ecclesia, non pars alterius ecclesie. ... Et super ista consideracione dependet magna pars sensus scripture et servicii ecclesie. Nam ex fide erit una totalis ecclesia glorificata post diem iudicii, et illa secundum magnam partem est modo sponsa in celo, in purgatorio et in mundo." *DE*, p. 124.

[38] *Ibid.*, p. 7.

[39] "Ad quid igitur opportet contendere circa caput ecclesie? 'Ipsa' inquit Augustinus 'caro Christi est caput ecclesie' ..." *ibid.*

Unam Sanctam, which calls for the pope's head on the body of the church—Wyclif deftly denies it. [40] Christ is the head of the church; it is *His* community. Under these circumstances it (salvation) requires only His leadership and His law. Sufficient for salvation, Christ's leadership is sufficient for the governing of his spouse, the church. [41] Popes, cardinals, and bishops are superfluous—unnecessary accretions in the face of Christ's sovereignty.

Whereas there was no doubt concerning the leadership of Christ and the sufficiency of His law in the universal church, there was considerable doubt as to the identity of the predestinate in that part of church that manifested itself on earth as the Church Militant. [42]

This theological position gives Wyclif's whole conception of man's relationship to God a distinctively individualistic cast. Wyclif frees man entirely from the mediatory role of the institutional church with its sacramental priesthood. Wyclif ignores the church, placing the responsibility total upon Christ's shoulders—He shall determine the membership of the true church. [43] Man has nothing to do with election; Christ elects! Wyclif thereby secures the sovereignty of Christ over the church, His body, as leader and head.

The Church Militant, that portion of the church battling on earth, is an "ecclesia permixtum" of the elect and of the damned functioning together as a community on the basis of "present righteousness." Because of this, it cannot be the cleansed, spotless bride of Christ, the infallible and timeless church. While mixed it is stained and blemished, and contains not only the predestined but the damned. The damned are only *of* the true church; they are not *in* it, as are the elect. [44] The conspicuous feature of this almost inseparable admixture

---

[40] *Ibid.*, as cited by Kaminsky, "Wyclifism," p. 71, fn. 28.

[41] "Item caput Christus cum sua lege est per se sufficiens ad regulam sponse sue ..." *DCD*, I, 380, 394ff.; *DOR*, p. 226. All citations found in Kaminsky, "Wyclifism," p. 72, fn. 31.

[42] *DE*, p. 3. Here Wyclif quotes a long passage from Augustine's *Enchiridion* concerning the nature of the church.

[43] Workman, II, 12-13.

[44] There are many passages in Wyclif's works which contain this important and famous phrase. Two of the best, both used by Kaminsky, *Hussite Revolution*, p. 32, fn. 93, can be found in a tract called "De Fide Catholica" in the collective *OM*, pp. 99 and 112. After describing the three forms of Christ's Church, Wyclif goes on to say: "Sed in sancta matre ecclesia militante sunt multi dyaboli ut presciti, sicut in humano corpore sunt stercora, fleumata et multe superfluitates alie que nullatenus sunt de illo," which leads then naturally into p. 112 and the difference between being *in* the Church and *of* it (aliud est esse de illa ecclesia). A somewhat lengthy passage is *SS*, II, 399.

of good and evil is man's inability to determine the wheat from the tares. Consequently, the Church Militant gropes—with the uncertainty of election, with the limits of human knowledge, and with the ever-present danger of subversion. It mirrors the components of human existence.

The Church Militant actually is earthly, human society, a political community with an existence real in both time and space.

> ... it is false to say that the Church Militant is not circumscribed as to place, since it is a body having one place that circumscribes it, just as it has one faith, and thus it is an animated, rational body, for it is a sensible body, performing vital actions .... [45]

As a community, the Church Militant has the rights, privileges, and prerogatives of other communities. As the imperfect humanly state of the true church, however, it is blemished. Because these blemishes are the result of original sin and never can be eradicated, totally, they necessitate the development of coercive power in the form of human institutions to regulate relationships within human society.

One method of regulating society within the Church Militant is to establish particular orders or estates, each with functions, that are specific but that "in toto" are complementary and beneficial to the whole. These estates with their corresponding roles are instituted by God; thereby Wyclif, dividing his tripartite Church Militant, creates a diversified functional hierarchy. [46] Wyclif follows long tradition to

---

[45] "Sic enim ex beatis viantibus et dampnatis fit unum genus humanus, unde quod dicitur ecclesiam militantem non esse circumscriptive alicubi, falsum est, cum sit corpus habens unum locum circumscribentem, sicut habet unam fidem, et sic est corpus animatum racionale, nam est corpus sensibile exercens actus vitales ..." *DE*, p. 423.

[46] "Ecclesia autem militantium ex approbacione Cristi expressa vel tacita dicitur communiter tripartita, scilicet ecclesia clericorum, qui debent esse propinquissimi ecclesie triumphanti et iuvare rediduum ecclesie militantis, ut sequatur Cristum propinquius, qui est caput tocius ecclesie ... Secunda pars militantis ecclesie dicitur esse militum ita, quod, sicut prima pars istius ecclesie dicitur instruencium oratorum, ita secunda pars ecclesie dicitur corporalium defensorum. Tercia vero pars ecclesie dicitur wlgarium vel laboratorum. Et in armonia ista trium parcium ad imitacionem trinitatis increate consistit sanitas corporis istius ecclesie militantis." *PW*, II, 654. For the general composition of the Church and its division according to estates see *SS*, II, 22-26, 337-338, 354; *OM*, p. 249; *Dialogus*, pp. 2-4. For respective roles within their hierarchy see *SS*, II, 175-176. A general treatment of the tradition of the threefold division of the Church is provided by Owst, *Preaching in England*, p. 329f. and Owst's companion work, *Literature and Pulpit*, p. 550f. Not only does Owst deal with the history of the threefold division of the church but also with the long tradition of the three orders working together by reason of love.

divide the Church Militant into three orders: the clergy, "who are called the priests of Christ;" the temporal lords, "who ought to be the vicars of deity;" the commons, "who are divided up into workers, merchants and stewards." [47] The bond among these three parts is the "caritas," the love and mutual aid, that they have for one another as members of one body, the church. [48] In the tract, *De Christo et Adversario suo Antichristo*, Wyclif again admonishes what he, in effect, calls the prayers, fighters and laborers to work together, to help one another to share both peace and unity. [49] In so doing each in his own way will compensate for the wrinkles and stains; eventually, together they will triumphantly overcome. [50]

Thus the church is an organic whole that is infinitely more important than any of its constituent parts for it exists prior to and over them. This is the mystique of the political community. It has a strong tradition which Wyclif draws upon and uses as a perfect corollary to his previous commitment to philosophical realism. [51] The church,

---

[47] "Dividebam autem meam militantem ecclesiam in tres partes quarum prima foret clerus meus, qui vocantur sacerdotes Christi ... Secunda pars mee militantis ecclesie forent domini temporales, qui debent esse vicarii deitatis ... Tercia autem pars militantis ecclesie sunt vulgares qui in operarios, mercantes et iconomos multipliciter sunt divisi." *Dialogus*, p. 2, as cited by Fürstenau, *Wyclif's Lehren*, p. 15. For the functions of these estates see Johannis Wyclif, *Tractatus de Blasphemis* (henceforth *DB*), ed. Michael Henry Dziewicki (London, 1893), p. 227.

[48] *Ibid.*, p. 3.

[49] *Supra* fn. 46. This is very similar to Alfred the Great's men of prayer, men of war and men of work.

[50] Wyclif answers three objections of an opponent concerning the church, namely, that there is a difference between the Church Militant and the Church Triumphant, that these churches differ in essential perfection and that they do not form one, single Church. He does so by replying: "Nam quoad primum utraque est univoce ecclesia, ideo oportet quod sit eadem generalis racio utriusque. Quoad secundum patet, cum ecclesia militans erit ecclesia triumphans, contradiccionem claudit quod infinitum distent in perfeccione essenciali; eedem enim persone que iam sunt ecclesia militant erunt ecclesia triumphans (ut patet ex fide)." *DE*, p. 417, and especially pp. 420-421.

[51] Wyclif uses corporeal similes and metaphors incessantly. His description of the Church Militant (*DE*, p. 423) as "a body having one place that circumscribes it, just as it has one faith, and thus it is an animated, rational body, for it is a sensible body, performing vital actions ..." is exemplary. The Church is an organism in *DCD*, I, 358: "... quod tota est ecclesia, sicut est sponsa Christi et corpus Christo spiritualiter coniugatum, sic est una persona, quia corpus animatum racionabile, quod non potest esse multarum personarum ..." and *DCD*, IV, 457: "Totum enim corpus ecclesie quod tenetur se iuvare reciproce debet secundum partem sanam corripere huiusmodi sacerdotes." The point is that the whole is always prior to its parts. One part must correct the other parts for the benefit of the whole. This is the mystique of the political community and it has a long tradition that is dealt with in part by Michiael Wilks, *The Problem of Sovereignty in the Later Middle Ages: The Papal Monarchy with Augustinus Triumphus and the Publicists* (Cambridge,

consequently, is a political community; it is a body politic and an organic whole whose membership is segregated theoretically and practically into the three fundamental estates found in every European kingdom. [52]

What Wyclif has done is to pick up the very conventional ideal of the realm as a community of estates and apply this definition of England to his conception of the Church Militant. In the process, he restores a lost dimension to the church and identifies the realm with the church. Church and realm are coterminous: "The church or realm is one body of all the inhabitants of that realm." [53] Wyclif's interchange of terms fabricates an equivocation as potent and as useful for his own ecclesiology as the Roman equivocation had been for its development.

Wyclif then relates the earthly Church Militant in reference to particular political communities: each with boundaries, constellations of power, and historical traditions; each with rights, prerogatives, and privileges. So, just as there is no single all-comprehending realm, there is no single manifestation of the Church Militant. Rather there are a number of "militantes ecclesiae," all individuated by the same criteria as the realm. [54]

Normally Wyclif explicitly avoids using the specific term "churches militant." There are, however, several ways in which he refers to the multiplicity of the "militantes ecclesiae." For example, he notes that the Church Militant has various names according to its locality— in Rome it is the Roman church where St. Peter worked and suffered his martyrdom. Yet this in no way excludes or negates such institutions as the Indian, Greek, Gallican, or English church from participating in the bride of Christ. [55] Among these churches "we can and ought to

---

1963), p. 20f. For an interesting discussion of this organic conception as applied to the church see *DCD*, I, 358-361, where Wyclif notes that the church is all of its members, but none of them severally. And in general, individual objects or parts cannot be apprehended except in that they form one species.

[52] This is nowhere more obvious than in *SS*, I, 252-253.

[53] "Unde pro liberiori locucione in ista materia suppono quod ecclesia sive regnum sit unum corpus omnium incolarum inhabitancium ipsum regnum ..." *SS*, IV, 7, as quoted by Fürstenau, *Wiclif's Lehren*, p. 18.

[54] *DE*, p. 424, as cited by Kaminsky, "Wyclifism," p. 72, fn. 36.

[55] "Ipsa autem sponsa secundum loca que inhabitat caput nomen, et precipue post passionem beati Petri vocatur Romana ecclesia, quia tempore suo et longe post ibi peregrinatur. Ideo sicut quartum imperium ... est imperium Romanorum, sic consenserunt sancti et iura canonica vocare dictam sponsam, secundum quandam excellenciam, Romanam ecclesiam; non negando quin sit ecclesia Indica, Greca, Gallicana, Anglicana, ..." *DCD*, I, 381. Wyclif supports this by referring to the New

believe that the Roman pontiff is head of a particular church to whom obedience is due on earth before others." [56] The emphasis is upon "particular." Subsequently in this treatise, Wyclif maintains that just because the church ought to be believed, it does not follow that bishops or colleges of particular places should. He then actually employs "militantes ecclesiae."

> Nevertheless among the churches militant we occidentals ought principally to believe the Roman pontiff with his college ... if conforming their deeds to the name of their office, they teach or command nothing but what they elicit from scriptural reasons. [57]

The Roman pontiff is preeminent among the churches militant and yet he is only the head of a particular church. Then Wyclif further hedges this limited notion of the papal position for no one can assert himself as the head of even a particular church without fear and special revelation. [58] No one, including the pope, can know whether he is "in" the church or simply "of" it—whether he is among the predestined or the foreknown. Nevertheless, the condition of a particular "head" matters little, for "only Christ can claim to be the head of the whole church and no Christian can presume himself to be the head of the universal church." [59]

Wyclif conceives of the Church Militant as an aggregate, federated body made up of a number of particular churches. Written large, this invisible church absorbs all visible ones and incorporates them: "Just as members of the body are not that body, so particular churches are not that holy church, but members of it." [60] As distinguished as these

---

Testament which mentions the "generatio" of the just at one time residing in one tribe and one place and then in others.

56 "Verumtamen pie credere possumus et debemus quod Romanus pontifex sit caput particularis ecclesie, cui obediendum est in terris pre ceteris, de quanto in ipso Christus loquitur legem suam," *ibid.*, p. 382.

57 "... verumtamen inter ecclesias iam militantes nos occidui debemus precipue credere Romano pontifici cum suo collegio, si facta nomini sui officii compensantes nichil edocent vel precipiunt, nisi quod elliciunt ex racionibus Scripturarum," *ibid.*, p. 417.

58 "Ex istis colliqitur, cum solus Christus sit caput tocius ecclesie que non est pars ad aliam iuxta primam conclusionem, oportet concedere quod sicut nullus christianus debet presumere se esse caput universalis ecclesie, sic nec debet sine timore et sine speciali revelacione asserere quod sit caput cuiuscunque particularis ecclesie." *DE*, p. 17. See also *Trialogus*, p. 166.

59 *Ibid.*, p. 17. See *supra* fn. 58 for quotation.

60 "... 'sicut membra corporis non sunt ipsum corpus, sic particulares ecclesie non sunt illa sancta ecclesia sed (ut docet apostolus I Cor. XII, 12) membra eius'" This is a quotation from Gregory's *Moralia*, which Wyclif picks up and uses. *Ibid.*, p. 23.

"churches militant" are, they are but a part of the larger Church Militant—and even it is subsumed into the universal church under the leadership of Christ. The sole leadership of Christ is clear: "... for the dove (church) is the community of the predestinate, which is the bride of Christ, who alone is its head and groom." [61]

Although Wyclif refers to the Church Militant as an actual community, circumscribed as to place, this community is in fact Christendom or Christian society, itself an abstraction induced from the existing structures of the particular "churches militant." [62] Wyclif abstractly but persistently still touches the real world with his Church Militant and the nexus is the individual "churches militant" conceived as political communities.

The identification of realms with sections of the Church Militant emerges in other ways, especially when Wyclif comes to deal with the heads of these particular churches. Because the miserable individual is ignorant of his election or damnation, "it would be a great presumption," he writes, "for us to assert that we are heads of any particular church which would be a part of the holy, Mother Church." [63] It is not even fitting to believe that the Roman pope is the head of a particular church unless God had actually predestined him for salvation. [64] A "head" must be among the predestinate. [65] If, however, divine election were aplied to the pope and if it were demonstrated conclusively (which is impossible), then the bishop of Rome could be head of part of the Church Militant. [66]

Nevertheless, such a capital designation would apply to only a part

---

[61] "... columba enim est universitas predestinatorum, que est sponsa Christi qui solus est caput eius et sponsus." *DCD*, III, 226.

[62] See *SS*, IV, 179, where Wyclif notes that the seven churches of Asia Minor signify the "universitas ecclesie militantis." Also consult *DE*, p. 30, as cited by Kaminsky, "Wyclifism," p. 72, fn. 33. Here Wyclif, in speaking of the particular churches existing before the Incarnation and yet comprising one and the same church, now triumphant, now militant, says that there is "no doubt but that these churches are distinguished from the universal church and other particular churches; therefore, there are many particular churches and consequently, the one universal church is collected from these ..."

[63] "Cum ergo nos miseri ignoramus si sumus ad celestem Jerusalem predestinati ... patet quod nimia presumpcio foret nobis pertinaciter asserere quod sumus capita cuiuscunque particularis ecclesie que foret pars sancte matris ecclesie, quia notum est ex concordi testimonio sanctorum quod nullus precitus est vel membrum ipsius ecclesie." *DE*, p. 18.

[64] *Ibid.*, p. 37.

[65] *Ibid.*, p. 17. For quotation see *supra*, fn. 63.

[66] *Ibid.*, p. 21.

of the Church Militant, for the Roman church is not the Roman
pontiff with his cardinals. Instead it is "the whole Church Militant,
whom God loves more than any of its parts" and it is dispersed in
all races and languages. [67] However, within this Holy Roman Church
—that is, the whole Church Militant with all its parts—the pope and
his college hold a preeminent position of dignity so long as they
follow Christ. [68] Still the Roman bishop is not the head of the universal church. Wyclif recognizes that sometimes the pope is referred
to as such, but this, stems from ignorance of the efforts of certain
doctors to equivocate—as when he is called head of the universal church,
meaning head of only the Latin churches which he rules. [69]

Predestination alone, however, is not sufficient qualification to
be considered head of even a particular church. One needs divine
election and the God-given dignity of office, for the head of a
particular church is: "the person who rules it in spiritual and temporal
things as the pope or emperor and other captains of particular churches.
Consequently, each church has a single head." [70] Again, if the pope
is among the predestinate and if he exercises his personal office
according to Christ's law, then:

> ... he is head of so much of the Church Militant as he rules, so
> that if he already rules chiefly the entire Church Militant according

---

[67] Quoting Jerome's description of the Holy Roman Church as being without
spot or blemish, always immaculate and indefectible, Wyclif then continues: "Hic
non potest intelligi quicunque papa cum suo collegio ... Cum ergo iuxta decreta
Romana ecclesia habet primatum et dignitatem quoad Deum super omnes alias,
patet quod illa est totalis ecclesia militans quam Deus plus diligit quam aliam eius
partem. Et sic manifeste sequitur ex fide quod non illud collegium sed tota mater
in omni gente et lingua dispersa sit illa sancta Romana ecclesia de qua iura loquuntur
cum sanctis doctoribus," *ibid.*, p. 87. Kaminsky, in his *Hussite Revolution*, p. 27,
has an interesting discussion on this point, a discussion in which he draws on the
ample criticism of the Decretists. See also Tierney, *Foundations*, p. 41f.

[68] "Unde non dubium oratur pro principalissima ecclesia militante quam suppono
esse Romanam ecclesiam, verumptamen inter partes eius in comparacione ad quantitatem sunt papa et suum collegium pars precipua dignitate, dum tamen sequantur
Christum propinquius et deserendo fastum atque primatum serviant matri sue
efficacius atque humilius," *ibid.*, p. 88.

[69] "Quando ergo doctores sic loquuntur ex circumstanciis, potest perpendi equivo-
caciones sue deteccio, ut vocando episcopum Romanum caput universalis ecclesie
intelligitur quod sit caput tante Latine ecclesie quantam regit," *ibid.*, p. 93.

[70] "Et patet quod caput unius persone ecclesie non est caput eiusdum ecclesie,
sed persona que regit eam capitaliter in spiritualibus ac temporalibus, ut papa vel
imperator ac alii capitanei particularium ecclesiarum; et per consequens quelibet
ecclesia habet unicum caput sublime racionis." *DCD*, I, 367.

to the law of Christ, then he is a particular captain of the Church Militant under the arch-head, Lord Jesus Christ. [71]

Just as there are many particular "churches militant" making up the Church Militant or Holy Roman Church, so there are many individual heads and captains ruling these various sections under the sovereignty of archhead Jesus Christ. [72] While this Church Militant is an abstraction and its "genus of captains" is a real universal, Wyclif pins both down to the concrete realities of people and place.

> It seems to me that reason dictates that the people set up a head for themselves, not just one genus of captains in political religion, but that each people take a single head for itself, as for example we English have one blessed king, to whom, according to the doctrine of the Gospel ... we must render secular obedience. And so it is with other greater or lesser realms, even up to the Empire. [73]

By conceiving of the church, whether universal or Roman, in his own peculiar manner and by withdrawing the sting of papal interpretation and absolutism through a federated conception of the Church

---

[71] "... sequitur quod dominus papa, si predestinatus est et exercet pastorale officium, est caput tante militantis ecclesie quantam regit, ut si sic regit capitaliter secundum legem Christi totam iam militantem ecclesiam, tunc est eius particularis capitaneus sub archicapite domino Jesu Christo." *DE*, p. 19.

[72] In addition to *DE*, p. 19, just quoted, see p. 22 where Wyclif notes that just as the people have many heads, one subordinate to the other, so the church has many heads ordered in the same way. "... sicut idem populus habet multos dominos, unum subordinatum alteri (sicut patet in materia civili). Et sic videtur dicere quod eadem ecclesia habet multa capita ordinata secundum inferius atque superius."

[73] "... videtur mihi quod racio dictat ut ipsi faciant sibi caput, nedum unum genus capitaneorum in religione politica, sed quod quilibet populus appropriet sibi simplex caput, ut nos Anglici habemus unum regem benedictum, cui secundum doctrinam ewangelii ... debemus inpendere obsequium seculare. Et ita est de regnis aliis maioribus sive minoribus, eciam usque ad imperium." *DOR*, p. 249, as quoted by Kaminsky, "Wyclifism," p. 62, and Fürstenau, *Wiclifs Lehren*, p. 48f. The Latin word "capitaneus" can be translated as captain and according to E. Habel and F. Gröbel, *Mittellateinisches Glossar*, 2. Aufl. (Paderborn, 1959), p. 47, means generally "durch Grösse hervorragend; Anführer, höherer Lehnsmann." Haberkern und Wallach, *Hilfswörterbuch*, p. 96a, point out that the term was used primarily in Italy. They also note, however, that the term can mean vicar. Wyclif employs the word in any number of ways; in *DPP*, p. 196, he has Christ electing the apostles to himself and one "capitaneus," Peter, among them. *DCD*, III, 62, states that it is fitting to constitute one "capitaneus" or king over the Church and this must be Christ. Another time Wyclif, in speaking of the depredations of the Friars, states: "Nec dubium, qui tunc limitator (Friar licensed to bed within a certain area) et sui capitanei negociabuntur de illis per media nimis subdola ..." *PW*, I, 33. Seemingly "capitaneus" is never used in any totally consistent fashion, but it is an important word in Wyclif's vocabulary and does need study.

Militant, Wyclif managed a unique feat. He at once decapitated the Roman pontiff, redefined the notion of Roman preeminence to an earlier reality, and rediscovered the original conception of the biblical church as a people. He did so while conforming to and echoing contemporary English opinion that the "ecclesia Anglicana" was the realm of England, distinguished by its own traditions, experience, and laws.

In setting up a federal church, composed of several "churches militant" identified with political realms possessing geographic and cultural frontiers, Wyclif reflected a long English process. As early as 1290, an official document paraphrased the "ecclesia Anglicana" with the words "Ecclesia de Regno Angliae." [74] By the mid-fourteenth century, this type of documentation increased and included the ubiquitous phrase "defensio ecclesiae et regni Angliae"; it had special significance for Wyclif. [75] Moreover these are only the official or at least semi-official utterances. They appear late in the development of the concept as a tardy response to an earlier reality. [76]

It is thus clear that not only Wyclif, but a large number of his contemporaries, ecclesiastical and lay, assumed themselves and their realm, including the English church, to be something peculiar. While they did not deny the Roman church, they evermore stridently proclaimed this Roman church to be composed of independent national churches such as their own. It was a view and a remembered tradition that Wyclif could represent. Marrying it to his own ecclesiology, Wyclif used this alliance of English fact and reality with his uncompromising realism and biblical exposition as a prototype for future development.

---

[74] See Denys Hay, "The Church of England in the Later Middle Ages," *History*, 53 (1968), 48f, where he gives this quotation from the *Rotuli Parliamentorum*, I, 57b.

[75] *Ibid.*, quoting *Rotuli Parliamentorum*, II, 12; III, 26 and 48.

[76] *Ibid.*

CHAPTER THREE

HISTORICAL DECLINE AND THE NECESSITY OF REFORMATION

As Wyclif's philosophy pushed him into a particular conception of Christ's Church, so this notion of the church as found in the Bible led him to reform. Mirroring the eternal truths and reflecting the universals of law, the words of scripture were preceptive. [1] Truth and law for Wyclif were interchangeable, with both directing man in the service of God. [2] Scripture, however, does not simply contain God's truth and harbor His law—it is His law. [3] In the process of this identification, both law and truth are absolutized beyond time; the law of God, Christ's law is archetypal and unchanging, [4] as Wyclif noted often. "Sacred Scripture which is the law of Christ contains in itself all truth; since all law is truth, it therefore contains in itself all law." [5] As the benchmark from which all Christian life is measured, the Bible is "one perfect word, proceeding from the mouth of God, whose single parts are the joint cause of the entire authority or efficacy of the law of Christ." [6] As the repository of all truth and confutation

---

[1] *SS*, ¶III, 263: "Dixi enim sepe quod universalia legum hominum, immo ipse leges hominum, sunt veritates eterne in scriptura planius implicate. ... Et sic de multis aliis principiis legum civilium, que leges non possunt justificari nisi ab eternis principiis et per se necessariis orirentur" and *DE*, p. 173: "Omnis lex utilis sancte matri ecclesie docetur explicite vel implicite in scriptura ... Omnis veritas est in scriptura sacra ..." Not only does the Bible contain all truth, but confutation of error as well: "Omnis veritas et omnis erroris destruccio est in ecangelio ..." *OE*, I, 91, and *VSS*, I, 8f.

[2] *Ibid.*, pp. 263-64: "... et sic dixi quod lex in sua generalitate est veritas directiva hominis ut debite serviat Deo suo, et hoc genus legis est generaliter lex divina cuius una pars in scriptura sacra absconditur. Et applicant explicite, ut debite serviant Deo suo, sunt heedem leges humane ..."

[3] Benrath, *Bibelkommentar*, p. 324.

[4] *DB*, p. 262: "Nec valet dicere quod oportet legem istam mutari; quia est lex Cristi eterna, cui non est superior successera." See also *DCD*, 396: "Pro dicendis in ista materia suppone quod lex Christi includat omnem legem quam Christus docet suum discipulum facere vel implere, cuiusmodi est lex cuiuscunque virtutis faciende et lex vicia puniendi; et eadem est lex Scripture, lex caritatis, et lex Dei."

[5] *Ibid.*, p. 397: "... Scriptura sacra (que est lex Christi) continet in se omnem veritatem, omnis lex est veritas, ergo continet in se omnen legem." See also *VSS*, I, 100; *DCD*, I, 347-350, 469; *SS*, I, 376; *DOR*, p. 222.

[6] "... tota lex Cristi est unum perfectum verbum, procedens de ore dei, cuius singule partes concausant totam auctoritatem vel efficaciam legis Cristi ..." *VSS*, I, 268.

of all error, this work manifests God's every wish, His every ordin-
ance. 7 Confirming Augustine's opinion, Wyclif agrees that all law,
all philosophy, all logic, and all reason are to be found in Holy
Scripture. 8

Viewing the Bible this way, Wyclif reasoned that what obtained
in God's word, should obtain in His Church, whether its condition
be militant, sleeping, or triumphant. What is true for the Bible is
true for the church because "the law of the Scripture is the law of
reason and consequently the law of Christ and His Church." 9 Scripture is, as Wyclif so nicely puts it, "the charter of Holy Mother
Church"; it cannot be contrary to the church 10 and with truth, so
with its alter ego, law: "All law useful to the Holy Mother Church
is taught explicitly or implicitly in Scripture." 11

Found in the Bible, all true law stands revealed by Christ, its
author and "our legislator." 12 As the "summus legifer" and the most
prudent lawgiver, Christ is at once creator and guarantor of the
eternal, the natural, and the written law. 13 And since no empire,
realm, city or community can live without the regulation of law,
even Christ's empire, the world and His realm, the Bride, must have
its law. 14 Just as the emperor founded civil law and the king the

---

7 "Omnis veritas et omnis erroris destruccio est in evangelio ..." OE, I, 91, and
DS, p. 66: "Oportet ergo ad iudicandum aliquid esse ordinatum consulere legem dei,
in qua omnis dei volucio vel ordinacio est contenta; nichil enim est licitum nisi de
quanto ordinacioni et volucioni dei fuerit conformatum."

8 VSS, I, 22.

9 "Cum enim lex predicta sit lex racionis et per consequens lex Christi et sue
ecclesie ..." VSS, III, 29.

10 "Veritas scripture sacre non potest esse ecclesie sancte contraria, et solum
illud dogma est hereticum, quod est contra ecclesiam. Solum igitur illi, qui contra
scripturam sacram, que est carta sancte matris ecclesie, conspirant et senciunt,
sunt censendi heretici, eo quod solum illi sunt contra ecclesiam." VSS, I, 370.

11 DE, p. 173: "Omnis lex utilis sancte matri ecclesie docetur explicite vel implicite in scriptura ..."

12 (Scriptura sacra), "cum ipsa sit autor summus et prima regula," VSS, III,
48, and DCD, I, 404: "Quamvis autem Legifer noster 'illuminat omnem hominem
venientem in hunc mundum, inprimendo primo omnium in eo noticiam transcen-
dentis, et per consequens docendo eum omnia."

13 "... et sic vita virtuosa moraliter est habitu vel actu memorari, noscere, velle,
agere vel pati in voluntariis rebus secundum diffinicionem legislatoris prudentissimi."
DEP, p. 267. For Christ as "summus legifer" or "noster Legifer" see DEP, p. 118,
and Dialogus, p. 7. Benrath, Bibelkommentar, p. 324, treats Christ as the creator
and guarantor of the law.

14 "... cum ergo nec imperium nec regnum, ymmo nec civitas nec societas potest
consistere sine lege, patet, quod oportet credere de provida bonitate dei, quod dedit
sue ecclesie quandam legem. Non enim deficit corporibus inanimatis, vegetabilibus

law of the land, so Christ, "noster Legifer," authored the law of
nature, the evangelical law, for His subjects. [15] With the erection of
His community came the foundation of His law, the Old and New
Testaments. [16]

This law of Christ overwhelms all others, reflecting as it does the
perfection of its craftsman. [17] It is the product of perfection, and
therefore as superlative as its maker. [18] "That law ... is the sacred
scripture and the immaculate law of the Lord, which one is to accept
from faith because it is the best law and consequently truest, most
complete and most salubrious ..." [19] As early as his *Commentary*
on the Bible, Wyclif adjudged Christ's law to be superior to all
others, arguing that it is "clearer, shorter, more noble and more
useful." [20] Much later in the *Sermones*, Wyclif comes back to this

---

vel sensitivis, quin ordinat eis legem; multo magis non deficeret sponse sue." *VSS*,
I, 155.

[15] "Christus autem convertit aquam in vinum, quando revocavit populum a ritu
gentili vel pharisaico frigido instar aque, ut gustet legem sapientem caritatis dulce-
dinem. Et oportuit Christum hoc facere, cum constat quod nec imperium nec regnum
nec civitas nec quevis communitas potest legitime conversari sine lege regulante;
et hinc imperator condidit legem civilem, rex legem terre sue, civitas legem suam et
breviter quelibet communitas cleri vel populi militat sub lege. Ex quibus sequitur
quod Deus cuius imperio subiacet totus mundus, cuius regnum est ecclesia sponsa
sua, cuius civitas est pusilus grex clericorum, dedit subditis istis legem nature, legem
evangelii et legem consilii." *SS*, IV, 233-234.

[16] "Ad primum suppono ex fide quod Christus instituit unam legem, que est
Vetus et Novum Testamentum ad ecclesiam catholicam regulandum ..." *DCD*, I, 118.
Benrath, *Bibelkommentar*, p. 261ff. sets out a number of passages in the *Commentary*
demonstrating the essential unity of the Bible, i.e. how the two basic testaments were
for Wyclif dependent upon one another.

[17] *VSS*, II, 142.

[18] "Suppono secundo id quod in primo argumento supponitur, scilicet quod omnia
debent esse communia; patet ex dictis superius, capitulo xiv. Ex istis argumentatur
sic: Summe potens, sciens, et benivolus non ordinat inperfecte aliquid (cum eque
perfecta sunt opera recreacionis, sicut creacionis, ut patet supra capitulo x.); sed
Christus cepit constituere novam legem ...; ergo sequitur quod ipsam consumavit."
DCD, I, 118-119.

[19] "Ista lex, quecunque fuerit, est scriptura sacra et lex domini inmaculata, quam
oportet ex fide capere, quod sit lex optima et per consequens verissima, completissma
et saluberrima, quam omnes homines tenentur cognoscere, defendere ac servare, cum
secundum illam tenentur sub obtentu eterni premii domino ministrare." *VSS*, I, 155.

[20] "... lex evangelica excellit alias leges adhuc causa multicipli primo propter
planiciem, secundo propter compendiositatem, tercio propter subiecti nobilitatem,
et quarto propter sui utilitatem. (2. Prolog zu Mt) WI d.)" Benrath, *Bibelkommentar*, p. 98, n. 29. Wyclif repeats this, as was his wont, some pages later in his
Commentary. "... cum lex ista excellit omnes alias, ut patet in prologo, et doctrina
debet excedere omnem aliam in compendiositate, claritate, efficacia et sufficiencia.
(W 18c)" p. 112, n. 94.

point; it ought to be obvious, he writes, "that Christ's law is short, useful and light, not burdening the sons of God as the ceremonies of the Old Testament nor consuming its legists in tedious study as the caesarian laws." [21]

Wyclif further asserts that the estate which Christ instituted is "more perfect in these three aspects; it is more secure, more meritorious and easier." [22] Christ's law, as the work of perfection, is not defective —it could hardly be so—and therefore is neither superfluous nor inadequate. [23] It stands alone and without the cooperation of man. If human additions are not at least implied in Christ's work, then they are hostile, repugnant, and evil.

Another category includes those laws of men that are neither implied in nor opposed to Scripture; that is, laws that are simply impertinent. Wyclif challenges these too: If they are not relevant to God's law, he argues, then they connote an incompleteness in Christ's law. To be incomplete is to be imperfect and to assert this is blasphemy. [24] The sufficiency of the law of Christ is pointed out repeatedly. [25] In

---

[21] "Princcipium autem debet esse fidelibus quod lex Christi est levis, brevis et utilis, non onerans Dei filios ut ceremonie veteris testamenti nec consumens suos legistas in studio tedioso ut leges cesarie, sed in opere brevi ac delectabili reficiens sibi fideliter adherentes." *SS*, III, 401.

[22] "Nam status quem Christus instituit est perfeccior in hiis tribus: est securior, meritorior atque facilior. Securior quidem, quia auctor nature pro salvacione perpetua corporis et anime ipsum instituit. Est meritorior, quia ordinacioni Dei conformior et statui innocencie propinquior. Et est facilior, quia inducta salute anime delectabilior et ab arte humana distancior." *OM*, pp. 218-219.

[23] "In Christo autem vel sua scriptura secundum fidem Apostoli non fuerunt *est et non*, sed oportet supponere ex fide catholica quod lex Christi non sit superflua, diminuta vel aliter defectiva." *SS*, II, 57.

[24] Item si legem Christi posset homo supplendo perficere, cum talis supplecio se haberet per modum formalis complementi, sequitur quod perfectissimum legis Christi posset eius vicarius ordinaire: consequens impossibile ... Confirmatur: Vel esset lex superaddita in lege evangelica inplicata vel inpertinens vel repugans ... Et ne fiat equivocacio ex amplo ambitu signi legis, suppono quod lex evangelica sit lex a Christo pro tempore sue viacionis exposita ad regimen militantis ecclesie requisita. Quo supposito, videtur blasphemium dicere quod illa lex Christi sine nova humanitus superaddita non sit sufficiens; tum quia quodlibet eius particulare observare sufficeret, tum eciam quia doctrina humana et eius ordinacio foret doctrina et ordinacione Christi perfeccior, tum tercio quia ante edicionem illius legis addite, non foret ecclesia debite regulata, quod dictum quilibet catholicus pius abhorreret." *DCD*, I, 120. See also for the sufficiency of Christ's law, *DCD*, I, 391, 427; *VSS*, I, 395, 399, 402; *VSS*, II, 181-184; *PW*, I, 257; *SS*, I, 83.

[25] "Ex dictis septimo colligi potest quod non licet Christiano post plenam publicacionem legis Christi extraneas leges sibi condere ad regimen Christi ecclesie. Patet primo tripliciter de virtute sermonis. Nam omnis bona lex est lex Christi ergo nulla est sibi extranea. Similiter nemo citra Christum est proprie legis conditor, sed

Wyclif's effort for reform, it becomes a talismanic averter of evil.

The governance of the church necessitated a law. "Scripture, execu-
ted duly according to its primary sense ought to suffice for the
universal rule of the Church Militant without the addition of human
laws." [26] Because of this divine sufficiency, "the clergy either dege-
nerate in accepting unfounded traditions or, if the traditions have
foundation, they should go straight to their source." [27] Wyclif's
admonition was to return to the evangelical law instituted by God
alone and explained through the word and work of Christ. [28] Anything beyond Christ's word and work was superfluous and profane. [29]
And if this was too general, Wyclif spelled out the law's sufficiency
in practical terms: receiving and distributing alms, determining obediences, and making ordinances beneficial to the church. Christ's law
was plenary. [30]

Christ required His law. It is unchanging and yet, according to
Wyclif, man fails it constantly. The little fire of the law of love that

---

legis primus connaturalis, et per consequens conditor, promulgator; ergo conclusio.
Similiter cum lex Christi pure per se sufficit ad regimen universalis ecclesie, super-
flueret ad hoc novas leges condere quod non licet; omnes ergo leges humane legitime
non sunt nisi lex Christi humanitus promulgata." *DCD,* I, 424ff. See also note above.

[26] "... cum tunc scriptura secundum suum sensum primarium debite executa per
se sufficeret sine superadditis tradicionibus hominum ad regimen universalis ecclesie
militantis." Benrath, *Bibelkommentar,* p. 357.

[27] "Patet ex hoc quod lex Christi est gravissima, quia dei sufficientissima et
completissima cuiuslibet hominis directiva. Ideo clerus, qui attendit tradicionibus aut
consuetudinibus humanis in dei legibus non fundatis. Vel si fundantur implicite dei
legibus clerus non degenerans debet aquam fontalem illius sapiencie de fonte illo
omninio habiliori accepere, et aquam stagnalem humanam postponere. Et servato
illo modo laudabili purificaretur lex dei et purgaretur ecclesia ab istis erroribus per
diabolum introductis." *Dialogus,* p. 78. For the "oldest is best" argument, see the
examples used by Wyclif in establishing an English tradition as quoted or cited by
Edith Tatnall, "John Wyclif and Ecclesia Anglicana," *The Journal of Ecclesiastical
History,* XX (1969), 20. See also *De Eucharista,* p. 279, where Wyclif notes that
the decretum of Nicolas II was more probably more authoritative than a later one
"not only," he says, "because there were more bishops, or because it was older,
closer to the fount of Christian faith, but ..." Proximity to source counted.

[28] "Ius divinum est ius a solo Deo institutum, per Christum verbo et opere expla-
natum, ut lex ewangelica." *DCD,* I, 125. See also *DCD,* I, 118; *Dialogus,* p. 78.

[29] "Nec dubium quin lex Christi, secundum formam qua ipsam edidit, conpen-
diosius ducit illum finem quam humanitus superaddita; ergo, etc. Item non licet
condere leges inutiles, superfluas, et prophanas ad onus ecclesie; huiusmodi forent
omnes leges tales extranee; ergo conclusio." *DCD,* I, 426, 401.

[30] "Sufficit enim lex Christi ad suscipiendum et distribuendum quascunque elemosinas, ad faciendum quascunque legitimas obediencias et ad faciendum quascunque
ordinaciones ecclesie edificatorias. Nonne credimus, apostolos omnia ista secundum
legem ewangelii perfeccius complevisse, quam complentur hodie secundum tradiciones
hominium introductas?" *VSS,* II, 270.

Christ set aflame should convert and consume all Christians. Instead, His fire gradually has grown tepid from the apostles to the martyrs, and from these to the "confessors" and from this time "the love of many grew cold down to the most manifest traitors of the Lord." [31] Yet contemporary conditions forced Wyclif to agree with Ezekiel: "Behold in peace my bitterness is most bitter." Again and again, in work after work, Wyclif returns to this phrase; in each case, from the *Commentary* forward, it functions as a statement of departure.

> It was bitter indeed from the Tyranny in the time of the martyrs, more bitter from the obvious heresy in the time of the confessors, but most bitter from the hypocracy, simony and ambition of worldly honor in the time of the traitors; and this came after the mortifying poison was spread in the Holy Church of God. [32]

The church initially had flowered under the tyrant's sword but, from the time of Constantine, the church had fallen away—its leaders had forsaken God and instead had placed their trust and confidence in their worldly riches. [33]

To Wyclif the motive force behind this ecclesiastical failure was the emperor Constantine. With imperial endowment came the addition of human laws which were mixed with the purity of Christ's law. The church that had thrived began, as a result of this miscegenation, a long and continuous decline. [34] Endowed now with secular holdings,

---

[31] "Lex igitur Christi manet immobiliter per se sufficiens, sed deficiunt exequentes. Si enim paucus ignis legis amoris, quem Christus venit mittere in terram ut ardeat, suffecit tantam conversionem secularem consumare in primitiva ecclesia, et alios ad religionem Christianam convertere, alios consumere; quanto magis eque incensus ignis difusior in materia tam capaci? Sed heu, iste ignis graditime tepuit ab apostolis ad martires, ab eis ad confessores, et abhinc 'refrigescebat caritas multorum' ad manifestissimos Domini proditores, ..." *DCD*, I, 296.

[32] "... sic quod mater ecclesia potest illus dictum Ezechie, Ysa. xxxviii. 17, 'Ecce in pace amaritudo mea amarissima.' Amara quidem fuit ex tiranide tempore martirum, amarior ex patenti heresi tempore confessoru, sed amarissima ex ypocrisi, symonia, et ambicione honoris mundani tempore proditorum; et hoc postquam diffusum est venenum mortificans in ecclesia sancta Dei." *Ibid.*

[33] "Unde post dies multos visitaberis, id est punieris, quia oportet maliciam crescere et ecclesiam malignancium per antichristum personaliter visitari, quod erit prope finem mundi, quia in novissimo annorum venies ad terram, que reversa est a gladio, quod tunc erit, quando seducet gentes terrenis inhiantes, ut iam facit ecclesia postquam reversa est a persecucione gladii post eius dotacionem, quia 'in pace' est eius 'amaritudo amarissima.' Nam ecclesia primo fuit florens sub gladio tirannorum, sed a tempore Constantini habens pacem a gladio reversa est. Hec inquam ecclesia de populis gencium educta est, qui habitaverunt in ea confidenter universi post tempus Constantini quo dimittentes timorem dei confidebant in diviciis. (Hes 38, 8) N 170 a b." Benrath, *Bibelkommentar*, p. 86, n. 201.

[34] "Cum itaque lex caritatis sufficit, ergo lex Scripturarum. Confirmatur ex facto:

the clergy lost its commitment to a spiritual charge and instead encroached upon the prerogatives and duties of the other estates making up the church. Chaos resulted: God's order and God's law were disregarded and made ineffective. Although the church was emancipated under Constantine, and although it gained in wealth and material position, this accommodation caused it to lose its spiritual life. [35] The bitterness grew. For Wyclif, Constantine's action was a source of constant brooding and he spent many pages documenting proscriptive lists of Constantine's crimes. [36]

There was a medieval tradition that thought of Constantine and his donation as at best "insalubrious." Many reformers actually considered it destructive of the true church and toxic in its effect. The alleged diabolical nature of Constantine became progressively apparent as criticism of the institutional church intensified. In the heat of such criticism, an apothegm emerged; when Constantine had endowed the church in the fourth century, an angel of the Lord was heard to say, "Today poison has been vented into the Holy Church of God." The story was used widely and to good effect. [37]

---

nam, quando ecclesia crescebat ab uno supposito usque ad gradum eius maximum inter tot adversantes, sine regimine iuris civilis sive canonici, regulata fuit lege simplici caritatis; et expost, quando istas duas immiscuit, ut asserunt considerantes status ecclesie, continue decrescebat." DCD, I, 121. This same volume, p. 431, expresses a similar sentiment: "Et iterum quia pure per observanciam legis Christi sine conmixtione tradicionis humane credit ecclesia celerime, et post contradiciones humane provocant secularia desideria, que sunt legi Christi contraria."

[35] See DPP, p. 198, where Wyclif quotes Ralph Higden's Polychronicon, V, 130. Writing of Constantine's donation, Higden says, "whence Jerome wrote in the lives of the Fathers, when it (ecclesia) grew in possessions, it declined in virtues." (Unde Jeronimus scripsit in vitis patrum, ecclesia ex quo crevit in possessionbus, decrevit in virtutibus.) See also OM, p. 23f.

[36] Having castigated an opponent who attempted to use the donation of Constantine as found in the Decretum, XCVI. dist., c. 13-14 (Friedberg, I, 342-345), Wyclif continues with even more invective: "Hic iste doctor insipide balbutit suam stulticiam, cum probabiliter creditur, nec scit iste doctor probare oppositum, quin iste Constantinus ex hoc, quod Christo fuit tam stolide adversatus, sit iam profundius dyabolus condempnatus. Ideo si sit catholicus de Christo cogitans, assumeret cum isto quod vel facto probare non poterit quod dictus Constantinus in hoc opere habuit licenciam a domino capitali, quia nec ex fide evidet; aliter crimen Constantini in hoc fuit dampnabile et non accipiendum a catholico vel a fidelibus approbandum." OM, p. 226; DB, pp. 54-55, 61.

[37] In the DPP, pp. 197-198, Wyclif speaks of the "diminution of the church," the reasons for this and then asserts that the chronicles confirm this opinion: "Narrat enim Cestrensis libro 86 cap. quomodo 'ex tunc ecclesia Romana quanto plus cepit ditari, facta est magis instabilis, adepta plus sollicitudinis et subieccionis, quam spiritualia devocionis, plus exterioris assecuta pompositatis quam interioris ut creditur felicitatis. Proinde et hostis antiquus facta per Constantinum hac publica

Whatever its genesis, the theme of the poisoned church became current, if not catholic, in the fourteenth century. Wyclif remarks in the tract *De Civili Dominio* that the *original* state of the church was more secure, more meritorious, and more perfect than that of the contemporary church because it was instituted by Christ. "For this reason, many chroniclers note that, with Constantine's gift, an angelic voice was heard in the air: 'Today poison was inserted into the holy church of God.'" [38] That angelic voice became for Wyclif a favorite litany. [39] Constantine—by drawing the church into the web of secular affairs and by overburdening it with lands and riches—had poisoned the church and had created an estate less perfect than that of Christ's institution. [40] "The devil, by seducing Constantine, mixed in venomous glue by endowing the church." [41]

---

largicione ecclesiis legitur publice in aere proclamasse 'hodie infusum est venenum in ecclesia.' Unde Jeronimus scripsit in vitis patrum, ecclesia ex quo crevit in possessionibus decrevit in virtutibus."

[38] "Ex istis colligitur quod licet dotacio ecclesie clericorum per temporalia sit licita et meritoria utrobique, tamen status primevus fuit securior, meritorior atque perfeccior. Patet primo ex hoc quod Christus primevum statum instituit; secundum autem errabilis humana devocio. Ideo cronicantes notant quod in ista dotacione ecclesie vox angelica est audita in aere: 'Hodie diffusum est venenum in ecclesia santa Dei." *DCD*, III, 232-233.

[39] *Ibid.*; *Trialogus*, p. 309ff.; *DPP*, p. 168, 198; *DE*, p. 369, 317ff.; *OM*, p. 243; *DCD*, III, 233. Occasionally, Wyclif identifies his source; *DE*, p. 317-318, gives the source of the legend as Henry de Gandano: "Unde contendimus instancius circa iurisdiccionem et secularem dominacionem tamquam nobis privilegium requisitum, quod tangit Doctor Solempnis, VI quolibeto q. XXIII, sed cum formidine: 'quod', inquit, 'ecclesiastici temporalium habeant jurisdiccionem forte non multum expedit et erat forte venenum quod legitur cecidisse in ecclesia Dei tempore Constantini qui in iurisdiccione sua dotavit ecclesiam, sed non assero." Wyclif was not afraid to, and often when he did so, he quoted or cited Ralph Higden. *OM*, p. 243: "Ideo sicut factum diaboli non hoc opus iustificat, sic factum huius cesaris non iustificat istud opus; nec aliqua cronica istud temptat, nisi quod cronicator Cistrensis narrat quomodo tempore huius dotacionis audita est vox evangelica ita dicens: 'Hodie effusum est venenum in ecclesia sancta Dei." In *DPP*, p. 198, Wyclif also acknowledges Higden as his source. Johann Loserth, "Johann von Wiclif und Guilelmus Peraldus. Studien zur Geschichte der Entstehung von Wiclif's Summa Theologiae," *Sitzungsberichte der Kaiserlichen Akademie der Wissenschaften zu Wien*, philosophisch-historische Klasse, 180 (1917), 14, 43, takes the position that Wyclif dredged up this story out of Peraldus' *De Avaritia*. Supporting his contention, Loserth gives the following quotation: "Quare Deus in primitiva ecclesia noluit temporalia coniuncta esse spiritualibus." Continuing some pages later, he adds: "Sed magis occupata est hodie ecclesia in temporalibus quoad magnam partem sui quam fuerit synagoga; unde quanto datum fuit a Constantino occidentale imperium ecclesiae Dei." Again, while it is quite possible Wyclif had read of the proclaiming angel in Peraldus, there is no reason, given the catholicity of the legend, to assume that he in fact did. Accessibility is not usage.

[40] "... et clerus inclinabitur ad statum pristinum, quem Christus instituit clero

4

Because of the donation, Constantine was "a contemptible devil" and the donation itself was characterized as the work of the Antichrist. [42] Of course this gift had been accomplished by both "laymen and theologians, as is clear from Constantine with his council and Sylvester." [43] Nevertheless, the "crime" of Constantine's endowment "was damnable and not accepted as catholic nor aproved by the faithful." [44]

Wyclif perceived one of the more odious results of Constantine's donative act to be the introduction of the concept of jurisdiction into the tradition of the church. It was, in Wyclif's words, "a poisonous term, knowing pride, sloth and cupidity" and, like the donation, it had been "introduced by the devil's craft" through the vehicle of Constantine. [45] Moreover, this "power of jurisdiction" stems not from the authority of Christ but from "Caesar Constantine." [46] Such jurisdiction is truly repugnant: [47] It is in contrast to Christ's authority, for there are but "two orders of authority of the church, namely the jurisdictional and the evangelical. [48]

On the basis of this Constantinian authority, bishops were elevated

---

suo, vivendo exproprietarie in comuni. Qui status est indubitanter perfeccior quam status dotacionis, quam Constantinum cum suis instituit." *VSS*, III, 56. See also *DPP*, pp. 168-169, 247.

[41] "... dyabolus Constantinum seducens dotando ecclesiam viscum immiscuit venenosum." *SS*, IV, 132. Wyclif also compares Constantine to Nebuchadnezzar, see *DE*, p. 369.

[42] *OM*, p. 226; *DPP*, pp. 321, 328; *PW*, II, 700.

[43] "... sicut dotacio ecclesie cepit a laicis atque theologicis, ut patet de Constantino cum suo consilio et Silvestro, sic oportet, quod rectificatur per laicos operantes et theologos instruentes." *VSS*, III, 29. See also *OM*, p. 226, and *DE*, p. 361. These passages are a paraphrase of the *Decretum*, XCVI. dist., c. 13-14 (Friedberg, I, 342-345) containing the donation of Constantine. Kantorowicz, *The King's Two Bodies*, p. 152, n. 188, notes that legislation for both Canonists and Legists rested on counsel and consultation. Gerhoh of Reichersberg is quoted, claiming that Constantine could not have endowed the church "nisi consultis consulibus ceterisque regni maioribus."

[44] "... aliter crimen Constantini in hoc fuit dampnabile et non accipiendum a catholico vel a fidelibus approbandum." *OM*, p. 227. See also *DB*, pp. 54-55, 51.

[45] "Et quantum ad iurisdiccionem videtur quod sit terminus venenosus superbiam, ocium et cupidinem sapiens, ex cautela diaboli introductus." *OM*, p. 136. This passage is quoted in Kaminsky, "Wyclifism," p. 60.

[46] *Ibid.*, p. 133, and *DPP*, p. 232. Interestingly enough Marsilius of Padua, *The Defensor Pacis*, trans. A. Gewirth (New York, 1956) II, 93, 305, attributes the acquisition of coercive jurisdiction by the papacy to Constantine's donation.

[47] *DPP*, p. 75.

[48] "Nec offenderet ista sentencia pias aures cuiusquam episcopi vel prelati. Sunt enim duo ordines in ecclesia dignitatum; scilicet iuridiccionalis et evangelicus." *DCD*, III, 369.

above priests and the Roman bishop came to reign over all other bishops. [49] The papal authority that developed from the donation could not have been derived from a source other than Constantine —not from Christ, Peter, nor Clement. None of these men had possessed the papal title; it was impossible for the very term "pope" had been invented in the course of Constantine's donation. Not found in Scripture, "it seems that in the donation of the church the term was invinted." [50] In Wyclif's opinion, this was hardly novel, for Canon law stipulated that Constantine had given Sylvester imperial power, vigor, and honor "by determining that he should have primacy over the four apostolic sees and be the prince of all the priests of the world." [51] Of all the bishops of Christendom, Constantine decided that he would constitute his bishop, the bishop of Rome, more dignified. [52]

For Constantine, however—at least according to Wyclif—dignity was equated with superiority in "wordly glory" (a heretical notion to be sure) and the Antichrist, "following in this error, amplified that heresy." [53] Wyclif also notes how such chroniclers as Higden repeatedly relate the imperial creation of the papacy: That Constantine elevated the Roman bishop above all others. [54] For Wyclif and others

---

[49] *PW*, II, 669; *VSS*, III, 232; *DE*, p. 232: "... et isto modo constituit Constantinus quod episcopus Romanus sit dignior aliis, ..." See also *DPP*, p. 177.

[50] "Quantum ad istud, sepe est dictum alibi quod ex nulla auctoritate legis gracie papatus potest concludi, cum Christus non fuit papa, nec Petrus, nec Clemens, nec aliquis ante dotacionem ecclesie. Unde cum nomen pape non est terminus scripture, ..." *OM*, p. 262. *The Dialogus*, p. 49, states: "Et sic cum hoc nomen papa sit terminus extra fidem scripture, videtur quod in dotacione ecclesie presumpta per cesarem est inventum." *PW*, II, 678, as quoted by Fürstenau, *Wiclif's Lehren*, p. 98, repeats this: "... sed iste terminus papa et hec sompniata sentencia non sunt fundata ex racionibus vel scriptura."

[51] "Unde notet homo formam dotacionis, XCVI dist. Constantinus, quomodo imperator tribuit Silvestro potestatem, vigorem et honorificenciam imperialem, 'decernendo quod habeat primatum super quatuor sedes et princeps sacerodibus tocius mundi existat'." *DE*, p. 361. Here again Marsilius of Padua agreed that "it was Constantine who gave to the Roman bishop and church this leadership or priority." *Defensor Pacis*, p. 305.

[52] "Ex quo notandum est quod ad reges pertinet statum sacerdotum et ministrorum ecclesie ordinare; sic enim licet perverse ordinavit Constantinus suum sacerdotem Romanum super omnes sacerdotes christianismi prepone; ..." *SS*, II, 96. Another example would be *SS*, II, 184: "Constantinus autem qui civiliter instituit suum episcopum esse summum non est allegandus tamquam fidem faciens, ..." See also *DPP*, p. 215; *DE*, p. 323.

[53] *Ibid.*, p. 299: "Nam licet Constantinus imperator decrevit suum eqiscopum atque clerum esse superiorem in mundana gloria quam reliquos in privatis aliis provinciis ..."

[54] "In qua materia credendum est cronicis. Narrat enim Cestrensis libro IV,

"the origin of the name and its excellence" was easily discerned for it was set down "in the donation of the church as specified in the *Decretum*." [55]

Although the donation stemmed from Constantine, the motivation was from Rome; the Roman bishop had sought this endowment, had desired to be elevated. The emperor might have been the means, but the motive force was clearly Roman. [56] The popes then have usurped their power not from Christ but from the emperor Constantine. [57] What an "irreligious presumption" it was for the emperor "to have decreed that generally his bishop would be the head of the whole church." [58] Certainly the papacy and its line of successive popes constituted a Constantinian institution, an institution whose imperial foundation found ample testimony in the law of the church itself. [59]

Papal authority rests on a single legal foundation, the jurisdictional system established by Constantine. It is a human tradition that rests on caesarian domination and the concessions of a "frivolous Constantine." [60] Polarization had set in: God's law and human tradition are now antipodes. Constantine's creation of papal primacy and bestowal of jurisdiction did not introduce a "new article of faith" necessary for the efficacy of the redemptive process. It was not necessary to be subject to the Roman pope; it would in fact be intolerable to have an individual's salvation predicated upon papal dominion. [61] Wyclif pointed out decisively and historically that prior to Constantine and his endowment "there was neither an endowed Roman church nor had it been decreed that the bishop of that church should have primacy over others." [62] Constantine's gift was perhaps many-splendored, but it was not included as an article of faith.

---

cap. XXXVI, quomodo excellencia Romani imperii adinvenit papatum sui pontificis super alios ..." *DPP*, p. 177f.

[55] "Origo autem istius nominis et excellencie fuit in dotacione ecclesie, ut specificat Decretum XLVI distinccione 'Constantinus.'" *Ibid.*

[56] *Ibid.*, p. 179.

[57] "Immo certum videtur ex cronicis quod non a Christo sed a Cesare Constantino Romanus episcopus usurpavit huiusmodi potestatem. Et patet historia in Decretis XCVI, dist. 'Constantinus'." *OM*, p. 133.

[58] "... quanta irreligiosa presumpcio in cesare statuere, quod generaliter suus episcopus foret caput tocius ecclesie aut quod maioritatem civilem sub pallio privilegii contra decretum Christi in ecclesiam suam induceret?" *DPP*, p. 319. See also *DOR*, pp. 18-19.   [59] See *DPP*, p. 246; *OM*, p. 133; *DE*, p. 361, and *DOR*, p. 36.

[60] *SS*, II, 324.

[61] "Dotatio ergo ecclesie non introduxit novum articulum fidei, ut sit necessarium ad salutem cuiuslibet christiani sic subici Romano pontifici." *DE*, p. 35.

[62] "Item tempore Constantini fuit sacerdocii translacio, et exhinc successit regni

In addition to the creation of the papacy, however, the gift did call for the formation of a hierarchy within the developing institution of the church. Bishops were elevated over priests and these, in turn, stood under the bishop of Rome; above all other priests and bishops reigned the Roman bishop. Wyclif could only view this development with concern: "It is doubtful," he said, "if it is permitted to establish degrees of dignity within the church, like pope, archbishop, bishop and archdeacon ..." [63] Later he was sure. Hierarchical modalities within the church were aberrant forms that had been invented by "caesarian pride." [64] It was pride that led Constantine to set up his bishop above all others, for just as he ranked over all secular lords, it was only fitting that his priest would stand higher than the priests of other lords. [65] Even Wyclif's opponents argued that, just as earlier the church had been ruled through Peter and his companions, "so likewise from the ordination of Constantine, it is fitting that the church be ruled by grades of caesarian prelates." [66] Naturally Wyclif concurred; that was exactly what he had been saying. Wyclif, however, pointed his accusatory finger at Constantine and turned papal argu-

---

sui stabilicio. Prius quidem nec fuit ecclesia romana notabiliter dotata, nec fuit decretum, quod episcopus illius ecclesie haberet necessario primatum in alios, ut hic supponitur." *VSS*, III, 232.

[63] "Secundo dubitatur si licet statuere gradus in ecclesie dignitate, ut papa, archiepiscopi, episcopi, archidiaconi officiales sese respiciunt hodie ut domini seculares; confundere autem hos ordines esset maiorem partem legum ecclesie perturbare." *SS*, II, 184.

[64] "... unum audacter assero quod in primitiva ecclesia ut tempore Pauli suffecerunt duo ordines clericorum scilicet sacerdos atque diaconus. Secundo dico quod in tempore apostoli fuit idem presbyter atque episcopus. ... Et idem testatur ille profundus theologus Hieronymus, ut patet XCV dist. cap. "Olim," tunc enim non fuit adinventa distinctio papae et cardinalium, patriarcharum et archiepiscoporum, episcoporum et archidiaconorum, officialium et decanorum cum ceteris officiariis et religionibus privatis, quorum non est numerus neque ordo ... Sed ex fide scripturae videtur mihi sufficere, esse presbyteros atque diaconos servantes statum quod superbia Caesarea hoc gradus et ordines adinvenit; ..." *Trialogus*, pp. 296-297, as quoted in Fürstenau, *Wiclif's Lehren*, p. 100, n. 181, with other examples. An interesting passage is found in the *Dialogus*, p. 83: "et sic, quasi ut legem nature similem, introduxit diabolus quod necesse est papam et prelatos alios taliter prepollere. Et totum istud est falsitas ipocritica infundabilis et religioni Christi contraria, per quam ecclesia militancium est seducta."

[65] "... sicut papa dat regi regnum sic rex terrenus facit suum episcopum esse papam, ut patet de Constantino, et generaliter imperatores fecerunt quod romani episcopi forent tante preeminencie super alios episcopos, ut patet in Cronica Cestrensi ..., ubi dicitur quod nicena synodus hoc privilegium contulit romano pontifici, ut sicut Augustus pro ceteris regibus ita Romanus pontifex pre ceteris haberetur episcopis et papa velud principalis pater vocaretur." *DOR*, p. 146.

[66] *DPP*, p. 319; *SS*, II, 96.

ments for legitimacy around. Whereas he agreed that Constantine was the source of such innovation, he categorically denied the necessity of the papacy for the governance of the church: "No pope with his college of cardinals, short of Christ, is absolutely necessary to rule chiefly the church of Holy God." [67] In fact, the Church Militant would be more secure and more perfect if this caesarian hierarchy were removed. [68] Hierarchical orders, established through caesarian ordination were an invention of the "diabolical Constantine"—"For after the donation of the church too many aspired to the rank of pope, bishop or caesarian prelate and through this, the devil incited many to be canons, monks and friars ..." [69] Wyclif wanted to see this hierarchy removed. [70]

The Constantinian endowment, then, introduced several factors into the church: the concept of jurisdiction, ecclesiastical possessions, and the creation of the papacy with its hierarchical authority. These elements prompted, or at least allowed for, the institutionalization of the Roman church. All shifted the allegiance of Christians away from the scriptural precepts of Christ's law. Men relied more and more on their attempts to absolutize human traditions.

The results were catastrophic and all too obvious; the church had been poisoned. With Constantine, the evangelical progression of the church stops. Up through that first Christian emperor, the church had flowered, prospered, and grew—it did so even in the early years

---

[67] "Ex istis colligi potest quod nullum papam cum cetu cardinalium citra Christum sit absolute necessarium capitaliter regere ecclesiam sanctam Dei." *DCD*, I, 380. See also *DPP*, p. 245, and Loserth, "Studien," II, 50.

[68] "... ymo patet ex dictis quomodo corpus Christi militaret securius atque perfeccius subducto tali ordine cesareo; nam vivendo omnino exproprietarie, sicut ante dotacionem tempore quo crevit ecclesia, quando pure regulabatur per legem Christi et regebatur per sacerdotes socios sine preeminencia humanitus instituta, melius et perfeccius vixit quam modo ... Tolle igitur dotacionem et tradiciones humanas, quibus preter scripturam sacram occupatur ecclesia et oriretur ecclesie prior status, qui foret indubie similior et disposicior ad ecclesiam triumphantem." *DPP*, pp. 246-247.

[69] "Per hoc enim post dotacionem ecclesie nimis multi ad statum papalem, episcopalem vel prelati cesarei aspirarunt et per hoc diabolus incitat multos esse canonicos, monachos atque fratres, quia quidam viventes modernis valde difformitor ex fallaci signo sunt beati in patria reputati ..." *OM*, p. 187. See also Fürstenau, *Wiclif's Lehren*, p. 101.

[70] "Omnis occasio scismatis, apostasie et blasfemie debet tolli ab ecclesia. Sed precipua occasio omnium istorum est prelatorum graduccio humanitus adventa; ergo racionabiliter debet tolli." *DB*, pp. 49-50. See also *DE*, p. 463; *Trialogus*, pp. 424, 447; *SS*, II, 299; *SS*, III, 453-454.

of Constantine—but then it declined. [71] Wyclif looked repeatedly to one biblical quotation "in peace was my bitterest bitterness." Now endowed with jurisdiction, hierarchy and property, the church turned from God's law to man's, inaugurating centuries of decline. Decline came, then, with human laws, human accretions, and excrescenses, with abuse and interpretation. Jerome said: "as the church grew in possessions, she declined in virtue," and Wyclif added: "Christ's state of expropriation is undoubtedly more perfect than the state of donation which Constantine instituted with his people." [72]

Constantine created a watershed. His endowment of the church, wrongfully accepted by Pope Sylvester, meant the acquisition of jurisdiction and temporal power. [73] As well-meaning as this might have been and however innocent the motivation, it was a violation of Christ's teaching. Sylvester should have rejected the donation. [74] Now, because he had not spurned the gift, both he and his followers in the papal office were not Christ's successors, but Constantine's. The church had fallen away. Accordingly, those true followers of Christ must disassociate themselves from these human growths, these aberrant forms and must return to the evangelical church as founded by Christ.

This view was hardly new. It had been an ever-recurring theme from at least the middle of the eleventh century. The Waldensians had used it, as had others. [75] Christ's Church was set against the Roman church and whatever differences emerged could be placed at the feet of Constantine. Historically, a causal relationship could be established. Constantine was the historical divide, sending the pure, clear stream of evangelical tradition into one watershed, the poisoned, muddied tradition of man into another. Differentiated through Constantine, the history of the church had but two periods. Wyclif found both periods admonitory.

The history of the church from the donation of Constantine became, for Wyclif, a table of decline, a line of increasing deviation from an earlier norm. In Constantine's donation, Wyclif saw the loss of the original pattern. Distortion set in. With the donation there began a series of apostasies, including the creation of the papacy with its jurisdiction, hierarchy, and possessions, which Wyclif assiduously

---

[71] *DE*, p. 299.   [72] *VSS*, III, 56.
[73] *SS*, II, 37-38; *OM*, p. 23.
[74] *DE*, pp. 368-369.
[75] Leff, *Heresy*, I, 9, 193; II, 457-458.

recorded. They were disfigurements—corruptions intruding deep into the church. Consequently the history of the institutional Roman church could only be a history of mistakes and deformation; it was the history of a human community set up in opposition to Christ's Church. Ecclesiastical history therefore became a pedagogical tool, if not a club, whose usefulness was limited to tracing the configurations of decline or to urging a negative comparison.

As Wyclif saw it, the true history of the church is the history of the evangelical period. [76] Its sources of authority were the revelations of Christ's law, supported and buttressed by the revelations found in the Fathers. [77] In effect Wyclif meant that Christ's law was His history—better, His revelation: "Moreover, Christ's every action is our instruction." [78]

The point again was that there was no reason to think theologically in terms of what had developed since Constantine's donation. That would be degenerative. Disregard ecclesiastical history; what transpired subsequent to Constantine can only be the history of the institutional church. Concentrate instead on what is timeless and abstract; concentrate on the record of the archetype, the Bible. It, as the mirror of perfection, was prescriptive, normative, and legally binding. Only the Scriptures can illumine the true Church of Christ; only the Bible can reveal the eternal and omnipresent. Set loose from time, Christ's Church is extra-historical!

The Church Militant had been buried under the accumulations of human novelty. The historical process, in Wyclif's mind, pointed up the contrasts between Christ's foundation and the institutional Roman church. The latter had been introduced in time; it would perish in the same medium, leaving true Christians to live by the eternal law of God. When Wyclif spoke, he spoke not as an historian, but as the proclaimer of the apostolic tradition, when the Church Militant paid its allegiance to God's law. The Church Militant became burdened with the human, the historical, and the innovative, and had fallen away. As proof of this phenomenon, Wyclif reached not only into

---

[76] *Dialogus*, p. 16.

[77] *OM*, p. 220; *DB*, p. 164.

[78] Wyclif uses the phrase "omnis Christi accio est nostra instruccio" as early as his *Commentary*. It certainly was not original with him. Lyra has used it, as had others, and in Benrath's opinion, this phrase already belonged to the general exegetical tradition of the fourteenth century. For Wyclif's usage of this tradition in his *Commentary* as well as a short, historical treatment, see Benrath, *Bibelkommentar*, pp. 184-185, and especially fn. 389. See also *DCD*, I, 199; *DCD*, IV, 457; *VSS*, I, 89.

the mixed historical bag but into contemporary practice as well. In both he found adequate support.

Yet the contemporary clergy stood in contrast to Christ's instruction and in opposition to His law. Failing to follow Christ's example of denigrating wealth and possessions, ecclesiastics and Christians disregarded and rendered ineffective God's law, opting instead for Constantine's. Moreover, the reason was clear to Wyclif—avarice, "the unnatural appetite of temporalities." [79] This sin, Wyclif decided, was the "special temptation of the clergy." [80]

Its pertinence to the clergy revolved about its inescapable effect, idolatry. [81] This gravest of clerical sins was infinitely "more dangerous than carnal luxury," for it was "the root of all evil for the church." [82] This had always been so. Just as avarice had precipitated the decline of the Jews, so it would bring the downfall of Christ's Church. Already its pernicious influence has pervaded every level of the church. [83] Wyclif advised that this was not what Christ wanted; for the clergy to return to Old Testament avarice would be "like a dog to return to its vomit." [84]

An avaricious clergy brought decline—mothered it and made it inescapable. Look at Constantine. At first the privileges granted by Constantine were of value and use, endowment and donation were welcome. But then, in peace and approval came the "bitterest bitterness;" for having once received the taste for possessions and jurisdic-

---

[79] "Ex isto evangelio notari potest primo quomodo avaricia pharisaica ac ypocritica est dampnanda. Quamvis enim omnis avaricia sit ydolorum servitus, tamen prelatorum avaricia quorum gradus debet esse dignior, contemptus mundi intensior et racio ex certitudine temporalium debet esse ab illis distensior, est apud Deum dampnabilior. Et patet huius racio in sermone ante proximo; cum enim avaricia sit appetitus innaturalis temporalium, ..." *SS*, I, 328.

[80] *Ibid.*, p. 126.

[81] *PW*, I, 120; *SS*, I, 90, 328.

[82] "Nam dictum est superius proximo capitulo, quomodo avaricia cleri est peccatum periculosius quam carnalis luxuria et radix omnium malorum ecclesie, ut dicit apostolus." *VSS*, III, 32. See also *VSS*, II, 264-265; *VSS*, III, 162; *Dialogus*, p. 16; *DE*, p. 129.

[83] "Nota tamen quod ypocrisis et cupiditas phariseorum fuit causa subversionis Judaismi ut patet Mt 23. Et ita timendum est de ecclesiasticis nostris onerantibus ecclesiam sive generali sive speciali onere statutis aut iniquis legibus que plus sonant in pompam coactivam et avariciam quam in Christi honorem aut subditorum edificacionem ..." Benrath, *Bibelkommentar*, p. 231, fn. 558. This charge is also to be found when Wyclif comments on the Old Testament, *ibid.*, p. 44, and in *VSS*, III, 94.

[84] "Si enim Christus tam diu et tam dure reprobavit hoc peccatum in sacerdotibus legis veteris, quomodo sacerdotem legis gracie nove movet redire ad dictam avariciam sicut canis redit ad vomitum." *Dialogus*, p. 16.

tion, priests turned from Christ's law, made up their own, and inaugurated decline. In their avarice they squeezed the laity for money, demanded temporalities, and when obstacles slowed their ingestion, they resorted to incessant litigation. [85] Nor did they shrink from the use of secular power as a means of implementing their greed. [86]

A further consequence of this unbridled greed, initiated through Constantine's gift was the total disruption of the God-given order within the Church Militant. [87] The estates of the church, Wyclif thought, once instituted by Christ, had been brought "out of order," with all elements chafing and working against each other. The result was disorder and disarray, [88] and again the cause was avarice. The clergy was enticed to "remain on earth" and remaining they sought constantly to reach into the secular sphere. Failing to stay in their place in God's order, they built upon their own intelligence instead of following the regulations of the Bible. [89] Consequently all parts of the church confusedly and irregularly moved to transgress their normal activities in oposition to one another. [90] Indeed, there could be no God-given order without God's law. As early as the *Commentary*, this idea had been developed by Wyclif in response to the chaos of the contemporary church; it became a hobby horse that he tenaciously rode the rest of his life. [91]

Criticizing the greed of the prelates, the clergy and the church, Wyclif fell back on the traditional sermon literature then so available

---

[85] Benrath, *Bibelkommentar*, pp. 57-58, 328f.; *DM*, ch. VIII; *DOR*, p. 212; *DPP*, pp. 197-198 speaks of the diminution of the church which continually grew stronger. See also *DCD*, I, 121, 396, for decline.

[86] *Ibid.*, p. 61.

[87] This view was not unique with Wyclif. Laehr, "Die Konstantinische Schenkung," p. 128, writes: "Allerdings glaubten manche zu erkennen, dass zu diesen päpstlichen Übergriffen und schliesslich auch zum Schisma die Cupiditas geführt hatte, die seit der Verlehung von weltlichem Besitz, also zuerst und vor allem durch die konstantinische Schenkung, in die Kirche eingedrungen war." See also Haller, *Papsttum und Kirchenreform*, I, 329, and the notes in Laehr for historical usage of this idea before and after Wyclif.

[88] *DOR*, p. 23; Tatnall, *Church and State*, p. 127; Benrath, *Bibelkommentar*, p. 58.

[89] Benrath, *Bibelkommentar*, p. 58, 132: "Si enim sit superbus, tunc presumit quod statui suo non congruit, quod est contra deum qui vult omnia esse ordinata ...," p. 121: "Unde radicalis causa regnacionis dyaboli est peccatum superiorum ecclesie, W12 a; ... per aspectum retro ad temporalia, W12 a," p. 330.

[90] *DOR*, p. 6.

[91] "Et nichil sensibilius conturbat ecclesiam vel inducit in eam morbidam discrasiam quam quod una ejus pars accipiat ministeria alterius, et correspondenter officia et per consequens simittat officia sibimet limitata." *Dialogus*, p. 4. See also Benrath, *Bibelkommentar*, p. 121, n. 130. For quotation see *supra* fn. 89.

and so appropriate. One of the leitmotivs that emerged from his excavations was the prophecy of Isaiah 24:2: "And it shall be, as with the people, so with the priest." St. Bernard hastened to add "but would that they be no worse," for "this, chiefest of all, destroys the church, namely, that we see the laity are better than the clergy." [92] Wyclif thought they were. He further believed that the totality of the clerical estate was primarily concerned with secular affairs and beset by avarice; "it is more deformed than any lay condition." [93] A sub-prior of Durham, Robert Rypon, also thought the clergy worse than the laity. "As the people, so the priests; the people are insolent," he noted, "but the priests are more so." [94] This opinion was not uncommon. [95] Wyclif used it as early as his *De Ente*: "an evil community deserves to have evil prelates." [96] Yet previously—in his first work, the *Commentary*—the emphasis was different: bad priests brought about the ruin of the people. [97]

This notion became an ever-recurring theme in the orchestration of Wyclif's reform movement. "The holy doctors and especially St. Gregory says that 'the greatest ruin of the people has been from the guilt of the priests.'" [98] And not only does the sin of the clergy ruin the people as Christians in the Church Militant, but it ruins the state as well, for "the state stands first and principally in the secular priesthood." [99] The character of the clergy is determinative, for in them rests the merit or the sin of the people, the church and the

---

[92] Owst, *Literature and Pulpit*, p. 268.

[93] "... et sic gradatim per subtilissimas cautelas diaboli, sophisticatur ecclesia a gradu altissimo pure apostolico in sacerdotibus usque ad gradum vilissimum sophistice agregatum. Unde et illud de statu agregato turpissimo considerarent tractantes de maioritate et obediencia, et tunc forte cognoscerent quod status totalis quem sic magnificat sit turpior quam status aliquis laicalis." *DOR*, p. 276.

[94] Owst, *Literature and Pulpit*, p. 271.

[95] *Ibid.*, fn. 3: "Immo multotiens sunt sacerdotes pejores laicis," and numerous other examples.

[96] "Mala communitas meretur habere malum prelatum ..." *Summa de Ente*, pp. 269-270.

[97] "Nam sedando turbaciones passionum ... adquiritur sacrarum noticia scripturarum ... Causa ruine populi sunt sacerdotes mali." Benrath, *Bibelkommentar*, p. 81, fn. 187.

[98] "Super quo dicunt sancti doctores et specialiter beatus Gregorius Omelia XXXIX libri II; quod 'maxima ruina populi ex culpa sacerdotum fuit', ideo primo omnium arguere illos cepit; omnis autem Christi accio est nostra instruccio." *DCD*, IV, 457. This phrase can also be found in *OM*, p. 55; *DOR*, p. 134; *FZ*, p. 262; *VSS*, III, 86, 94, 236.

[99] *Ibid.*, p. 436: "Ex quo processu philosophico videtur primo quod policia stat primo et principaliter in sacerdocio seculari, hoc est in personis laicis honorabilioribus et eroycis docentibus sacras leges ..."

realm. [100] Writing of his contemporaries, Wyclif remarked that now instead of following Christ the clergy ruin whatever they touch with their damning "caesarian avarice." This was why human traditions were attended to while the awareness of God's law was lost, why the "norma rectitudinis" had been subverted and why the decline in the church could be corrected only through a reversion to the law of Christ. [101]

The necessity of reform forced Wyclif to accept a notion of institutional and clerical decline. Not regarding the historical, empirical institution of the Roman church as Christ's Church, he could deal with it only as a human phenomenon introduced by Constantine. It was a temporal institution that was developed "in the process of time"; its clergy, "by declining more from life of innocence, declined more to terrestrial living." [102] Poison was poured into the church with Constantine's donation and whatever its form, avarice, jurisdiction, hierarchy, or the rejection of God's law in favor of fallacious human tradition, the result was the same—decline. [103] Undaunted, however, by the accretions of the past, Wyclif sought to rediscover in the Primitive Church a consciousness of God's law and a relative freedom from innovation. [104]

Was Christ's law to last but three centuries, he asked, and that of the Antichrist forever? [105] His answer, strewn throughout his work, was an emphatic no! Nevertheless, this question must have weighed heavily, for the longer the decline was permitted to continue, the more difficult would be its eradication. The pattern had to be broken immediately and thus a certain urgency attended Wyclif's labors. Still

---

[100] "Ideo totum peccatum regni sicut eius meritum redundat causaliter in eius prepositos spiritales." *VSS*, III, 97. See also the remainder of this rather long passage for further elucidation of this idea.

[101] *DOR*, p. 212.

[102] *Ibid.*, p. 254: "Narratur autem quod Cristus comendet hec quinque dominia secundum ordinem eversum illi ordini quo succedeunt, quia in processu temporis plus declinando a vita innocencie plus declinant ad conversacionem terrestrem."

[103] *DOR*, p. 171, and *DB*, p. 23. Interestingly enough, F. Graus, "Social Utopias in the Middle Ages," *Past and Present*, XXXVIII (1967), 15, has pointed out that people in the Middle Ages tried to connect "the concept of a happy age with the reign of a particular ruler. This had the advantage," Graus contends, "that it was possible to locate the end of that age exactly and explain it." Seemingly, the same could be said negatively or at least Wyclif did.

[104] See Loserth, "Studien," I, 107, fn. 1.

[105] *Dialogus*, p. 16.

there persisted the model of the Primitive Church, Christ's institution, and it was available to all. [106]

Reformation was needed and for Wyclif such a reformation meant a series of erasures, wiping out the human, historical marks inaugurated by Constantine. [107] Reduce the church to its primitive estate, reform the clergy to the state that God had constituted; return to the lost, but ever-present archetype. The traditions of Constantine had to be renounced. Christ's Church had to be released from its historical error and repristinated to its superhistorical purity. But how? Whereas the Scriptures defined Christ's Church and gave shape to the Primitive Church, they were void of regenerative programs.

----

[106] For the purity of the early church and the desirability of its restoration, see *DOR*, pp. 42, 65, 211, 213; *Dialogus*, p. 49, and *DE*, p. 56. This certainly is not a complete list, simply a representative one.

[107] Adolf von Harnack, the noted historical theologian, wrote in his *Wesen des Christentums*, p. 160, that he was convinced that "every really important reformation in the history of religion was primarily a critical reduction." This passage is quoted in Wilhelm Pauck's *Harnack and Troeltsch* (New York, 1968), p. 24.

CHAPTER FOUR

THE RELIGIOUS POLITY

John Wyclif's unequivocal rejection of the historical church as it had developed under papal claims to spiritual and secular sovereignty forced him into a radical reassessment of the relationship between church and state. In doing so he emphatically denied the formidable apparatus of the "Hildebrandine" church which had had as its theoretical goal the "libertas ecclesie." Essentially that "libertas" had meant the establishment of a papal theocracy with the political community subsumed into the church. Wyclif rejected this out of hand; not only did it provide the clergy with a justification for its involvement in the totally secular interests of society, but papal monarchy flew in the face of existing fourteenth century political realities. Instead, John Wyclif offered an alternative. Turning the papal argument on its head, his desire was to integrate the church into the actual political construction of the realm. To do so he retained the Gregorian notion that there existed a fundamental unity between *ecclesia* and *mundus*, while changing the emphasis. In the past this unity had been proclaimed through an identification of the two. The secular sphere bore the cost of this merger absorbed as it was into the spiritual. Christ's Church prevailed, embracing the whole world; between the sacred and the profane there were to be no artificial boundaries, indelible marks or segregated activities. [1]

Wyclif's reformatory template had to conform to this view, which denied the existence of separate entities or spheres for church and world. Moreover, the desired reformation of the church had, of necessity, to involve the whole of the political community. And if the realm or body politic was coterminous with the individual church militant, then its reformation required the support of all its estates, ecclesiastical and lay. What was true practically was even more valid theologically. Hence the true church had been designated as the community of the predestinate, then even within the individual church militant "the distinction between clergy and laity lost its basic

---

[1] Norman F. Cantor, "The Crisis of Western Monasticism, 1050-1130," *The American Historical Review*, LXVI (October, 1960), 57, and Kaminsky, "Wyclifism," p. 62ff.

ecclesiological significance." [2] What has been termed the "vicarate of Christ" replaced the divisive, ecclesiastical distinctions. [3] In this vicariate each individual Christian, whether lay or clerical, was expected to contribute positively to his church in an imitation of Christ; insofar as he did so "he is a vicar of both Christ and of Peter." [4] The foundation of this vicariate was the notion that Christ's every action was our instruction. [5] Every Christian, regardless of estate, had the opportunity to cooperate with Christ in the redemptive process through His imitation. And being incumbent upon all, this same *imitatio* gave an extra, spiritual dimension to all human activity, however secular. [6] The measure of that additional dimension was to be found in the mirror of Scripture, illustrating the normative precepts of God's truth for all of human life. [7] What Wyclif envisaged, therefore, with his identification between the union of the Church Militant and the political community or realm on the one hand and the "vicariate of Christ" on the other, was a thorough-going theocracy. Within the structure of the political church, all estates of the realm were to perform their "imitation" in a manner appropriate to their respective functions.

This proposed evangelical community, which was both political and ecclesiastical, would contain three basic estates: clergy, workers and defenders. [8] Each of these divisions, Wyclif reasoned, would have specific tasks and their interdependence, quite naturally, forced specialization in the proper ordering of the Church Militant. [9] As teachers, laborers and fighters these orders, though hierarchically arranged, would be integral parts of the realm having the responsibility of

---

[2] Kaminsky, *Hussite Revolution*, p. 31.

[3] Kaminsky, "Wyclifism," p. 63. See also Benrath, *Bibelkommentar*, pp. 226, 241-242.

[4] *DE*, p. 366. This quotation is also given by Kaminsky, "Wyclifism," p. 63, n. 39.

[5] For the concept of Christ's every action being for our instruction see above, Chapter III, p. 56, fn. 78. See also *DB*, p. 156, where Wyclif states that Christ's life, being best, ought to be the model for the clergy.

[6] *DPP*, p. 10: "Omnis enim potestas qua homo sanctificiat se vel tempus est potestas spiritualis." This inclusive definition, first pointed out by Kaminsky, "Wyclifism," p. 64, is crucial in the construction of Wyclif's theocracy because it erases so many of the segregating distinctions that emerged from the Gregorian period. For Wyclif's constant injunction to follow Christ through imitation, see *DA*, p. 77; *DB*, p. 91; *VSS*, III, 155f.; *DCD*, I, 76; *DCD*, III, 98.

[7] Kaminsky, *Hussite Revolution*, p. 31.

[8] In addition to the citations given above, Chapter II, fn. 49, see *DB*, p. 216.

[9] *DCD*, I, 185-186.

helping each reciprocally. [10] Complementing one another, these allied elements would constitute a single entity—the realm—under the direction of Christ's law. [11]

The divisions of Church and State, although God-ordained and revalued by Wyclif, correspond nicely to actual conditions of fourteenth century society. [12] The commons, for example, are to labor either with their hands or the mechanical arts; should they serve the laws of God and labor faithfully to maintain the other two orders of society, then they shall be secure. The temporal lords, on the other hand, have a greater responsibility to the community and one fraught with greater danger for they possess in this scheme an office beset with the worldly temptations of pride and greed. [13] This is necessary because of all the estates, they alone are to have wealth for the proper exercise of their office. [14] "Moreover, this office is to defend the law of God, to protect the servants of Christ and to subdue the ministers of the Antichrist." [15] And for this reason, Wyclif argues, they carry the sword. [16] The clergy who make up the third estate occupy the highest position, the one "nearest to heaven"; it ought "to relinquish the world, to vivify the church as the spirit ... and of all estates it should follow Christ closely." [17]

---

[10] "Sicut enim singule partes terre se ipsas et spheram suam usque ad centrum iuvant reciproce, sic regnum debet partes eius singules et specialiter se totum saltem spiritualiter adiuvare." *PW*, I, 242.

[11] *DOR*, pp. 58-59: "Ideo necesse est esse Ierarchias in regno que omnes unam personam unicordem consistuant, scilicet sacerdotes vel oratores, seculares dominos vel defensores, et plebeos vel laboratores ... Quando iste tres yerarchie comproporcionantur in quantitate et qualitate secundum dei regulas regnum procedet prospere."

[12] Fürstenau, *Wiclif's Lehren*, pp. 27-31, has argued, convincingly, that Wyclif's divisions not only reflect actual English conditions, but those operative in fourteenth century parliament.

[13] "Constat quod ecclesia integratur ex tribus partibus quarum prima generacione et infima perfeccione est vulgus vivens de laboricio vel arte mechanica; et ista pars est bona et secura, si servet Dei mandata et labori fideliter sit intenta. Secunda pars ecclesie melior sunt domini temporales, et illa pars perficiens quod incumbit suo officio est perfeccior sed periculosior. Officium autem suum est legem Dei defendere, servos Christi protegere et Antichristi ministros opprimere. Hec enim est causa cur portant gladium, et rex secundum Augustinum est vicarius deitatis. Est autem iste status periculosus et pronus, ut superetur superbia, cupiditate mundana et voluptate accidiosa." *SS*, I, 252-253.

[14] For greater treatment of these points, see *Dialogus*, pp. 2-5.

[15] *SS*, I, 253.

[16] *Ibid.*; see also *DB*, p. 33.

[17] "Tercia vero pars ecclesie optima est clerus dum perficit quod incumbit suo officio; debet enim mundum relinquere, ecclesiam vivificare ut spiritus (sicut notatur Luce IX) et omniquaque proxime sequi Christum." *Ibid.*

These functional divisions are often reiterated, but the discussion is usually prefaced with the concept of the essential vicariate of all. In the second volume of Wyclif's sermons, he writes: "It is fitting, moreover, to have three manners of ministers reciprocally helping each other." [18] And after again depicting the duties of these estates, he concludes that martyrs and saints are to be found in all three parts of this Church Militant. [19] All three estates are properly spiritual. Even laymen can be considered priests in this scheme exercising as they do the priestly obligations, whether absolving or hearing confession. [20] Nor was there any reason why a layman could not reign as Christ's vicar, that is as the pope. [21] Wyclif, in short, blurs the traditional distinctions between clergy and laity. Indelible, visible signatures do not appear. [22] Anyone following Christ's counsels has as much merit as a religious. [23] Each estate is to follow Christ and contribute to the welfare of the church, each in his own manner. [24] Their fruit, he says, will identify them; the commons producing the fruits of the earth; the clergy, virtue; and the nobility, peace by their authority. [25]

In this highly functional, highly integrated system, the realm's parts come to mesh in a rational, even mechanical pattern of support. Concluding one section on the division of the church with an admonishment to aid one another, Wyclif illustrates this principle, declaring that the common people should not be oppressed against the law of God because they are the realm's foundation. Accordingly, they should be stabilized by "the superior parts according to the law

---

[18] "Oportet autem in domo ista habere tres maneries ministrorum reciproce se iuvancium, ut clericos qui debent esse supremi et Deo dignissimi sed non ad honores vel lucra mundana attendere sed totam spem retribucionis future expectare in ecclesia triumphante." *SS*, II, 354.

[19] "Et de omnibus istis tribus partibus contingit esse martyres et gloriosos in ecclesia triumphante. Cum enim Deus non sit acceptor personarum sed dans graciam quibuscunque gloriose certantibus, patet quod quicunque de aliquo istorum trium statuum meritorious agonizaverit est apud Dominum plus acceptus." *Ibid.*

[20] See *DB*, p. 10, 140; *DE*, p. 577; *VSS*, III, 100.

[21] *DPP*, p. 272.

[22] *DPP*, p. 32. For the blurring of distinctions see *ibid.*, p. 10, which is discussed above in footnote 6.

[23] *DB*, p. 10.

[24] *PW*, I, 242. For the quotation see above, footnote 10.

[25] "Et 3: 'a fructibus eorum cognoscetis eos.' Est autem triplex fructus hominis secundum triplicem partem ecclesie, ut pars infima wulgi producit terre nascencia; pars media dominorum secularium pacificat potestative populum; et clerus plantat et rigat in ecclesia semina virtutum. Unde licet iste tres partes ecclesie iuvant se mutuo, et omnes debeant fructus meritorios in caritate producere, tamen in ordinata eorum comixtio mutuo se confundit." *DB*, p. 227.

of God, by the priests spiritually, by the lords temporally." [26] If this
is not done, the realm shall fall.

This artful arrangement was in essence a religious polity; it was to
unite all sections through charity, which, Wyclif said, would descend
from Christ like the ointment of Aaron's head to the clergy, then on
to the nobility and finally the common people. [27] In this fashion the
realm, defined as a religious polity, would become an organic whole
infused with the mystique of the political community with everyone,
including the priesthood, "subject to the political rules." [28] Already
Wyclif has shifted the focus from his earlier evangelicalism that
emphasized the individual imitation of Christ to one which centered
on the Christian community as a political body. In doing so, Wyclif's
religious polity met the problem of developing a reforming ideology
that would at once conform to his conception of the "evangelical"
church of Christ and the actual conditions found in the realm of
England. The nature and scope of this ideology can perhaps be best
illustrated by considering the task Wyclif assigns to theologian and king.

The science of theology was an absolute necessity for the religious
polity Wyclif envisioned. In fact, without it the republic cannot be
saved, the church cannot grow. [29] It is, Wyclif asserted, the most

---

[26] *PW*, I, 242. For the quotation see above, footnote 10.

[27] "Concedat igitur deus, quod totus populus sit unius religionis, exclusis istis
exalacionibus gelidis, ut vir unus; sic quod de illis verificetur istud psalmo 132.
'Ecce quam bonum et quam jucundum habitare fratres in unum. Sicut unguentum
in capite, quod descendit in barbam, barbam Aaron.' Aaron, inquam, figurat summum episcopum, qui supra mensuram habet unguentum gracie et caritatis; 'De cuius
plenitudine nos omnes accepimus,' ut dicitur joh. I. Ab isto, inquam, capite huius
abbatis descendit gracia in clerum Christi, ut apostolos et eorum discipulos, cum sit
barba Aaron superior. Et iterum descendit hoc oleum ad barbam inferiorem, quia ad
dominos seculares. Sed 3 descendit ad 3am partem ecclesie, scilicet populares, eciam
ad abiectissimum genus wulgarium, cum subditur, quod 'descendit in oram vestimenti
eius.'" *DB*, pp. 87-88; see also above Chapter II, p. 35.

[28] "Quinto et ultimo principaliter arguitur per leges ethnicorum philosophancium
supra dictam sentenciam. Nam Aristoteles septimo Politicorum, ut recitatur libro
quinto cap. octavo ponit, quod 'sacerdocium debet esse pars precipua policie.' Nec
dissonat hoc tempore legis gracie racioni imperatoris dotantis ecclesiam, igitur adhuc
dotata ecclesia, debet clerus subici regulis policie." *VSS*, III, 79. *Ibid*.: "Omnis enim
pars est inferior suo toto ..."

[29] "Ideo est sciencia theologica pernecessaria sine qua non potest salvari respublica,
quia per illam crevit ecclesia et post ex eius carencia minoratur. Unde errant notabiliter qui dicunt quod theologi sunt anglie inutiles, quia sine illis non potest pax
Dei ad hominem confirmari." *SS*, IV, 487, and *DB*, pp. 22-23: "Et ad magnam
utilitatem ecclesie, Cristus sic locutus est obscure atque equivoce, ut fideles mereantur
in sensus scrutinio, et ut ecclesia, detestans leges humanas, cognoscat se specialiter
indigere theologis qui interpretentur sibi fideliter legem dei; per illos enim tempore
apostolorum, martyrum et sanctorum doctorum crevit ecclesia."

useful of all the sciences. [30] In addition to being most useful, it was grander than any other form of knowledge. [31] Theology alone was to be the directive art of polity and like Christ's law, it was sufficient for this task because its author was God himself "who alone knows how to institute and instruct in this art." [32] Every other activity or art depended upon it and is subservient to it. [33]

As with Augustinus Triumphus, Wyclif's political writings are more theological than political. [34] For both of them theology is the "finis et domina omnium scientiarum"; both prefer theology over canon law, both emphasize its overwhelming virtues, and both underline the desirability of electing a theologian as pope. [35] They were not the only ones to develop this argument. [36] William of Ockham said as much when he attacked the decretalists with the charge, "the letter killeth, but the spirit giveth life." [37] In Ockham's eyes, the canonists were competent in law and its formal procedures, but limited when recognizing and elucidating the deeper meanings of the law. For this type of direction, one needed the theologian; only he could decipher the true intent of the founders. Theologians should lay out God's law, cut the pattern and then aid its realization in the

---

[30] "Cum igitur bonum non potest acquiri ecclesie sine doctrina huius sciencia, videtur, quod illa sciencia sit utilissima sancte matri ecclesie. Quecunque enim sciencia multiplicaverit in populo virtutes theologicas, hec est sacra theologia sine differencia ligwarum vel forma humanitus instituta." VSS, II, 144.

[31] ... sequitur, quod theologia quoad bonum delectabile exsuperat quascunque alias sciencias. Ipsa enim plus preparat in via ad fidem, spem et caritatem. Cum igitur oportet in predestinatis succedere claram visionem, comprehensionem et plenum amorem, sequitur, quod theologia disponit maxime ad hunc finem. Igitur hec sciencia propter certitudinem procedendi, propter nobilitatem objecti et propter racionem finis ultimi est honoracior cunctis aliis." Ibid., pp. 145-146.

[32] "Ex ista sentencia doctorum que collata est ex infringibili Scriptura, patet primo quod sola theologia sit ars ecclesie et in spiritualibus directiva; secundo patet quod ipsa sit sufficiens ad hoc, cum auctor illius sit Deus, qui solus scit instituere et magistraliter instruere in hanc artem ..." DCD, I, 124.

[33] Ibid.

[34] See Wilks, The Problem of Sovereignty, pp. 6-7.

[35] "Ex quo patet ulterius quod necesse est papam esse theologum; nam sibi ut huiusmodi committitur vicarium regimen in spiritualibus tocius ecclesie militantis, quod non potest cognoscere si non sit theologus; ergo conclusio." DCD, I, 124. For Augustinus Triumphus see Wilks, Problem of Sovereignty, p. 7, and the article by Martin Grabmann, "Die Erörterung der Frage, ob die Kirche besser durch einen guten Juristen oder durch einen guten Theologen regiert werde bei Gottfried von Fontaines and Augustinus Triumphus von Ancona," in Eduard Eichmann Festschrift (Paderborn, 1940), pp. 1-19.

[36] See E. F. Jacob, Essays in the Conciliar Epoch (Manchester, 1953), p. 93.

[37] C. C. Bailey, "Pivotal Concepts in the Political Philosophy of William of Ockham," Journal of the History of Ideas, X (1949), 199.

religious polity. Another theologian, Giles of Rome, had written at the turn of the fourteenth century that kings should respect theologians above all others. [38] What Giles of Rome said earlier, Wyclif repeated. Without the continuation of the theological faculty, Wyclif wrote in the *De Officio Regis*, "the realm cannot possibly stand" because "through it, the reputation of the king is extended and through this the subject is informed of the correct obedience to God and his magistrates." [39]

Given Wyclif's concept of the church as the political community, the importance of the theologian is hardly surprising. Nor was it unusual for Wyclif, after having postulated the necessity of theologians for the stability of the realm, to contend that "the king ought to have theologians helping him in the government of his realm." [40] Not only do theologians qualify to advise, counsel and influence kings on the basis of their biblical knowledge, but they have other definite functions as well. Kings, for example, are to remove heretics from their realms—it is part of their trust and stewardship—but how are they to accomplish this segregating task unless according to the doctrines and judgments of theologians, "who alone know what is contrary to scripture." [41] That is the crux of the issue; once Christ's law becomes the standard by which all else is measured, then its knowledge becomes absolutely obligatory. It becomes, indeed, a truly existential question. Since there is "neither king, realm nor people," Wyclif writes, "without faith and grade, it is clear that it is necessary to have in the realm, men who should teach faith and virtues and destroy errors contrary to these, because otherwise the people, king and realm

---

[38] Jean Dunbabin, "Aristotle in the Schools," *Trends in Medieval Political Thought*, ed. Beryl Smalley (New York, 1965), p. 81.

[39] "Sed ista exigunt continuacionem theologice facultatis, cum sine ipsa, ut dictum est, non est possiblile regnum stare. Per ipsum enim fama regis extenditur, per ipsam subditus de recta obediencia deo et suis prepositis informatur." *DOR*, p. 177. For a rather limited selection of passages concerning theologians and their activities, see L. J. Daly, *The Political Theory of John Wyclif* (Chicago, 1962), p. 59ff.

[40] "Et ex istis colligitur quod sciencia theologie est pernecessaria ad stabilimentum cuiuscumque regni, et per consequens rex in quantum huiusmodi debet habere theologos ad regni sui regimen se iuvantes." *Ibid.*, p. 72. See also p. 51 for the advisory role of theologians: "Debent ... sacerdotes assistere instruendo in hiis que sunt ad Deum, consulendo ad exemplar legis dei in iusticiis servandis ad proximum. Hoc anim est excellentissimum et necessarissinum officium regis legio deputatum."

[41] "Debet enim rex omnis, quantum sufficit, semovere a regno suo hereticos, quod non faceret prudenter nisi secundum doctrinam et iudicium theologorum qui sciunt quod solum illi sunt heretici qui sunt scripture sacre, que est lex dei, contrarii." *Ibid.*

shall be destroyed." [42] These instructors could only be theologians, true theologians. "How, therefore, should the realm remain without theologians?" Wyclif inquires. [43]

These theologians need not have any formal training. All that is necessary, Wyclif maintains, for qualification is correct teaching. Legists are eligible; even the laity, can be considered. [44] Earlier Wyclif had written that "every man ought to be a theologian and legist, for every man ought to be a Christian. That cannot be unless he shall know the law of God's commandments." [45] The emphasis here is upon the word "ought"; insisting upon each individual's obligation to be a theologian, Wyclif nonetheless realizes the difficulty of this precept for the secular estates. [46] He is also aware of the various levels of cognition to be found in any such study, for later he asserts that only men who devote themselves entirely to the knowledge and love of God as revealed in His law can properly be called a theologian. [47] Again, this did not preclude a layman from being a theologian. That was becoming increasingly difficult, however, especially since in Wyclif's opinion, "there are so many errors today in which our theologians stray in the Lord's symbol and speech." This declension, he went on to say, necessitated greater study on the part of theologians so that having acquired an orthodox faith, they could at once teach the people and defend the law. [48] It is difficult under the best of

---

[42] "Item cum nec est rex nec regnum nec populus sine fide et gracia, patet quod necesse est in regno esse homines qui fidem et virtutes edoceant, erroresque istis contrarios destruant, quia aliter destruentur populus, rex, et regnum." *Ibid.* See also *DCD*, I, 432.

[43] "Quomodo ergo sine theologis staret regnum?" *DOR*, p. 72.

[44] "Quomodo ergo sine theologis staret regnum? Quod si legista decretista vel eciam quicunque laicus habet habitum sic docendi, ipse est vere theologus." *Ibid.*

[45] "Ex estis tercio sequitur quod omnis homo debet esse theologus et legista, nam omnis debet esse Christianus; quod tamen non potest esse nisi legem mandatorum Dei cognoverit; sequitur quod omnis homo debet cognoscere legem istam: cum ergo omnis homo sit eo perfeccior theologus quo perfeccius cognoverit legem Dei, sequitur quod omnis homo debet esse theologus." *DCD*, I, 402. See also *DOR*, p. 77, where Wyclif holds that all Christians are theologians, more or less.

[46] *VSS*, I, 378; *VSS*, II, 141, 145, 166.

[47] "Licet autem omnis homo debet esse theologus, qui in quacunque arte sua principaliter intenderet Deum cognoscere; tamen ille qui dimissis curis seculi studet Deum diligere, secundum quod est omnia in omnibus, est secundum excellenciam quandam theologus." *DCD*, I, 403.

[48] "Quod si obicitur omnem fidelem eciam laicum esse theologum, certum est quod sic: sed cum sint hodie tot errores in fide scripture, in tantum quod nostri theologi errant in simbolo et oracione dominica, necesse est esse theologos doctores docciores qui simpliciores illuminent. Aliter enim sciencie lucrative cum fructu earum cecarent populum in heresim involutum. Nam vix sufficit quantumcumque dispositus

conditions to ascertain so many of the abstruse truths of the Bible and if this is true for theologians themselves, it is doubly true for men of the world.

Every man a theologian is a desirable program, but a disturbing practice with a predictable result. Theologians are created to interpret the scriptures according to reason and the testimony of the saints. And it would be best for laymen to follow this. [49] "This science is necessary for king and realm and consequently his theologians ought to be held in due reverence." [50]

Just as each individual within this Christian community has functions peculiar to his estate, so too the king. As the supreme secular power within the religious polity, his is "to defend the law of God by force," accomplishing this with "power regulated by reason." [51] This power given by God is more than sufficient to implement Christ's law through political activity. [52] In his *Sentencia de Summo Bono*,

---

in naturalibus qui ab ineunte etate laborat pure in facultate theolocya adquirere habitum orthodoxe fidei ad debite docendum populum obedienciam impendendam deo et regi et ad defendendum legem nostram contra adversarios legis dei, ..." *DOR*, pp. 72-73.

[49] *Ibid.* See also *DOR*, p. 49, quoted by Fürstenau, *Wiclif's Lehren*, p. 76, where Wyclif maintains that there exist "difficultates solis theologis reservatas ..."

[50] "Unde propter defectum et mutacionem theologorum necesse est esse multos hereticos. Item quam necessarium est esse theologos ad rectificandum populum, tam necessarium est esse theologos ad declarandum ius regis et famam sui ac regni, tam intrinsecus quam ad extra. Sed sine primo non prosperabitur regnum, cum non sit populus regni terreni nisi prius sit populus dei. Ergo nec sine secundo. Nam certificando de iure regis et eius iusticia in exequendo ministerium a deo sibi creditum debet doceri et declarari per suos theologos. Non enim est ius humanum nisi de quanto fundatum fuerit in lege Dei divina, nec fama regis nisi de quanto exercet iusticiam conformiter illi legi. Cum igitur fama et honor regis sint meliora quam omnia temporalia regni sui, et illa non possunt haberi sine sapiencia theoloyca, patet quam necessaria regi et regno est ista sciencia et per consequens theologi eius ministri debent haberi in debita reverencia." *Ibid.* Specifically, Wyclif writes in the *DOR*, p. 51, that theologians, especially bishops are to "instruant eum (king) secundum legem dei quid est catholicum et quid hereticum in hiis que concernunt regimen regni sui."

[51] The following passages were first cited by Kaminsky, "Wyclifism," p. 63, fn. 41: *Dialogus*, p. 2: "Secunda pars mee militantis ecclesie foret domini temporales, qui debent esse vicarii deitatis ... Eet sic secundum potentiam regulatam racione debent hii domini virtuose defendere legem dei." *DOR*, pp. 78-79: "Et patet sentencia quam dixi in xxxiii conclusione abreviata; quod officium dominorum temporalium et regum precipue est legem ewangelicam potestative defendere et ipsam in sua conversacione diligencius observare."

[52] Having stated that rulers should correct the clergy, Wyclif continues: "Item, eo ipso quo Deus prudentissimus committit regi potestatem ad regnum iuxta suam legem gubernandum, dat sibi potestatem ad faciendum omnia opera humana necessaria pro eodem quia aliter vel Deus impotens, invidens vel imprudens esset. Sed

Isidore of Seville set down the basic role of the secular power. Later this passage was incorporated into the *Decretum* (XXIII, v. 20) under "principes seculi" and the frequency of its quotation is a measure of Wyclif's agreement. And what Wyclif found in the *Decretum*, he reworked into a more satisfying statement:

> The temporal lords have power given to them by God, so that where the spiritual arm of the church does not suffice to convert the antichrists by evangelical preaching, ecclesiastical admonition, or the example of virtues, the secular arm may help its mother by severe coercion. [53]

Typically, Wyclif failed to mention that this admonishment was directed by Isidore at coercing erring pagans, not wayward ecclesiastics. No matter, the quotation is still a keystone in Wyclif's reforming thought. Not only does it provide the secular power with a justified freedom of action that can be independent of the clergy, but it renders that same clergy accessible to secular correction as well. [54] In the process, the temporal lord acquires another spiritual function, correction, and adding this to an already existing tendency, the lord's authority takes on an additional dimension that is fundamentally spiritual. But the reality that had corresponded to Isidore's opinion had passed with Isidore. For this reason alone its unalloyed rejuvenation by Wyclif was as creatively anachronistic as was his conception of the "just king," surrounded by a theocratic nimbus. Both ideas sprang from Wyclif's notion that "the king was the vicar of God." [55] In this, as in so much else, Wyclif followed Augustine, taking up his

---

Deus dedit regibus potestatem ad regni gubernacula secundum suam legem, ergo dedit illis omnia necessaria consequencia ad eandem. Sed potestative agere contra falsos prophetas et scribas est in casu pernecessarium ad regimem regni dati, ergo hoc est concessum a Deo regi." *SS*, I, 279-280. See also *SS*, III, 210, where once again following Augustine, Wyclif holds that God gave custody of the realm to the king and doing so, he gave him all that was necessary for the governance of the realm. This view was also expressed and used by canonists, conciliarists and royal lawyers; their version of this older idea was that God does not grant power without knowledge of how to use it. See Wilks, *Problem of Sovereignty*, p. 407, for Augustinus Triumphus' view along with the pertinent literature.

[53] "Dixi autem alias quodmodo domini temporales habent potenciam datam eis a deo ut ubi spirituale branchium ecclesie non sufficit convertere anticristos ewangelica predicacione, ecclesiastica correpcione, vel virtutum exemplacione, seculare brachium adiuvet matrem suam severa cohercione ..." *DOR*, p. 186, as quoted by Kaminsky, "Wyclifism," p. 72, fn. 45. See *ibid.* for further citations.

[54] For the significance of this in terms of correction and disendowment, see Chapter VI.

[55] *SS*, I, 233; *Dialogus*, p. 2.; *DPP*, p. 378.

formula of God's vicariate and making it his own. [56] And if kings and sometimes temporal lords were the vicars of God, it was left for priests to be the vicars of Christ. [57]

As the vicars of God it was natural for kings to be looked upon as paradigms of virtue; they were to be super-excellent, who because they were vicars of God, were superior in virtue, deriving their power directly from God. Because of their special vicariate, they must precede all others in virtue and righteousness and, as Wyclif said, "it is to the king that we must submit ourselves above all others." [58] This idea of virtuous superiority had its genesis for Wyclif in Aristotle's *Politics*: "Royal rule, if not a mere name, must exist by virtue of some great personal superiority in the king." [59] This notion

---

[56] "Igitur reges, qui secundum Augustinum sunt dei vicarii, debent rectificare dei iniuriam." *DB*, p. 265. "'Rex' enim secundum Augustinum 'debet esse Dei vicarius,' sed episcopus humilis vicarius Jesu Christi, et sic prior debet immiscere potenciam instar Dei et secundus debet vivere secundum paupertatem et summam pacienciam instar Christi." *SS*, II, 300. "Secunda pars mee militantis ecclesie foret domini temporales, qui debent esse vicarii deitatis. Ideo sepe meminit augustinus quomodo rex est vicarius deitatis. Sacerdos autem qui secundum humilitatem et pauperiem debet procedere est vicarius humanitatis domini jhu Christi." *Dialogus*, p. 2.

[57] *Dialogus*, p. 2, as quoted above, fn. 62. In a theocratic realm such as the one conceived by Wyclif it is hardly surprising to find him depositing God's vicariate upon the king. Nor is it unexpected, once the king has this office, to find him responsible for reform. See Ladner, *Idea of Reform*, p. 131; Michele Maccarrone, *Vicarius Christi, storia del papale* (Romae, 1957), *passim*, and esp. 41f. and Kantorowicz, *King's Two Bodies*, pp. 34, 77f., 116f., and 155ff. where he points out the reciprocity of law and king in Bracton's treatise. The king is "recognized as the vicar of God only when and where he acts 'God-like' by submitting to the Law which is both his and God's." God's vicariate, then, imposes demands of a moral character upon the king which can *severely limit* him in the exercise of his governmental functions. On the different meanings of the terms "vicarius Dei" and "vicarius Christi," see Kantorowicz, *passim*, and the interesting article by Wilhelm Durig, "Der theologische Ausgangspunkt der mittelalterlichen liturgischen Auffassung vom Herrscher als Vicarius Dei," *Historisches Jahrbuch*, LXXVII (1958), 174ff. as well as Walter Ullmann, *Principles of Government and Politics in the Middle Ages* (London, 1961), p. 121, and *passim*; Wilks, *The Problem of Sovereignty, passim*; Heinrich Heimpel's review of F. A. von den Heydte, *Die Geburtsstunde des souveranen Staates* in the *Göttinger Gelehrte Anzeigen* (1954), p. 197f. and Wiebke Fesefeldt, *Englische Staatstheorie des 13. Jahrhunderts. Henry Bracton und sein Werk* (Göttingen, 1963), *passim*. For the older literature, and an interesting article in its own right, see Adolf von Harnack, "Christus praesens—Vicarius Christi," *Sitzungsberichte der Preussischen Akademie der Wissenschaften*, phil.-hist. Klasse, XXXIV (1927), 415ff.

[58] "... et debet fieri ista subieccio non propter questum aut lucrum habendum ab homine sed pure et simpliciter propter Deum et potissime superioribus personam Dei representantibus, sicut 'regi' qui debet extollere in execucione iusticie feriendo iniustos et premiando iustos." *SS*, III, 215.

[59] Aristotle, *The Politics*, BK. IV, 1289G. See also Wilks, *The Problem of*

is repeated by Wyclif in the first volume of the *De Civili Domini* and elsewhere: "super-excellence in the king is the principal cause for ruling civilly." [60] Yet, super-excellence, however sufficient for ruling, has to combine "with the approbation of the people" if it is to rule civilly. [61] This was original. The notion of super-excellence as a criterion for lordship was not, of course. In addition to Augustine, both Giles of Rome and St. Thomas Aquinas had emphasized the importance of virtue in the king, had applied this standard to the king more than any to other individual and had forced the king to justify his position through a life devoted to moral excellence. [62] The king was to be the noblest of them all; he was to excel all others. [63] Viewed in this manner, the prime function of the king was moral leadership. Once this had been established, the virtue deposited in the office of the king would automatically bring stability to the realm. [64]

Deriving his power directly from God, affirming this through his moral preeminence, the king had the public right to approve, judge, and regulate. [65] Wyclif, opposing the prevailing doctrine established by Hugh of St. Victor, formulated his position clearly:

> It pertains to the kings to instruct their subjects in virtue, especially since the purpose per se of natural life is that it be adorned with virtues, and the realm or people can neither be nor lawfully live in any other way. [66]

Sovereignty, pp. 99, 142f.; Kantorowicz, *King's Two Bodies*, p. 268f. for a discussion of the role virtues play in late medieval thought.

[60] "Et patet ex sentencia Aristotelis, tercio Politicorum, capitulo xxviii. recitata, quod virtus superexcellens in rege est precipua causa regnandi civiliter." *DCD*, I, 212.

[61] "Ipsa enim per se sufficit ad regnandum ewangelice, et est sufficiens cum approbacione populi ad regnandum civiliter; unde, sicut titulus acquirendi non per se sufficit (ex xxi. capitulo) sed oportet precipue superaddere titulum caritatis, sic indubie nec successio hereditaria nec popularis eleccio per se sufficit." *Ibid.*

[62] Dunbabin, "Aristotle," p. 73.

[63] *DOR*, p. 80. See also Dunbabin, "Aristotle," p. 73. Even Matthew of Paris in his *Chronica Maiora*, H. R. Luard ed., Vol. II (London, 1874), 454-455, has something to say on this subject. He quotes from a much disputed speech that has been attributed to the Archbishop Hubert of Canterbury. The occasion was the supposed election of King John and the archbishop remarked that no one has the right to succeed another in kingship unless he would be preeminent in good qualities, for he who excells in all the kingdom should be set over all.

[64] For this idea in Giles of Rome, see Dunbabin, "Aristotle," p. 74.

[65] See Johannes Loserth, "Wiclifs Sendschreiben, Flugschriften und kleinere Werke kirchenpolitischen Inhalts," *Sitzungsberichte der Kaiserlichen Akademie der Wissenschaften,* philosophisch-historische Klasse, 166 (Wien: 1910), p. 91, where he translated or paraphrased a great many of Wyclif's smaller, less important works.

[66] "Sicut ad reges pertinet subditos suos in virtute instruere, specialiter cum per se

Furthermore, because kings are the vicars of God, they have the obligation "to destroy vices and establish and augment virtues in themselves and others." [67] On this basis the king is not only the vicar of God, but his works have to represent the justice of God; for "the office of temporal lords and of kings is principally to defend vigorously the evangelical law and observe this more diligently in his daily life." [68] And in this the king is bound to do justice for all because "he holds this commandment from God as His principal vicar." [69] As the vicar of God, preeminent in virtue and guardian of God's law, it is incumbent upon the king to be "priest and pontiff in his own realm." Fundamentally, "the law of the church is the law of the king." The reason for this is not because the king is a Christian, but because the custodianship of these laws is the foundation of the king's government. [70] Wyclif's point was that there was an almost total identity between God's law and that of the king. And kings were not only the vicars of God, but according to the laws of men, kings were "pontiffs" and according to the law of God, theirs was a "spiritual and evangelical power." [71] Wyclif's king, in other words, aproaches the classic example of what modern scholars have chosen to call the "pontifical king," whose functions were spiritual although non-priestly: his was "to rule, to judge, to correct, and, through these operations to guard the doctrinal purity and, in so far as possible, the temporal well-being of the church." [72] Sharing the episcopal

---

finis vite naturalis sit ut ornetur virtutibus, nec aliter est regnum vel populus, nec aliter vivit legaliter." *DPP*, p. 8, as quoted by Kaminsky, "Wyclifism," p. 64, n. 49.

[67] "Et tercio quia reges temporales habent spiritualem ad destruendum vicia et plantandum ac augendum virtutes in se et in aliis, 'quotquot autem receperunt Christum per fidem, dedit eis potestatem' racione filiacionis spiritualis, ad impendendum opera spiritualia misericordie que indubie est potestas spiritualis ..." *Ibid.*, p. 10.

[68] *DOR*, pp. 78-79.   [69] *Ibid.*

[70] "Nec dicat aliquis quod non pertinet ad regem, qui debet sacerdos et pontifex regni sui iuxta decretum 21 di. 'Cleros,' exequi istam legem, quia lex dei, et per consequens lex ecclesie, est lex regis, non solum sub racione qua cristianus, sed sub racione qua in istarum legum custodia stat precipuum regimen regni sui." *DOR*, p. 152.

[71] "... cum 'reges' secundum Augustininum 'sunt Dei vicarii' et secundum leges hominum sunt pontifices, ideo cum potestas eorum quam innuit Apostolus ad Romanos XIII non sit corporalis, quia in hoc excellit eos operarius, manifestum est quod est potestas spiritualis et evangelica ..." *SS*, I, 233-234.

[72] T. E. Mommsen and K. F. Morrison, *Imperial Lives and Letters of the Eleventh Century* (New York, 1962), p. 5. For a limitation of this view with respect to Saxon kingship, see K. F. Morrison, *Tradition and Authority in the Western Church, 300-1140* (Princeton, 1969), pp. 373-389. While this has little to do with

ministry, this king's office, his very character, bore a dual imprint.

Because of man's sin, the Church Militant as a religious polity needs this king just as it requires regulation by civil law. Simply put, monarchy is to be preferred over other forms of governance because it is most expedient. Civil law is obligatory, *ratione peccati*, in the governance of the church, but without an executor, Wyclif argues, such law would be useless. Clearly the best solution would be to select a single individual to direct that law, and that person is the king. [73] Likewise, gradation is a prerequisite for order within this polity. Hierarchically organized, the polity must have a head; if it did not, if the realm were composed of equals, "there would be no order in the execution of political acts." [74] Such political acts, dependent upon the civil law, included keeping the peace and restraining those rebelling against God's law. Consequently, the king, as the law's executor, is as necessary for the body politic as the law itself. Kings are necessary and this, Wyclif writes, can be confirmed not only with the example of Old Testament kings, holding their offices through God's election and approbation, but closer to home, Wyclif also finds numerous English paradigms of "glorious martyrs" and "devout confessors." [75]

The king's commitment to civil law does not mean, however, that his government is not to be guided by the laws of the Gospel. [76] The

---

Wyclif's conception of the kings, it does point up the dichotomy between theory and reality. In such a situation even Saxon kings opted for fact; so did Wyclif, translating his theological commitment into juristic modes.

[73] "... et questio supponitur, monarchiam vel regaliam esse licitam ac meritoriam. Fundatur illud tripliciter: primo ex hoc quod lex civilis est necessaria (supposito peccato) ad regimen ecclesie sed illa foret inutilis sine persona principaliter exequente, ergo talis persona est necessaria in ecclesia militante, et illa, ut huiusmodi, est rex; ergo regalia est necessaria." *DCD*, I, 185.

[74] "Item cuiuscunque ordinis est dare gradus, et per consequens infimum et supremum; sed policia civilis stat in quodam ordine, ergo illius est dare gradum summum: sed quamcuque personam in illo gradu positam in populo supponamus ipsam, ergo de racione naturali (supposita civilitate) sequitur regem esse. Si enim multi fuerint in populo dominantes, sed illis concurrentibus pro regimine reipublice, necesse est esse aliquem principalem; quia aliter non foret ordo in execucione actus politici, si omnes forent simpliciter equiparium potestatum." *Ibid.*, p. 186.

[75] Having posited the necessity of kings, Wyclif goes on to say: "Confirmatur ex hoc quod David, Ezechias, Yosias, et ceteri reges Veteris Testamenti fuerunt eleccione et approbacione Domini in illo officio ministri Dei precipui, ut patet ex processu libri Regum et Paralipomenon: ... Sed in lege nova fuerunt reges multi, gloriosi martires et devotisimi confessores, ut patet de regibus Anglie et regnorum plurium aliorum." *Ibid.*, p. 185.

[76] "Verumtamen sicut vita activa non valet ad meritum sine contemplativa vivifice, sic nec lex humana vel regis officium, nisi de quanto ex lege ewangelica est directum." *Ibid.*, p. 198.

two should correspond. [77] In fact, since the king is the "minister of God" according to his preeminence in virtue, "it is clear that the king is to rule the men of his realm according to the divine law." [78] Kings have their power from God, but theirs is a commission to promote justice among their subjects. The king's office, therefore, is a *beneficium* of rulership; God has entrusted the kingdom to him as a charge. The king is a servant of Christ, holding from Him and for that reason bound to govern according to Christ's law, [79] for he is charged with "the perpetual salvation of himself and of the people, whose government God entrusted to him." [80] Viewed as a trustee, imbued with spiritual as well as secular power, the king is to establish just laws conforming to scripture and then practice these in the observance of Christ's law and the utility of the realm. [81] Here again God's law and the king's merge and when civil law can be considered a part of God's power, then that same power can be pulled into the life of this world. In the accomplishment, royal law and evangelical law become identical. [82] Stated another way, "regalian rights of the king and all human laws of the king should be directed by the law of God," and they do so to such an extent that Wyclif can speak of the law of God actually "conserving the regalian rights of the

---

[77] Johannes Wyclif, *Tractatus de Simonia* (henceforth *DS*), ed. Herzberg-Frankel and M. H. Dziewicki (London, 1898), p. 32.

[78] "Cum ergo regis sit ministerium Dei, secundum eminenciam virtutis gradui correspondens, patet quod regis est regere secundum legem divinam homines regni sui; et cum partes iusticie sunt declinare a malo et facere bonum, patet quod rex debet rebelles divinis legibus et aliis subministrantibus cohercere, et factores iusticie secundum caritatis regulas promovere." *DCD*, p. 188.

[79] "Rex, cum sit servus et tenens Cristi, aliquid debet ut sic sibi facere; sed nichil, si non gubernare eius populum 2m legem suam; ergo illud officium 2m modum suum debet exequi propter Cristum." *DB*, p. 273.

[80] See Matthew Spinka, *Advocates of Reform from Wyclif to Erasmus*, "The Library of Christian Classics," Vol. XIV (Philadelphia, 1953), p. 60. The text Spinka translates is that of G. V. Lechler, *Johannis de Wiclif tractatus de officio pastorali* (Leipzig, 1863). "For this reason princes ought faithfully to note the decree of Isidore where the opinion is advanced that whether the Church increases or decreases, Christ will require a reckoning from them in the day of judgment, of how they have exercised in this ministry the power which he gave them ... Who, therefore, sober of mind, will be offended toward the secular arm because he is reasonably charged with the perpetual salvation of himself and of the people, whose government God entrusted to him?" Here again we find Wyclif citing his favorite passage from Isidore; cf. *Decretum*, pars II, C. XXIII, q. 5, c. 20, and fn. 52 and 53 above.

[81] "Si ergo regum est iustas leges scripture conformes condere et eas in observancia legis Christi religionis et utilitatem rei-publice practizare (ut patet capitulo secundi huius) ..." *DCD*, III, 313.

[82] *DS*, p. 32.

king." [83] Conservation, therefore, becomes identification and any departure from the royal position, whether in word or deed, becomes not only sedition but sacrilegious. [84]

Within this religious polity called England with its theocratic base, the king is to regard himself as a Christian steward regulating every sphere of activity within his kingdom or church, disregarding designations such as sacred and profane, secular and ecclesiastical. The king is now the head of the "church militant." [85] Or as Wyclif puts it: "every country has from divine ordination one interpreter." [86] Here in the *De Apostasia*, Wyclif leaves the identification of that interpreter open; earlier, however, he had said:

> It seems to me that reason dictates that the people set up a head
> for themselves not just one genus of captains in political religion,
> but that each people take a single head for itself, as for example
> we English have one blessed king, to whom, according to the doctrine
> of the Gospel . . . we must render secular obedience. [87]

Wyclif's intention in establishing this earthly "head" or "captain" in "political religion" is nothing more, nor less, than an attempt at reclaiming for the king and his polity the spiritual nimbus he had lost when the church achieved its *libertas* in the eleventh century.

---

[83] "Sed quantum ad primum, dicitur quod necesse est regaliam regis et omnes leges humanas regi per legem dei, licet sit suppeditata hodie; vel aliter sunt prophane. Ideo lex dei regaliam regis conservat precipue; et alie tradiciones consumunt adulatorie iura regis." *DB*, p. 198.

[84] "Et hec racio quare dixi superius quod oportet regem regulari per sapienciam theologicam, et quare est nimis impium atque sacrilegum impugnare verbo vel opere regiam potestatem dicente apostolo 'Roman xiii Qui resistit potestati, Dei ordinacioni resistit.' Ideo rex debet precipue cavere de talibus cum sint, ut ait, hostes Dei regis et regni." *DOR*, p. 78.

[85] For the king as the head of the church, see Fritz Kern, *Kingship, Law and Constitution in the Middle Ages*, trans. S. B. Chrimes (Oxford, 1948), p. 58f.; Kantorowicz, *King's Two Bodies, passim*, esp. pp. 124-126; H. Kaempf, *Pierre Dubois und die Geistigen Grundlagen des Französischen Nationalbewusstseins um 1300* (Leipzig and Berlin, 1935).

[86] "Sic igitur quelibet patria habet ex ordinacione divina unum interpretem, ita quod non opportet currere ad Romanum pontificem pro quibuslibet causis ambiguis decidendis." Johannes Wyclif, *Tractatus de Apostasie* (henceforth *DA*), ed. M. H. Dziewicki (London, 1889), p. 203.

[87] "Videtur mihi quod racio dictat ut ipsi faciant isibi caput, nedum unum genus capitaneorum in religione politica, sed quod quilibet populus appropriet sibi simplex caput ut nos Anglici habemus unum regem benedictum, cui secundum doctrinam ewangelii debemus inpendere obsequium seculare. Ex ita est de regnis aliis maioribus sive minoribus, eciam usque ad imperium." *DOR*, p. 249.

PART II

THE INSTRUMENTALITY OF
LEGAL REFORM

CHAPTER FIVE

THE METHODOLOGY OF REFORM

John Wyclif's effort to reassert a religious definition of rulership contrary to the prevailing papal theory was not unique. On the contrary, by the fourteenth century, as part of a frontal campaign to establish the sovereignty of lay leadership, a widespread effort was made to "transcendentalize" the emerging national state along with its ruler through the appropriation of ecclesiological language and ideas. [1] Wyclif became a participant in this struggle when he made his king the "head" of the English church, when he gave England's political "body" a religious legitimacy equal to that of the institutional church. Church merges with realm and Wyclif can pass from one organological conception of Christian society to another. This concept of religious polity then, becomes for Wyclif, as it had been for others, a vehicle in the transfer of values from church to monarchy, and, combined with Augustine's idea of the king's vicariate, it formed the basis of Wyclif's "political religion," [2] which itself was one theatre in an extended war. The king was the head of the church body; and although Wyclif does not specifically refer to priests as the soul, protecting the whole of the realm including the king through its advice, the tradition was there. [3] And just as Wyclif visualized a perfect kingdom directed by the vicar of God through the advice of theologians, so had others such as Gilbert of Tournai, but earlier. [4] Gilbert had termed this arrangement a "corpus mysti-

---

[1] Kantorowicz, *King's Two Bodies, Passim*, esp. 207ff.; Hans Liebeschutz, "Chartres und Bologna, Naturbegriff und Staatsidee bei Johannes Salisbury," *Archiv für Kulturgeschichte*, L (1968), 18ff.; Wilks, *Problem of Sovereignty*, p. 237f.; Ewart Lewis, "Organic Tendencies in Medieval Political Thought," *American Political Science Review*, XXXII (1938), 849ff. For a brief, but highly suggestive summary of the growth of the organological concept of the state, see Ernst Kantorowicz's article, "Pro Patria Mori," which first appeared in the *AHR*, LVI (1951), 472-492, and has now been reprinted in Ernst Kantorowicz, *Selected Studies* (Locust Valley, 1965), pp. 318-320. For further literature, see below.

[2] *DOR*, p. 249.

[3] If Wyclif left this unsaid, others did not. See Liebeschutz, "Naturbegriff und Staatsidee," p. 19f. for John of Salisbury's position and anatomical comparisons. Moreover, Robert Pullen, with whom John of Salisbury had studied had a very similar view. See in addition to Liebeschutz, F. Courtney, *Cardinal Robert Pullen: An English Theologian of the Twelfth Century* (Romae, 1954), *passim*.

[4] Kantorowicz, *King's Two Bodies*, pp. 207-209.

cum," while Wyclif decided upon "political religion." In both cases it was a theological polity functioning as a distinct entity within what Kantorowicz called "the traditional mystical body," and this "state within the church" was only another way of expressing Wyclif's conception of particular realms making up the single Church Militant. [5]

Autonomous, England as a land and as a polity would live under the direction of its theocratic king, who instituted laws in conformity with Christ's commandments. This king, having been restored to his theocratic position, was the kingdom's divine representative, ruling in accordance with God's law, exacting obedience by virtue of God's appointment, his "evangelical lordship," and the acceptance of his own people. [6] In fact, both realm and subject depend upon the righteousness of this king's rule. [7] Serving justice, the king "knows he is the whip of God for coercing his rebels," for establishing and maintaining peace. [8] These functions are in Wyclif's opinion crucial. Moreover they combine with Augustine's four-fold definition of cardinal functions to restore and emphasize the king's sacerdotal dimensions. First the king ought "to found just laws consonant with the law of God; secondly, he should destroy those laws contrary to God's; thirdly, he ought to compel the people to placate God; and fourthly, this theocratic king ought to appoint the secular branch to pacify his people. In these four elements consists the justice of the king." [9] The emphasis here, as elsewhere, is upon the administration

---

[5] *Ibid.*, fn. 45.

[6] See *DE*, p. 342; *DCD*, I, 212; *DOR*, Ch. 4, *passim* and esp. p. 69. According to Kantorowicz, "Kingship," *Select Studies*, p. 158, jurists in seeking to support the imperial foundation had long tried to combine divine origin of imperial power with that of the popular origin. The *Glossa Ordinaria* of Accursius attempted this same task and in combining the authorities of "God" and "people," it came very close to John of Paris, "populo faciente et Deo inspirante," and Wyclif's own formulation. See, for example, *DCD*, I, 212.

[7] King and realm are so closely identified as to resemble the marriage of the bishop to his diocese. What affects the one, affects the other. "Constat quod sic, cum secundum Augustinum ut alias diffuse exposui, rex et regnum in virtutibus et viciis sibimet reciproce, ut plurimum, correspondent." *DA*, p. 61. See also *DCD*, I, 189.

[8] *OM*, p. 400.

[9] "Ex isto textu apostoli ellicit Augustinus, epistola xxxvii. ad Macedonium predictum regis officium. Unde, epistola xxxiii. ad Bonifacium, hoc idem expressius declarat, recolligens totum officium regis in quatuor: primo, leges iustas legi Dei consonas sanxiendo; secundo secundum dictas leges divino cultui contraria destruendo; tercio, ad placandum Deum populum compellendo; et quarto, ad pacificandum populum tam extrinsecus quam intrinsecus seculare brachium apponendo. In istis quatuor consistit iusticia regis." *DCD*, I, 189.

of the law that must be one with God's, or the use of the king's power is not just. There can be no friction between the secular and spiritual aspects of the king's obligations. Secular administration, service to the realm and the furtherance of God's service, all form one organic whole. This, in other words, is an English theocracy under the direct leadership of the king with each of the realm's estates contributing in the nature of its own vicaritate. [10] Wyclif himself states that:

> The king of England should first and principally give a work for regulating his clergy and especially bishops in order that they should live similar to the law of Christ; for the whole realm is one body which to watch and heal belongs to the office of the king .... [11]

Again, relying upon Isidore's formulation of the corrective role of the theocratic king, Wyclif has his "king and priest" bearing the cardinal responsibility of "recognizing, according to the law of Christ, what is useful for his mother [the church]." [12] This recognition, often enough, is a divine mandate to intervene coercively in the conduct of ecclesiastical affairs when the spiritual branch is found wanting. [13] Even here, the king in his supervisory capacity will determine the time, place and extent of that failure. [14] Operating extraordinarily in spiritual affairs, the king defined the shape of Wyclif's theocracy. Under his direction, all segments of the Church Militant are to work harmoniously together, each pulling its load in unison for the fulfillment of the realm's religious duties.

The restructuring of this community on the basis of the model above necessitated a revival of the study of Christ's law, for:

> the law of Christ, when perfectly executed, teaches most rightfully, how every injustice must be extirpated from the commonwealth, and

---

[10] See above Chapter IV, pp. 63-66.

[11] After setting out Jerome's concept of royal functions, Wyclif continues saying: "Et ex istis primo patet quod rex Anglie primo et principaliter daret operam ad regulandum clerum suum et specialiter episcopos ut vivant similius legi Christi; totum enim regnum est unum corpus, quod tueri atque mederi spectat ad regis officium, ut dicit iste sanctus. DPP, p. 377. The unity of the realm as one body composed of clerics, lords and community is also touched upon in FZ, p. 258.

[12] DB, p. 110, as quoted by Fürstenau, Wiclif's Lehren, p. 94: The king has the responsibility "secundum legem Cristi cognoscere quid est utile matri sue."

[13] DOR, pp. 121-122: "Necesse est matrem ecclesiam habere seculares dominos, ut reges, dei vicarios, qui potestative ipsam defendant ubi vicarii Cristi deficiunt, et illam potestatem immediate habent a deo." See also DE, p. 13; SS, I, 230, 234; DB, pp. 56-57, 136; DOR, pp. 6, 22, 186.

[14] See Fürstenau, Wiclif's Lehren, p .94, and the support for this argument, DOR, p. 137.

> how those offending against the law should be chastised .... The
> law of Christ teaches most completely how every sin should be des-
> troyed and avoided; but since it is not possible that a commonwealth
> deteriorate except on account of sin, therefore if justice (of the
> law of Christ) be observed by every person, the commonwealth will
> prosper. [15]

Such an awareness of Christ's law was especially incumbent upon the
king. [16] The rationale for this was made perfectly clear in one of
Wyclif's tighter syllogisms: "No one," he writes, "without wisdom is
suitable for ruling, but there is no wisdom, unless in the law of the
Lord. Therefore," he concludes, "without knowledge of this law, no
one is disposed for ruling." [17] And having concluded that royal
government was most expedient for England's theocracy, Wyclif went
on to say that such a government, including the office of the king,
cannot be right "unless when directed from evangelical law." [18] This
injunction was particularly important in the light of Wyclif's decision
to have an "interpreter" of the divine in each royal polity, who
would, in fact, be a repository of virtue.

Christ's law must be implemented. Nor will the realm stand unless
the king's governance be legitimate and his person just. To this end,
the king must be beneath God's law; he had to pattern his works on
the justice of God. Consequently, "it is fitting that the king be
regulated" not only through his own knowledge of Christ's law, but
"through the wisdom of theologians." [19] If God's law is to be the

---

[15] "Item lex Christi perfecte executa docet rectissime quomodo omnis iniusticia
debeat a republica extirpari, et quomodocunque offendens in legem debet castigari;
docet insuper quomodo quecunque iusticia viantis foveri debeat et finaliter premiari;
sed cum declinare a malo et facere bonum due partes adequantes iusticiam, sequitur
quod lex Christi plene iusticiam docet rempublicam regulare. Argumentum patet eo
quod lex Christi docet completissime quomodo omne peccatum debet destrui et
caveri; sed non est possibile quod deterioretur respublica nisi occasione peccati; ergo,
observata a quacunque persona illa iusticia, sequitur eius prosperacio." *DCD*, I, 432.

[16] "Patet quod necesse est omnem regem precipue cognoscere legem Christi, eo
quod in quolibet predictorum quatuor oportet eum secundum legem Christi principaliter regulari ..." *Ibid.*, p. 191.

[17] "Nemo sine sapiencia est ydoneus ad regnandum, sed non est sapiencia nisi in
lege Domini, ergo sine huiusmodi legis noticia nemo disponitor ad regnandum." *Ibid.*

[18] "Sic est expedicius ecclesie, supposito peccato populi effreni ex rebellione
divinis legibus durius cohercendi, quod sint reges civiliter punientes, quam quod cum
illis paribus sint soli apostolici, pure secundum legem ewangelicam populum regu-
lantes ..." *Ibid.*, p. 198.

[19] *DOR*, p. 78; see also p. 51. This need on the part of the king has also been
shown indirectly by Fürstenau, *Wiclif's Lehren*, pp. 42-45, when dealing with
Wyclif's concept of the standard two-sword theory. Commenting upon the secular
sword, Wyclif writes: "Sacerdos autem habet, si sciverit, illum gladium obiective ad

measure of truth, righteousness, legitimacy and justice, then absolutely no one is in a better position to apply this standard than Christ's theologians. If rulers are dependent upon the Bible to fulfill their trust, then theologians, as students of that law, must provide the proper instruction. [20]

This need for theological guidance is perhaps most apparent when Wyclif deals with the use of privilege in the Westminster case discussed in his work, *De Ecclesia.* Falling back upon his divinely appointed interpreter and the *Decretum*, Wyclif maintains that the use of privilege is to be determined and interpreted by the king on the authority of the maxim—it belongs to him to interpret laws and privileges, who founds them. [21] In this matter of interpretation, however, the king should be guided by theologians. Determinations, whatever their interpretation, whatever their source, are only valid when actually grounded upon scriptural foundations. [22] There are other examples of the need for theological direction. Since the security of the realm, in fact, its very existence depends on combating heresy, theologians are for Wyclif a *sine qua non* for they alone "shall be able to discern what is heretical." [23] On this point Wyclif is emphatic: "Only he knows what is heretical, who knows it to be contrary to scripture." [24] Nor does Wyclif leave the question at the level of simple recognition; instead, beating in effect his own drum, he categorically proclaims that heresy increases in direct proportion as theologians

eius [king's] officium regulandum." *DE*, p. 315. It is Fürstenau's view that the parenthetical "si sciverit" refers to the correct teaching from the Old and New Testaments mentioned in the same text. The meaning then is that the king, in order to rule correctly, has to be advised by theologians, which gives them a limited access to the secular sword.

[20] See *VSS*, II, 143-144.

[21] "Igitur inprimis, cum illius sit interpretari leges ac privilegia cuius est condere (ut patet XXVa, q. I, 'Ideo permittente,' et V Decretalium, De Sentencia Excommunicacionis, 'Inter alia'), rex autem Anglie debet concedere et condere leges tales privates de suo regali dominio ad edificacionem ecclesie: ideo capiendum est tamquam per se notum quod regis est illas leges privatas ac elemosinas interpretari et in rectitudine sua defendere." privates ac elemosinas interpretari et in rectitudine sua defendere." *DE*, pp. 227-228. The correct citation from the *Decretum* is II Pars, C.XXV, q. 1, c. s vi. The use of this principle becomes a maxim for Wyclif, see *DCD*, III, 30: "Cum ergo eius sit legem exsequi cuius est condere, ..."

[22] *Ibid*. See also *DE*, pp. 328-329, where scholastics and bishops were held to advise the king of danger to himself and to the realm.

[23] "Et patet ... quod necesse est ad stabilimentum regnorum esse theologos qui soli sciunt discernere quid sit hereticum ..." *DOR*, p. 125.

[24] "Ex quibus patet quod solum theologus debet hereticare dampnabile; solum enim iste scit quid est hereticum, qui scit esse Scripture sacre contrarium." *DCD*, I, 437.

decrease. [25] These heretical categories run the gamut from simple heresy to the extremely subtle forms of apostasy and blasphemy. Theologians were indispensible here too. Wyclif holds them responsible for advising the king of his proper jurisdiction and power, especially with respect to the "blasphemous excesses" of the Roman papacy. [26] In another context, Wyclif is even more direct: "it is clear that a theologian is necessary for the governance of the realm." [27] For Wyclif theologians are plainly necessary; and this requirement inexorable "because it is incumbent upon these [theologians] to destroy errors and protect the king and realm from such danger." [28]

Advised by theologians, both virtuous and knowledgeable in terms of sacred scripture himself, the king possesses a power that is at once "spiritual and evangelical." He is, for Wyclif, a modified reincarnation of the pontificial king who bore himself in the royal image of God. [29] Considered as king and priest, graced with a sacred royal power, which no one but God can give, Wyclif's king quite naturally calls synods on the basis of his own God-given authority, [30] and demands doctrinal declarations from his clergy. [31] "Since they are among the

---

[25] "Unde propter defectum et mutacionem theologorum necesse est esse multos hereticos." *DOR*, p. 73.

[26] It is necessary to have theologians to determine what is heretical and: "quorum est detegere potestatem regum nimis diu sopitam et blasfenum excessum potestatis vendicatum a pretenso Cristi vicario." *Ibid.*, p. 125.

[27] "Et patet quam necessarius est theologus ad rempublicam gubernadum." *DCD*, I, 437.

[28] *DE*, pp. 330-331.

[29] *DOR*, p. 5: Kings "gerunt regalem ymaginem dei." *SS*, I, 233. For the quotation of this text, see above. The form of the modification is set out in part in Kaminsky, "Wyclifism," p. 64. See also *DOR*, p. 128: "Papa igitur et alii Cristi vicarii habent auctoritatem participative vel subautentice ad faciendum opera Cristi in quantum sacerdos et rex, ac alii seculares domini habent a deo potestatem auctoritativam ad faciendam vindictam et alia opera Cristi, in quantum rex et sacerdos. Et hinc vocantur reges dei vicarii atque pontifices, que auctoritas quodammodo precellit aliam tam tempore quam natura." And *ibid.*, p. 52: "non pertinet ad regem, qui debet esse sacerdos et pontifex regni sui ..." Both citations found in Fürstenau, *Wiclif's Lehren*, p. 85.

[30] *DOR*, p. 71: "Sacra potestas regalis ... quam non nisi deus secundum apostolum potest dare." Quoted by Fürstenau, p. 50. "... rex debet auctoritate sua sive ecclesie facere, quando oportet, synodum congregari et auctoritate Christi et apostolorum corrigere et ad hoc leges statuere ..." *OM*, p. 408. Also *DCD*, IV, 484. Without fully developing a canonical base, Wyclif does call upon the examples of Pope Leo IV and St. Gregory.

[31] "Nam primo videtur quod reges et potentatus seculi quererent instanter ab hiis sectis quator quid naturaliter et quid figuraliter sit hostia consecrata." *OE*, p. 412. Elsewhere Wyclif speaks of royal scrutiny, saying: "Cum ergo rex Anglie cum suo regno multa milia marcarum expendit circa huius sacramenti ministerium annuatim,

faithful of the church," kings ought "to discuss ecclesiastical causes," be these doctrinal, as above, or jurisdictional, as when they relate to "adultery, rape and other injuries to God." [32] Moreover, because the king's power is bipartite, spiritual in character as well as temporal, it is obligatory for this theocratic king to cooperate with the episcopacy for the betterment of the clergy. "It is plain," Wyclif asserts, having first quoted Gregory the Great's famous letter to the king of France, "that this most holy pope desired seculars, together with bishops to correct crimes of the clergy." [33] And in this effort, neither bishop nor king is to act wholly on his own authority, but rather jointly. [34]

Again, Wyclif's conception is that of a religious polity, a community of estates working in concord, each according to its vicariate and the law of Christ. [35] This conception also gave definition to Wyclif's king—who was the outstanding vicar of God, possessing both secular and spiritual power, guiding his polity through spiritual as well as carnal fear. [36] The basis for this Wyclif found in the tradition of the Apostolic Church and its successor, the Imperial Church, when ecclesiastical decrees were harmoniously blended with imperial law, when there was advice and consent between ruler and ecclesiastic. [37] Then Christ's ideal had been near perfection. Endowment, unfortunately, had destroyed this harmony and had become in its turn the source of all trouble. [38] Once the church had been endowed, and cooperative effort abated, the church left its spiritual essence to become involved in secular affairs, destroying the theocratic foun-

---

racionabile foret tam in regni fidelibus quam in vocatis clericis et prelatis quod certificent regi et regno suo quid sit illus sacramentum quod tam sumptuose consecrant et regno tam salutifere sicut dicunt." *OM*, p. 256.

[32] "... patet quod reges cum sint fideles ecclesie debent ecclesiasticas causas discutere, ymmo ... debent adulteria rapinas et ceteras iniurias Dei et hominum in regnis suis destruere ..." *SS*, II, 422.

[33] "Ecce quam plane iste papa sanctissimus voluit seculares cum episcopis compunire crimina clericorum." *OM*, pp. 408-409.

[34] "Verum tamen nec reges nec episcopi debent ex sua sola auctoritate hoc facere sed auctoritate universalis ecclesie et per consequens auctoritate Christi domini Dei nostri." *Ibid.*, p. 409.

[35] *DB*, p. 216.

[36] *DOR*, p. 5: "Istis premissis secundo generale praeceptum huius pape sanctissimi cuilibet servo domini saecularis, cum tam timore carnali quam timore spirituali ... Timore namque spirituali debet subditus subici regi secundum racionem qua principalius deo subicitur, et sibi tanquam persone in qua relucet maiestas sume regie potestatis." Quoted in Fürstenau, *Wiclif's Lehren*, p. 50.

[37] Benrath, *Bibelkommentar*, p. 58.

[38] *DB*, pp. 83, 264. For further references and Wyclif's conception of decline see above Chapter IV, *passim*.

dation of the state. That this had occurred there could be little doubt; that the visible church was in need of a reformation elicited widespread agreement. But if the necessity of reformation enjoyed universal recognition, the means of effecting it remained a mystery to most.

There was very little mystery in the world for John Wyclif. Certainly neither the methodology of ecclesiastical reform nor its agency fell into this category. Focussing upon the mirror of Scripture and right reason, Wyclif delineated a reformatory dream in which biblical precept, functioning as Christ's law, was to order contemporary English society as the Church Militant. Pushed by Wyclif to the forefront of reform, this notion of the law served as a guide for the daily practice of government as well as an exemplar for life. In effect, Christian doctrine was now applied to the problems of secular government in the hope that once this law influenced and structured human society, it would make inevitable a return to the pristine liberties of the Apostolic Church; it would force clerics out of secular affairs, thereby resuscitating the imitation of Christ within all orders of society. The executor of this testament was to be the secular lord, whose duty it was "to defend the evangelical law." [39]

Unmindful, then, to the mysteries of reform, Wyclif called upon the laity to realize his dream. Just as the endowment of the church had begun with the cooperative efforts of laymen and theologians, "as is clear from Constantine with his council and Sylvester," so, Wyclif says, "it is fitting that it be rectified through functioning laymen and instructing theologians." [40] This must be the path of reform, for "unless God shall act through the secular branch, the destruction of the Christian people shall follow." [41] Repeatedly, often stridently, Wyclif plead for reform; "the most noble work of Christian charity," he says, is the return of the church to that condition ordered by Christ. But because of the present condition of the clergy, it would be foolish to expect them to lead in this reform. The secular lords, however, are able to do a great deal and that which is most important. Because of this the reformation must proceed from

---

[39] *Trialogus*, p. 298; *DE*, p. 383.

[40] "Hoc autem verissimiliter coniecturo, quod, sicut dotacio ecclesie cepit a laicis atque theologicis, ut patet de Constantino cum suo consilio et Silvestro, sic oportet, quod rectificatur per laicos operantes et theologos instruentes." *VSS*, III, 29.

[41] "Et sic, nisi deus in brachio seculari adiuverit, sequetur dissipacio populi cristiani ..." *DB*, p. 83.

them. [42] The onus for reform, therefore, rests with the secular powers. It is to them alone that "all ecclesiastical possessions belong by right" and they alone possess the power and responsibility "to coerce the clergy." [43] According to faith, Wyclif asserts, the clergy are to be without possession; kings, therefore, as the vicars of God, must redress this injury to God. [44] This does not mean, however, that reformation can be effected through the sole agency of the lords; instead "the whole church must remedy this." [45] Everyone had to be involved in the reformation of the church if the theocracy was to be correctly repristinated. This most certainly included the clergy.

One of the most important precepts voiced in the New Testament was the evangelical poverty of Christ's institution. Following the example of Christ, His clergy were exhorted to live "exproprietarily." As an integral part of God's scheme, it became man's when biblical precept became the principle of the political communities' organization. Wyclif was adamant; in this religious polity, the clergy should be free from unnecessary wealth, the source of all evil. [46] This was not true for all segments of the church. Temporal lords, for example, should possess temporalities in moderation if for no other reason than to strike fear in those spitefully opposing Christ's law. [47] Likewise, those in the community of labor and trade could possess moderate wealth. The clergy, however, ought to be freed from wealth's contamination.

---

[42] See Loserth, "Wiclifs Sendschreiben," pp. 66-67, for a resume of the tract "Exposicio super Matthei XXIV," with the transcription: "Temporales domini possunt studere evangelia in lingua eis cognita et reducere ecclesiam ad ordinacionem quam Christus instituit. Et istud foret opus precipuum caritatis." This same position can be found in *DS*, p. 45. This was but an extension of the "onus gubernandi regna sive domina" which "tam reges quam domini" have assumed for God. *FZ*, p. 261.

[43] "Sed cum notum sit quod huiusmodi defectus stat magis in clero, tota ecclesia debet correccioni isti intendere. Ex parte autem brachii secularis, patet quod ipsum habet precipuum interesse. Nam omnia illa temporalia dominia que clerus occupat, debent alteri brachio pertinere; et suum est bona sua requirere, tum, quia dedit illis deus potestatem coactivam ad talia requirendum, tum eciam quia talium excommunicatorum ministerium inficit ecclesiam, et specialiter ex consensu." *DB*, p. 265f.

[44] "Item constat ex fide, quod Cristus sic ordinavit clerum suum totum vivere vitam pauperem exproprietarie, et illa ordinacio plurium est eversa, clero occupante dominia que ex dei ordinacione debent adiacere brachio seculari. Igitur reges, qui secundum Augustinum sunt dei vicarii, debent rectificare dei iniuriam." *Ibid.*

[45] *Ibid.*

[46] *Ibid.*, pp. 33-34.

[47] "Deus enim wult quod seculares domini moderate habundent temporalibus, ut potestative incuciant timorem discolis contrariis legi Cristi." *Ibid.* For this idea, see *Dialogus*, p. 4; *DB*, p. 33; *PW*, I, 243.

Clearly the vicariate of the laymen was not that of the clergy—theirs was to follow Christ most closely, to be nearer to God; theirs was to provide a living witness, and theirs was to be supported by voluntary offerings of the laity. [48] Wyclif thought this to be patently obvious, and having difficulty accepting the opposite view, constantly cited biblical passages to substantiate his view that evangelical poverty was not only the most perfect estate in the church, but also nearest to the state of innocence. [49] It was a position he never abandoned. Excessive wealth affected every Christian for it vitiated the admonishment "come follow me"; but nowhere was wealth more pernicious than with the clergy.

Unfortunately the hallowed example of Christ had been lost. Instead of living in His imitation, the clergy had become avaricious, beset with violence and forever grasping in the hope of usurping secular power. "Instead of shepherds, they want to be lords." [50] The cause of their avarice, the source of their greed, for Wyclif was endowment, poisoning the vascular system of the church. This had not subsided in the course of the years, but had grown. As a result the church had, in Wyclif's eyes, declined. Churchmen no longer followed Christ, and again drawing the parallel between Pharisees and the prelates of his own period, Wyclif pronounced decline. Like the Pharisees the contemporary clergy burdened the church with their laws, cultic forms and orders, all of which rested not on Christ's example, but on secular drive of the "Hildebrandine" church to establish its worldly "libertas." [51] The Church Militant had declined from the ascension of Christ. It will continue to do so until such time as the clergy's greed and desire for secular power has been eradicated and poverty and humility reestablished. The simplicity of this was for Wyclif a truism: "the root of all perturbation in the world is the decline of the clergy from the law of Christ to civil and traditional life." [52] In such a state, the solution had to be as radical as the

---

[48] "Est enim fides quam magnificare debet catholicus quod prior status cleri quam Christus instituit est perfectissimus, scilicet quod secluderetur a mundo, recipiendo a laicis alimenta et tegumenta necessaria ad laborem quibus tribueret necessariores elemosinas spirituales." *OM*, p. 171. See also *DE*, p. 281, and *DB*, p. 268.

[49] See *DCD*, III, 88; *DCD*, IV, 492.

[50] Benrath, *Bibelkommentar*, p. 330.

[51] *Ibid.*, p. 231, and above, Chapter III.

[52] "Non enim cadit auctoritas vel racio dispensandi; unde verisimile est quod radix tocius perturbacionis in seculo est cleri declinacio a lege Christi ad vitam et tradiciones civiles." *DE*, p. 189.

problem, fire had to be met with fire, and Wyclif's radicalism was disendowment.

If the agency for reform lay primarily with the secular lords, the means was a radical dispossession of ecclesiastical temporalities, thereby forcing the church to return to its spiritual essence. In the "De Fide Catholica," Wyclif writes: "... it is clear that the faithful can and ought to help to reduce the priesthood to that first order of Christ." [53] For Wyclif the capability of effecting just such a reduction to the pristine state obviously existed in the removal of clerical temporalities. Again, and from his first biblical expositions found in the *Commentary* to his very last sermons, Wyclif wielded the hammer of clerical dispossession. [54] Again and again, from the brilliance of his student career to the harmless, bitter days of decline, Wyclif attempted to persuade and finally demand that the church revert to the order of the Primitive Church. [55] In all of this, Wyclif absolutized a form of historical Christianity, divesting it of any temporal or ephemeral element, making it authoritative and normative for all time.

Wyclif felt that only the return to the primitive order of the church could bring adequate reform. [56] Relieve the church of its excessive endowment and the church will be restored to its primitive condition. [57] "Every man," he wrote in the *De Potestate Pape*, "should honor the Holy Mother Church, but the highest honor would be to remove from it the blot of turpitude by serving it in a dignified and noble way, by returning it to pristine liberty." [58] Simplistic perhaps, but Wyclif compellingly argued that if the church would only allow its landed holdings to be removed, then it could begin the long progres-

---

[53] "... patet quod fideles possunt et debent iuvare ut sacerdotium ad primam Christi regulam sit reductum ..." *OM*, p. 102. See also Loserth, "Sendschreiben," p. 26, where this passage is quoted.

[54] See Benrath, *Bibelkommentar*, p. 44, and Smalley, "Wyclif's Postilla super Totam Bibliam," p. 193ff.

[55] "Unde confidenter prenostico quod ante correccionem nostram secundum statum primevum non deficiet regnorum perturbacio." *DE*, p. 56. Wyclif even calls this church an exemplar: "Quantum ad assumptum, patet quod pusillus grex apostolorum secundum formam quam Cristus instituit, debuit esse exemplar et origo tocius posterioris ecclesie cristiane ..." *DB*, p. 265. See also *Dialogus*, p. 49, for a return to the Primitive Church.

[56] In addition to the citations above, see *DE*, pp. 56, 189.

[57] *DOR*, pp. 182, 189, 210-211, 275-276, 280f.

[58] "... omnis homo debet honorare sanctam matrem ecclesiam, sed honor eius precipuus foret auferre ab ea turpitudinis maculam, servando in ea statum tam dignum et nobilem et tuendo pristinam libertatem ..." *DPP*, p. 373.

sion back to apostolic life. [59] Only through dispossession could the church return, only through clerical disendowment could Christians in general learn again to spurn excessive possessions in their attempt at redemption. This return to poverty would constitute the chief means to general reform. Nor was there danger in this method; dispossession would only affect the greedy and the thieving, not the pious. It would relieve good men "from the burden of land-owning"; it would incline the clergy toward "the original state, which Christ instituted for His clergy, living exproprietarily in common." [60]

Wyclif clearly thought that ecclesiastical dispossession was the way, the only way, to reform the church and Christianity in general. Yet as articulated as this reforming principle was, there is a certain confusion and conceptual growth as to the identity of the reforming agent. Commonly this reform would be accomplished by the secular lords, most notably the king. While this is certainly so, it is a later development in Wyclif's thought; it also disregards many examples where Wyclif emphasized the cooperative nature of the enterprise. Surely the secular lords were most responsible, but as already noted, there existed any number of injunctions for the laity in general to participate in any reforming movement. As early as 1371, that is, in the year of his earliest commitment to reform through dispossession, Wyclif saw in the "community of the laity," the "chain" which, in conjunction with the king, would tear the temporalities of the church from the "unrighteous Mammon." [61]

While the agent for reform varied at times within the polity of

---

[59] Benrath, *Bibelkommentar*, p. 197, fn. 449: "Sed indubie minus malum esset, quod ecclesia privetur toto dominio temporali, quam quod persona vel communitas foret scismatica occasione oblacionis temporalium, vel quod onus ecclesiarum particularium ex lege evangelii debitum sit substractum, tunc enim rediretur ad vitam illam apostolicam."

[60] "Nec est periculum in dissolucione prudenti furum vel sociorum eorum, cum exhinc boni alleviabuntur a sarcina terrenorum et clerus inclinabitur ad statum pristinum, quem Cristus instituit clero suo, vivendo exproprietarie in comuni." *VSS*, III, 56.

[61] "Tercii vero exponunt istud de temporali domino auferente ab ecclesia possessiones quibus abutitur, talis enim foret missus de celo et haberet potestatem super divicias aureorum que sunt claves abisse, et cathena est communitas laicorum confederatorum cum eo ab abstrahendum mammona iniquitatis ab ecclesiasticis, sub illis enim latitat diabolus adversans homini sicut Behemoth sub umbra Job 40, unde ablatis illis ligaretur potestas diaboli que seducit gentes per ecclesiasticos et hoc usque ad tempus antichristi (Apok 20, 1) B 170 b." Quoted from Benrath, *Bibelkommentar*, p. 308, fn. 848.

England, [62] normally the responsibility for disfranchise rested squarely on the shoulders of the secular lords. There was good reason for Wyclif to swear: "may God intervene so that they [the clergy] bring the secular powers on themselves," if his reform was to be successful, if his England was to be prosperous. [63] He could and did invite the clergy and especially the bishops to voluntarily divest themselves of all temporalities, but he had little faith in them and for this reason consistently called upon the nobility. [64] Theirs it was to purge the church of its ancient blasphemy, [65] to restore it to "its first perfection," [66] to rid the church of its "diabolical poison." [67] And the "medicine necessary" for this task "would be to expropriate the entire clergy and renew the former order of Christ" with respect to His church. Then all the clergy, whether bishops, clerics or monks "would live purely exproprietarily, just as formerly, accepting neither dignity nor ecclesiastical benefice on account of cupidity of temporalities nor honor." [68] If possible this revocation should be accomplished peacefully; if not, force was an acceptable alternative. [69] However implemented, reformation was to be carried out prudently, systematically, politically. Practically, withdrawal of ecclesiastical temporalities could be used to alleviate ecclesiastical involvement in secular affairs. Kings and clerics had long argued that exploitation of ecclesiastical offices was necessary for the administration of the realm. [70] Like Wyclif, they

---

[62] *Ibid.*, pp. 333, 351f.; see also John Wyclif, *Select English Works of John Wyclif*, ed. Thomas Arnold (Oxford, 1869-1871), III, 351, who poses the question, who can and should undertake the reformation of the church. His answer is clear: everyone should, each in their own way. Further, *Dialogus*, pp. 80-81, for same sentiment.

[63] *Ibid.*, p. 330, and *VSS*, III, 239: "Nam regni prosperitas stat in rectificacione cleri sui secundum statum suum originalem, quem Cristus instituit."

[64] *Dialogus*, pp. 80-82.

[65] *DB*, pp. 6-8.

[66] "... et temporalium appropriacio posset verisimilius esse eorum correccio, ecclesie ad primam perfeccionem restitucio et tam vivorum quam mortuorum melioracio." *DCD*, IV, 478; *DOR*, pp. 210-211, 275-276.

[67] "Quarta conclusio: Medicina necessaria ad extinguendum venenum diaboli foret totum clerum exproprietarium facere et ordinacionem Christi primevam quoad suam ecclesiam innovare." *SS*, II, 269.

[68] "Tunc enim viverent omnes episcopi, religiosi, possessionati et clerici pure exproprietarie sicut olim nec acciperent dignitatem vel beneficium ecclesiasticum propter cupidinem temporalium vel honorem." *Ibid.* See also *SS*, III, 21; *DE*, pp. 203, 308.

[69] Benrath, *Bibelkommentar*, pp. 308-309.

[70] W. A. Pantin, *The English Church in the Fourteenth Century* (Notre Dame, 1962), pp. 30-42.

too saw entanglement and exploitation, but this time for the convenience of the secular government. In both cases involvement rested on a conception of Christian society which allowed the identification of Church and State. [71] The issue was which of the two, Church or State, would subsume the other. For Wyclif this question posed no problem; all issues had to be revalued in terms of Christ's law and His polity. And in this religious polity the withdrawal of ecclesiastical temporalities could be used for stipendia, enabling the king to employ secular administrators rather than complicating bishops and curates in the secular affairs of the realm. [72] Using ecclesiastical lands in such a way would allow literate laymen, "so necessary to the office of the king and the administration of the realm," to be supported and encouraged. No longer would the king be forced to rely upon ecclesiastics for the competent administration of his realm; no longer, argued Wyclif, need the clergy be infected with simony and sacrilege, so often accompanying secular responsibility. [73]

Theoretically, practically, rulers must relieve the church of its endowment, not in order to despoil it, but to revive it. [74] Only a return to Christ's order could bring adequate reform and such reform required clerical dispossession. [75] If reform was the goal, dispossession through the agency of the king, as the guarantor of spiritual orthodoxy, was the way; if deprivation was Wyclif's panacea, the laity was his tool.

---

[71] *Ibid.*, p. 44.

[72] "Minus malum esset quod expropriata forent omnia temporalia quibus ecclesia Anglicana dotatur, ut pro eorum proventibus darentur stipendia servitoribus regis nostri quam quod episcopi et alii curati forent adeo secularibus regni negociis implicata." *OM*, p. 51.

[73] Ideo alias dixi, quod minus malum foret, ut expropriata forent omnia temporalia, quibus ecclesia Anglie est dotata, ut ex eis darentur stipendia laicis literatis, necessariis ad officium regis et secularium dominorum ..." *VSS*, III, 85. This is a very common theme; in addition to the previous note, *OM*, p. 51, which is almost verbatim, see *DE*, p. 180; *DB*, p. 63, 155; and *PW*, I, 98.

[74] *DE*, pp. 189, 340.

[75] *Ibid.*, p. 56.

CHAPTER SIX

THE CONDITIONALITY OF ENDOWMENT

Presupposing, the correctness of the apostolic ideal and the necessity of lay correction to effect meaningful reform, John Wyclif sought desperately to establish the right of the secular nobility to dispossess the church. To underpin this corrective role for the nobility legally, Wyclif contended that all ecclesiastical endowment had been granted conditionally. He attempted to make that conclusion compelling and clerical dispossession feasible by first establishing the historical conditionality of all endowment and then describing the legal consequences of this arrangement.

In the twenty-fifth chapter of the *De Veritate Sacrae Scripturae* Wyclif embarked on this task, baldly stating that the realm has a right over temporal property of the church. Should the church be negligent in the exercise of its function, he continues, then its temporalities should be withdrawn by the secular loads. [1] Out of the almost innumerable ways in which Wyclif might possibly have sought to establish his argument, he immediately decides to determine the factual nature of the question in historical terms. There is nothing so unusual here in either Wyclif's approach or manner of working. Both were typical of the legal reasoning prevalent among crown lawyers whose concern in land-law was to determine origin, nature of tenure and method of acquisition. But this avenue was strikingly atypical for a theologian. It was especially unorthodox for a reformer interested in the spiritual resuscitation of the evangelical church. [2] Nonetheless, by employing this historical method to pry into the tangled question of ecclesiastical possessions, Wyclif securely grounded his inquiry on empirical evidence. This made his approach all the more persuasive to those interested in, and capable of, effecting a radical change in the disposition of church temporalities.

---

[1] *VSS*, III, 1: "Ex istis colligi potest sentencia, quam sepe inserui, licet sit mundo odibilis, scilicet, quod licet in casu tam subtrahere quam auferre bona ecclesie a suis prepositis."

[2] The following quotation is from Bracton, *De Legibus et Consuetudinibus Angliae*, ed. Travers Twiss (London, 1878), I, 84, and it illustrates this method of systematic assessment: "... quis donare possit, et quis non. Item quae res possit donari, et quae non, et cui dari possit, et cui non. Item quae exigantur ad hoc,

Wyclif began by arguing that historically all property belonging to the church had been initially conferred by the laity as alms. 3 Committed to this stance, he proceeded with his formal argument. In the evangelical church Christ and His followers were paupers, holding and possessing nothing of their own and exercising absolutely no civil authority. 4 This was the historical reality of the apostolic church. The secular endowment of the church, therefore, could neither rest on, nor find its jurisdictional authority in, the principle of hereditary right. That was certainly clear; but even if hereditary right were accepted as a justification, according to the view that Christ was Lord and possessor of the whole world with the clergy succeeding to this total, universal lordship, there would still be difficulties. For in that case the emperor Constantine, by means of his donation, would have granted away or kept for himself temporalities which were

---

quod valeat donatio. Item qualiter acquiratur possessio, et qualiter transferatur ab uno ad alium, et cum fuerit acquisita, qualiter amittatur, et cum amissa fuerit, qualiter restituatur." Another, perhaps even more pertinent example of determining or buttressing one's case in historical terms, is that of the crown jurists of Oxford and Cambridge, who drew up a learned disquisition at the behest of Edward I. Their purpose was to prevent the papacy from interfering in the feudal relationship between England and Scotland. The basis of their argument was the numerous historical precedents from Brutus through King Arthur and then subsequent English history. For the report, see Walsingham, *Historica Anglicana*, ed. Henry Thomas Riley (London, 1863-1864), I, 87-95. See also Loserth, "Studien zur Kirchenpolitik Englands," pp. 14-15.

3 *VSS*, III, 16: "Et per consequens ex diffinicione elemosine posita libro quinto capitulo ... sequitur, quod omnia talia bona ecclesie sunt elemosine corporales." Buddensieg, the editor, remarks in a footnote his inability to find the reference. My research has also been fruitless. The notion, however, that the English church had been secularly endowed in its totality was a commonplace for Wyclif and his contemporaries. See A. Hamilton Thompson, *The English Clergy and Their Organization in the Later Middle Ages* (Oxford, 1947), p. 10, where he informs us that "as early as the last quarter of the thirteenth century we find an enunciation of the theory, embodied afterwards in the preamble of the Statute of Provisors, that the English Church as a whole had been founded and endowed by the kings of England and others of Christ's faithful people for the spread of the orthodox faith, for the remission of their sins, for the increase of divine worship, for the keeping of hospitality, the distribution o alms to the poor and the supply of suitable and resident ministers to individual churches." See also Howell, *Regalian Right in Medieval England*, p. 192: "Ultimately ... even the wealth which attached to cathedral prebends had been given to the church either by the king or by some other lord or donor. All patronage was in origin lay patronage. And the king, as 'Advowee Paramount,' the patron of bishoprics, was the natural defender ..." Lay foundation of all ecclesiastical possessions is also referred to in *Rot. Parl.*, I, 219; II, 144-145, 162, item 35, and 172.

4 Item Cristus et sui clerici ex primaria institucione erant pauperrimi, non habentes quidquam in proprio, ut superius ostensum ..." *VSS*, III, 17.

not his to endow, grant or keep, and similarly, all lords holding "the church's heritage" would have been heretical or sacrilegious for whatever land they held really belonged to the clergy. [5] Because of the poverty of Christ's institution, because of the righteousness of secular lords, this was obviously not the case. It was necessary, therefore, for the clergy to concede that all the temporal lands of the church stem from the "pura elemosina" of the secular lords. [6] Sliding into his transition, Wyclif wrote:

> Thus there remains from all this evidence that the entire donation of the church is from the alms of lords. Which, lest it be forgotten, is stipulated in the charters of our realm of England: how the king and other founders gave in pure and perpetual alms such lordships to the church. From which the corollary seems to follow that all clerics are mendicants, not only to God, but with respect to men. [7]

Having begun with the historical reality of Christ and His Church, Wyclif quickly moved on to the touchstone of English history. Once

---

[5] "Igitur dotacio ecclesie non potest ex iure hereditario vendicari eo, quod tunc quilibet presbiter foret dominancior imperatore ex iure hereditario patris Cristi. Quod si foret verum, omnes civiles domini forent excomunicati detinentes hereditates ecclesie sicut et Constantinus, antequam dotavit ecclesiam, et cum non libere concessit ecclesie, quod antea non erat suum, sed limitavit sibi officium, quod erat suum, retinens sibi et successoribus suis magnam partem, sequeretur, quod ipse et omnes tales seculares domini remanerent sacrilegi atque heretici, quod foret summa demencia anticristi." *Ibid.*

[6] "Oportet igitur, clericos nostros concedere, quod habent omnem dotacionem ex pura elemosina dominorum ..." *ibid.*, pp. 17-18. Wyclif also indicates the origin of all ecclesiastical properties in using the parable of the owl, first stated at a London parliament. See *DCD*, II, 7. Further consult *DOR*, p. 139, and Walsingham, *Historia Anglicana*, I, 314.

[7] "Relinquitur igitur ex quolibet evidenciis, quod tota dotacio ecclesie sit ex elemosinis dominorum. Quod, ne tradatur in oblicionem cavetur in cartis regni nostri Anglie, quomodo rex et alii fundatores in puram et perpetuam elemosinam donarunt talia dominia ecclesie. Ex quod videtur sequi corellarie, quod omnes clerici nedum ad deum ut omnes homines, sed quoad homines sunt mendici." *Ibid.*, p. 18. The presumption of apostolic poverty, upon which Wyclif bases his argument, was a hotly debated principle as was the dependent question of Christ's mendicancy. When Wyclif draws his corollary, he is referring to the religious orders and their controversy at Oxford with the mendicants. See M. D. Knowles, "The Censured Opinions of Uthred Boldon," *The Proceedings of the British Academy*, XXXVII (1951), 130; A. Gwynn, *The English Austin Friars* (Oxford, 1940), and Wyclif's "Determinatio ad argumenta magistri Outredi de Omesima monachi," *OM*, pp. 405ff. An interesting side-note is that Fitzralph, the archbishop of Armagh, assumes a position quite contrary to the stand of Wyclif in this question; namely, that Jesus Christ was a poor man, but that he did not practice begging and taught no one to beg. On the contrary, mendicancy was actually disapproved of by Christ. See Gerhard Lechler, *John Wycliffe and His English Precursors*, pp. 65-57.

there he called upon the evidence of royal charters to document an English tenure, frankalmoign, knowing full well that this form of tenure was an integral part of the feudal land-law of England, at once so assessable, so respective of custom, memory and history. The type of tenure known variously as frankalmoign, free alms or "libera elemosina" was essentially a land tenure, which had been granted to ecclesiastics in return for the performance of some form of spiritual service such as prayers and masses for the souls of the grantor and his subsequent heirs. Because the service performed was of a spiritual nature, characterized by the absence of any temporal service, the grantee was not required to swear an oath of fealty. [8] This peculiar form of tenure was further distinguished by the condition that the spiritual service called for, be uncertain. If this were not the case, if indeed specific service was prescribed, such as the definite stipulation to sing *one* mass a year, then the tenure was not spoken of as being tenure by frankalmoign, but rather tenure by divine service. [9] The distinction is important. A writ of "contra formam feoffamenti" cannot be brought against land held in frankalmoign because no certain service is required. [10] It could be brought against land held in divine service and the land could be recovered by the secular donor through the agency of the English law. Later Wyclif will use this distinction to legitimatize the recovery of church temporalities on the part of secular lords.

Can Wyclif's assertion that the king and other founders gave the entire endowment of the church in "pure and perpetual alms" be actually documented in the extant charters of the realm as he states or is this simply an attempt to overlay his argument with a veneer of legitimacy? The Statute of Carlisle, a statute issued by Edward I in 1306, states that the king and other founders of the realm gave lands and holdings in free alms and that a major cause of their donations was the performance of almsgiving. [11] This same statute is

---

8 F. Pollock and F. W. Maitland, *The History of English Law Before the Time of Edward I* (2 vols., 2nd ed.; Cambridge, 1923), I, 240ff. Further, Edward Coke, *The Institutes of the Laws of England* (3 vols., 1st Amer. ed.; Philadelphia, 1812), I, sect. 135, 136 and 137.

9 *Ibid.*

10 See Coke, II, bk. 1, 18.

11 *Rot. Parl.*, I, 217, 'Statutum Karliol': " Nupur ad noticiam Domini Regis, ex gravi querela magnatum, procerum, et aliorum notilium regni sui, pervenit, quod cum monasteria, prioratus, et domus religiose ad laudem et honorem Dei et exaltationem sacrae ecclesie per regem et progenitores suos, et predictos magnates et nobiles et eorum antecessores fundata fuissent, et terre et tenementa quam plurima essent data

later referred to, repeated and elaborated upon in 1350-51 and again in 1376 under Edward III. The later issues are even more specific in content than the first, and they register precisely the tradition Wyclif is so anxious to use:

> You nobles, let us think and reconsider how his noble progenitors, the kings of England and other great nobles of the same land, with the aid and the devotion of Christian people, founded in ancient times the churches in England; then through great devotion, various deeds and in the process of time, they gave possessions with diverse franchises and all the temporalities which the churches have. Such things, along with those which our Lord the king himself gave and granted to them, constitute more than the third part of his realm. [12]

Although these examples lend credence to Wyclif's position, documenting the fact that at least the king and a part of the nobility felt that the English church's temporalities had been bestowed by the king's ancestors as well as his nobles, they do not touch upon the condition or nature of the grants. [13] Consequently, there is an issue

---

per ipsos dictis monasteriis, prioratibus, et domibus, ac viris religiosis ... tam clerici quam laici admitterentur, et pro animabus predictorum fundatorum et heredum suorum fierent in eisdem."

[12] "Primes, lui; leise penser et repenser, coment ses progenitours nobles Roys d'Engleterre, et autres Grandes de mesme terre, ove l'aide et la devotion de poeple Cristien, en auncien temps fesoient les Esglises en Engleterre; puis par grande devotion par diversez foitz et proces de temps donerent possessions, ove diverses Franchises et toutz les Temperaltez q eles ont. Queles choses, ovesq ceo q nostre Sr le Roi mesme ad done et grante a eux, si amonent a pluis q la Tierce partie de son Roialme." This is a portion of the text of 1350-1351, *Rot. Parl.*, II, 232, whereas the 1376 formulation is *Rot. Parl.*, II, 337. Another section of the text of 1350-1351 alludes to the same condition. "Come jadiz le Parlement de bone memoire Sire Edward Roi d'Engleterre, ael nor Seignr le Roi q ore est, l'an de son regne trentisine quint, a Dardoill tenuz, oie la Petition mys devant ledit ael et son Conseil en le dit Parlement per la Communalte de son Roialme, Contenant, q come seinte Eglise d'Engleterre estoit founde en estat de prelacie deinz le Roialme d'Engleterre per le dit ael et ses progenitours, et Countes, Barons, et Nobles de son Roialme, et lour Auncestres, pur eux et le poeple enfourmer de la Lei de Dieu, et per faire Hospitalites, Almoignes, et autres oevers de Charite, et lieus ou les Esglises faurent foundez pur les Almes des Foundours et de lour Heirs ..." Perhaps an indication that Wyclif used this statute can be seen when in *VSS*, III, 88, he points out that more than one-third of the revenues of the crown are in the hands of the clergy—a fact noted in the text above. I say perhaps because that figure was common. See also Howell, *Regalian Right*, pp. 186-200: according to Statute of Provisors, all patronage in England was lay in origin.

[13] See *supra* fn. 2, as well as Johannis Haller, *Papsttum und Kirchenreform, Vier Kapitel zur Geschichte des ausgehenden Mittelalters* (Berlin 1903), I, 391: "Nach englischem Rechte ist das Gegenteil der Fall, sie [church] tragt ihren Besitz vom Staate nur zu Lehen, er ist ihr nur zu bestimmtem Zwecke und gegen Übernahme

of fact. Even though the king, his ancestors and other founders have endowed the church with all that it has, how do archbishops and bishops, not to speak of abbots and others, hold their land; what is the nature of their tenure—by barony or frankalmoign? Is the land obligated or not? Glanvil, when discussing alienation, simply states that neither a bishop nor an abbot can alienate any part of his demesne without the consent and confirmation of the king, because this is held of "elemosina" from the king and his heirs. [14] Yet holding land "de elemosina" without any additional appellation or such adjectives as "pure," "perpetual" or "free," is still very loose, if not nebulous. Nonetheless, even in Glanvill, one can discover, although circuitously, that at least bishops, archbishops and other prelates held temporalities "per baroniam." [15] This is borne out in the *Rotuli Parliamentorum*:

> From the speeches of the prelates, counts, barons and others, a certain petition in this parliament was set forth in these words: our lord the king and his council showed the archbishops, bishops, prelates, counts, barons and the other great lords of the land how they held their baronies, lands, tenements and honors in chief from our lord the king through military service . . . [16]

bestimmter Leistungen gegeben," and the following discussion. Haller also asserts, p. 377, in line with Thompson, that England retained an awareness "dass alles Gut, das die Kirche vom Könige erhalten hat, ursprunglich Staatsgut war ..." See also Thompson, *The English Clergy*, p. 10, fn. 2, where the author quotes a protest by Archibshop Romeyn of York against a papal plan to annex a prebend. The grounds for his defense are interesting: "Verumtamen non hec fuit pia intentio ac devota clare memorie catholicorum regum Anglie et aliorum Christi fidelium qui nedum prefatas nostras ecclesias sed et totam ecclesiam Anglicanam ad dilatationem fidei orthodoxe fundantes eas temporalium bonorum largitionibus dotaverunt amplissimis et libertatum immunitatibus munierunt sed ea nimirum consideratione constat sic eos eisdem ecclesiis fuisse munificos ut cum delictorum expiatione consequerentur per hoc salubre remedium animarum cultus divini nominis augeretur servaretur hospitalitas elemosine darentur pauperibus et per ministros idoneos ad quos pro tempore ex eisdem bonis ecclesiastica stipendia devenirent servire prefatis ecclesiis personaliter tenerentur."

[14] *Tractatus de legibus et consuetudinibus regni Anglie qui Glanvilla vocatur*, ed. G. D. G. Hall (London, 1965), p. 74: "Notandum autem quod nec episcopus nec abbas, quia eorum baronie sunt de elemosina domini regis et antecessorum eius, non possunt de dominicis suis aliquam partem donare ad remanenciam sine assensu et confirmatione domini regis."

[15] *Ibid.*, p. 106, states that homage is not due for a fief given in frankalmoign. Bishops-elect, moreover, are to do homage before their consecration. The obvious conclusion is that bishops do not hold all the temporalities of their bishoprics in frankalmoign.

[16] *Rot. Parl.*, I, 383, no. 114; *ibid.*, p. 456, allows: "... quod Archiepiscopi, Episcopi, Abbates, Priores, Comites, Barones, Milites et omnes alii cujuscumque

From this it seems certain that Wyclif's assertion that the king and other founders gave the church its entire endowment in "pure and perpetual alms" corresponded neither to the historical tradition nor the legal realities of the period. Granted, the king, his predecessors and the secular nobility firmly maintained the historical reality of their endowment, but the tenurial basis of that endowment—this is the crux of the question—was by no means solely frankalmoign. [17]

The direction of Wyclif's argument is clear. He portrays the endowment of the church, beginning with Constantine and more to the point that of the *ecclesia anglicana*, as stemming from the pious, personal donations of king and magnates. These secular gifts were made in free alms, made in return for service, spiritual service. Whether the owed service is certain or not, Wyclif leaves unsaid and unspecified. Because of this, the exact tenurial nature of the endowment is left precisely where Wyclif wants—in obscurity. Nonetheless, whether frankalmoign or barony, both are feudal tenures and as such both imply and depend upon a contractual, bilateral agreement, an agreement whose basis was "do ut facias." Should such a contractual agreement be broken, should owed services not be made, should some form of fraudulent use be made "contra formam donationis," then, as with other feudal tenures, the endowment should revert to its proper owner. Summarizing, Wyclif can say:

> For all possessions with which the church is endowed are alms of secular lords from the first supposition, which were given to clerics in order that they should observe original religion from the second supposition. Therefore, since capital lordship remains in their possession from the third supposition, it follows that the purpose having been frustrated through their actions, secular donations ought to revert to their owners. [18]

---

conditionis existant qui de Nobis tenent in capite per Servicium militare ..." This form of tenure is treated lucidly by Pollard and Maitland, *History of English Law*, I, 279ff.

[17] *Supra*, fn. 2.

[18] *VSS*, III, 21: "Suppositis igitur hiis tribus radicibus facile est, ostendere conclusionem propositam ab infimo episcopo usque ad romanum pontificem. Nam omnia bona, quibus dotatur ecclesia, sunt elemosine secularium dominorum ex supposicione prima, que donata sunt clericis, ut observent religionem primevam ex supposicione secunda. Cum igitur remanet penes eos capitale dominium, ex supposicione tercia, sequitur, quod frustrato per se fine dotacione seculares debent ad bona propria resortiri." A possible source for this opinion might be *Libri Feudorum in Authentica D. Iustiniani Imp. Avg. Novellearum Volumen* (Lugduni, MDL), Libri secundus, tit. XXIV, c. 6. It is a source sometimes used by Wyclif (*OM*, pp. 41, 413; *DCD*, IV, 454), and conceivably is referred to here.

Here Wyclif has not only blurred the distinction between frankalmoign and tenure by divine service, he has also changed the import
of both. The intent of frankalmoign was the exchange of tenurial
holdings for either certain or uncertain services, but always services
of a personal nature such as masses or prayers for the donor and his
heirs. The grounds Wyclif gives here for endowment remain uncertain, but they are hardly personal. Instead, he says, the intention
was to free the church from secular involvement, to enable the clergy
to pray more devoutly, and to concentrate more on the sacraments. [19]
In short, Wyclif subtly alters the purpose of secular endowment—the
donor's personal piety and profit—to fit his general argument while
still relying upon the foundation of feudal tenure in order to push for
reversion should the conditions of tenure not be met.

In support of this position, Wyclif appeals to fiscal or secular
law as well as the law of scripture.

> This is confirmed from the assumption of the Archdeacon, that these
> temporalities had not been given to those living secularly and con-
> founding the clerical office. Therefore, if clerics occupying the tem-
> poralities are wanting according to the form of the donation, temporal
> lords are held not only by the law of the fisc but by the law of
> scripture to provide [guard against the impoverishment] concerning
> their properties. [20]

Although the meaning of this passage is relatively unambiguous, the
authority it calls upon is not. The "lex fisci," while a commonplace
in the corpus of Roman law, [21] is not a standard reference in the
legal terminology of the fourteenth century. Again, what law does
Wyclif have in mind? The term "fiscus" appears often enough,
however, and it usually means fief or imperial treasury. [22] Both

---

[19] "Propterea dicunt sancti et leges concorditur, quod ea intencione dotata est
ecclesia, ut sacerdotes servantes priorem pauperiem orarent devocius, predicarent
liberius et ministrarent iustius bona pauperum et ecclesiastica sacramenta." *Ibid.*, p. 19.

[20] "Confirmatur ex assumpto Archidiaconi, quod non istis seculariter viventibus
et officium clerici confundentibus erant data hec temporalia. Si igitur desunt clerici
secundum formam donacionis temporalia occupantes, domini temporales tenentur
nedum ex lege fisci, sed ex lege scripture de bonis propriis providere." *Ibid.*, pp.
21-22. The editor of Glanville, G. D. G. Hall, notes in his appendix that "canon
law included prohibitions against all alienation of church lands (Decretals iii, 10,
1-3): the patron was under a duty 'providere,' i.e., to guard against all impoverishment
of the church." Glanvill, *Tractatus de legibus*, p. 185. This same sense is given in
Habel and Gröbel, *Mittellateinisches Glossar*, p. 318, and is the meaning I have
used in the above translation.

[21] D. 49.14; C. &.73; 10.1; 5.9.

[22] See R. E. Latham, *Revised Medieval Latin Word-List* (London, 1965); V. F.

meanings are appropriate here for although Wyclif employs the term "lex fisci" at no other time, he does cite with some frequency the laws of the emperor Conrad II included in the *Libri Feudorum*. Each time he does so, he cites them in precisely the same context—the withdrawal of church temporalities through the secular lords—as the "lex fisci." 23 This close association of context and citation as well as the general connotation of "fiscus," meaning pertaining to the affairs of the fief or imperial treasury, are compelling reasons to equate the "lex fisci," referred to above, with the imperial or feudal law of the *Libri Feudorum*, regularly appended to the *Corpus Juris Civilis* and especially with its title XL, "de capitulis corradi." 24 There are a number of reasons though for being dissatisfied with this interpretation. Although the text of the "de capitulis corradi" concerns itself with clerical crime, it does not deal with endowment directly.

> If a cleric, such as a bishop or an abbot, holding a benefice under crown grant, given not for himself but for the church, should lose that benefice because of his guilt, the benefice is to belong to the king so long as the cleric lives and holds his office. But after his death it is to revert to his successor. 25

Furthermore, the cause of deprivation, clerical guilt, is ambiguous in the extreme even if one disregards the difficulty of matching text with authority. Finally, this is imperial law, that is, foreign law. Admitting its applicability in some oblique way to Wyclif's argument, it still leaves unanswered the question as to whether its usage would have, in fact, any foundation in actual English practice.

A more plausible interpretation is to take Wyclif's "lex fisci" not as the codified imperial and feudal law of the *Libri Feudorum*, but simply as the feudal law, the "lex terrae" as it had evolved in England. Seen in this manner the "lex fisci" was the English feudal law that spelled out the rights of the royal fisc, using perhaps the legal provisions found in the *Libri Feudorum* as models to formulate existing

---

Niermeyer, *Mediae Latinitatis Lexicon Minus* (Leiden, 1957); C. T. Lewis and Charles Short, *A Latin Dictionary* (Oxford, 1879).

23 See *OM*, p. 413, and *DCD*, IV, 454.

24 *Libri Feudorum*, Liber secundus, tit. XL, 74-75. For a discussion of this law see Holdsworth, *History of English Law*, II, 108, 112-13, 258.

25 "Item si clericus, veluti episcopus, abbas, beneficium habens a rege datum non-solummodo personae, sed ecclesiae, ipsum propter suam culpam perdat: eo vivente, et ecclesiasticum beneficium vel honorem habente, ad regem pertineat, post mortem vero eius ad successorem eius revertatur." *Ibid.*

English practices. Secondly, that royal fisc was already being equated with "patria" and "respublica" and deemed a fictitious person [26] with rights and obligations of its own that in no way depended upon the person of the king. In other words, the fisc was the public treasury of the king [27] to be used for the common profit of the realm and its law was included in the general "lex terrae" that was at once feudal and common to both king and land.

Wyclif's contention, then, that temporal lords are bound by feudal law to protect the church against impoverishment can indeed be supported. This is especially so in the numerous prohibitions against clerical alienation. The second Statute of Westminster, issued under Edward I in 1285, sets down the principle that should lands be given to religious houses by the king or his progenitors be alienated by their abbots, priors, or others, then these lands shall be confiscated and held by the king. [28] If, however, the founder hapened to be an earl, baron, or "other person," then the process was somewhat different. In this case, a writ of "contra formam collationis" was to be issued on behalf of the founder in order that he might recover the alienated lands. The writ runs:

> Command such an abbot that he justly give up to B such a tenement, which was given to the said house in free alms by the aforesaid B or his ancestors, and which to the aforesaid B ought to revert, by the alienation which the aforesaid abbot has made of the aforesaid tenement, contrary to the form of the gift aforesaid, as he says. [29]

Moreover, if lands are alienated that have been given either as alms for the maintenance of a chantry or candles in a church or chapel, then, these too are to revert to the original founder. [30] While this is of interest, the subsequent portion of the clause is even more so:

> But if the land so given for a chantry, light, sustenance of poor people, or for the support and doing of other alms, be not alienated

---

[26] Kantorowicz, *King's Two Bodies*, p. 188ff.

[27] Post, *Studies in Medieval Legal Thought*, p. 374. See also Ullmann, *Principles*, p. 163ff.

[28] *Statutes of the Realm*, I, 91-92. This is the Statute of Westminister, II, c. xli. Later this particular clause was repeated and reaffirmed in 1376 by the Commons in a parliamentary petition under Edward III. See *Rotuli Parliamentorum*, II, 333.

[29] "Praecipe tali Abbati, quod juste, etc. reddat B tale tenementum quod eidem domui collatum fuit in liberam eleemosynam per praedictum B vel antecessores suos et quod ad praedictum B reverti debet per alienationem quam praedictus Abbas fecit de praedicto tenemento, contra formam collationis praedictae, ut dicit." *Ibid.*, p. 91.

[30] *Ibid.*

but such alms be withdrawn for the space of two years, an action shall lie with the donor or his heir to demand the land so given in domain, as it is ordained to in the Statute of Gloucester for lands leased to do, or to render the fourth part of the value of the land or more. [31]

This, therefore, applies not to baronial tenure by which the bishops or abbots hold from the king, but to tenure by frankalmoign or divine service. The basis for this action is the writ of "cessavit," a writ which has an interesting pedigree running back to Roman law with eventual inclusion into the corpus of Canon law. [32] Although Edward Coke mentions that he had read that this writ was used in England in the time of John, no trace has been found and it is not until Edward I that "cessavit" enters the law books in response to a growing need on the part of the landlord. [33]

Prior to Edward I, a lord was relatively limited in the courses of legal action he might take if his tenant failed, purposely or not, to perform the services for which he held his land. This was especially true when it came to removing the tenant from the land itself in order to regain actual possession. [34] Such difficulty in protecting the lord's interest in the land was partly remedied under Edward I with the development of the principle of distraint on the one hand and an action termed "cessavit per biennium" on the other. The writ of "cessavit," first set down in the Statute of Gloucester, held that if a tenant should neglect to perform the duties or services owed to the lord and had done so for two or more years, then he could be removed

---

[31] "Et si forte tenementum sic datum pro Cantaria, Luminari, potura pauperum, vel aliis elemosinis sustentandis, vel faciendis non fuit alienatum, sed subtracta fuit hujiusmodi elemosina per biennium, competat accio donatori vel ejus heredi ad petendum tenementum sic datum in dominico, sicut statutum est in statuto Gloucest', de tenemento dimissis ad faciendum vel ad reddendum quartam partem valoris tenementi, vel majoris." *Ibid.*, p. 92.

[32] According to Pollock and Maitland, *History of English Law*, I, 353, Justinian put into effect a rule that a tenant who had not paid his rent for three years may be evicted (Cod. 4.66.2). Later in Nov. 7.3.2, an exception is made for the church: when it is the landlord, the three year limit is reduced to two years, after which the tenant can be rejected.

[33] In discussing the writ of Cessavit, Pollack and Maitland write: "Coke says that he had 'read amongst ancient records' that a Cessavit was brought in the reign of King John. We have found no trace of any such action before the statutes." *Ibid.*

[34] The writ "ne injuste vexes, de consuetudinibus et serviciis" was normally used. Because this writ was a writ of right it was very slow. Even if the lord were successful in establishing the nature of the services and the tenant's failure to perform them, even then he could only destrain. Under no condition could he regain possession and this, unfortunately, was the crux of the issue. See *Ibid.*, II, 352.

from the land and the lord regain possession. [35] Yet the writ was not nearly as broad as first might appear. It applied only to a small segment of the cases involving failure to perform service, namely those in which the land had been let for a money rent combined with certain amounts of service. [36] What began in 1278 was repeated by 1285. Then the text of the writ was cited and extended to include heirs and in c. 41 of the same statute, it even included ecclesiastical property and tenants. [37]

As always the problem of tenants failing to perform services, of uncontrolled alienations and the inability of secular lords to legally control their lands, tenants and endowments was a pressing one. The writ of cessavit and its rapid extension from a timid and purely secular remedy to one encompassing ecclesiastical tenures epitomizes concomitantly a serious problem in the English land-law and an ever-mounting concern on the part of the lords.

In practice, the writ of "cessavit" was often applied to monastic institutions. Now founders and patrons or their heirs brought actions to bear for what amounted to breach of contract. English Benedictine chapters, for example, both provincial and general, repeatedly document the common complaint that alms were abused, fraud perpetrated and divine service discontinued. The service due patrons was either allowed to lapse or, more often, simply left unperformed. [38] The case of the abbey of Creake is typical. In 1341, a certain Margaret de Roos brought a complaint against the residing abbot of Creake for failure to perform the divine service agreed to in the endowment charter. These divine services included the singing of masses, matins and vespers in the chapel of Margaret's foundation and the daily gift of bread to a specified number of poor persons. The form of the complaint was the writ of "cessavit." It forced the case into the secular courts. There the decision of the case went against the abbot with

---

[35] *Statutes of the Realm*, I, 48.

[36] *Ibid.*, p. 83. The writ itself ran: "Praecipe A. quod juste, etc. reddat B. tale tenementum, quod A. de eo tenuit per tale servitium, et quod ad praedium B. reverti debeat, eo quod praedictus A. in faciendum praedictum servitium per biennium cessavit ut dicit." For the extent and the money rent, cf. T. F. T. Plucknett, *Legislation of Edward I* (Oxford, 1949), p. 90.

[37] *Ibid.*, pp. 91-92.

[38] W. A. Pantin, *Documents Illustrating the Activities of the General and Provincial Chapters of the English Black Monks, 1215-1540*, III vols., Royal Historical Society, Camden 3rd Series, vols. XLV, XLVII, LIV (1931, 1933, 1937), I, 10, 37, 76, 236; II, 10, 205; III, 127-128.

Margaret regaining possession of the land in question. [39] Other examples, particularly those found in the *Year Books*, show that this case was not extraordinary, [40] and we find that the writ of "cessavit per biennium" was joined by another writ, the writ of "cessavit de cantaria." [41] And both allowed that in cases of tenure by divine service, failure to meet obligations as embodied in the endowment charters could be legally adjudicated in the king's courts. [42]

In addition to monastic foundations, the thirteenth and fourteenth centuries witnessed a new development—the perpetual chantry. Chantries could be either ecclesiastical benefices or service foundations, [43] established to provide for the celebrating of mass but under a board of trustees rather than the bishop. In the latter case, it was quite common to have the chantry chaplain swear on the Gospels that he would abide by the conditions of the founding charter. Such charters were specific concerning the required services and, in conforming to past experience, "almost invariably included some provision for removal of a chaplain who seriously failed to do his duty." [44] The founders and patrons were concerned; they gave considerable attention to the problem of neglect, evil living, waste and alienation; problems that so often occurred in spiritual foundations. Priests, it was felt, should perform their contracted divine services and, in the event these services were not met, deprivation was normal. [45] Deprivation did not mean, however, that the property reverted to the founder. It did mean the founder's chantry and its chaplain were accessible to the patron. Either he or his successors could protect their interests, could ward off failure of service, alienations or a sullied reputation. [46] The patron could supervise; he maintained a proprietary interest and he did have definite rights. For minor offenses, he could distrain the chaplain

---

[39] *Year Books, Edward III*, ed. A. J. Horwood and L. O. Pike (London, 1883-1911), VI, 448. See also G. G. Coulton, *Five Centuries of Religion* (Cambridge, 1936), III, 77, where the author points out that earlier a priest could be deprived of his benefice under this when neglect or non-residence could be proven.

[40] See especially *Year Books, Edward I*, ed. A. J. Horwood (London, 1863-1879), pp. 262, 488.

[41] Pollard and Maitland, *History of English Law*, I, 240. See also Plucknett, *Legislation of Edward I*, pp. 89-93, as well as *Registrum Omnium brevium tam originalium quam iudicialium* (London, 1531), pp. 237-238.

[42] *Ibid.*

[43] K. L. Wood-Legh, *Perpetual Chantries in Britain* (Cambridge, 1965), p. 84; see also 14ff.

[44] *Ibid.*

[45] *Ibid.*

[46] *Ibid.*, p. 14.

by withdrawing the chaplain's stipend. If the abuse were more serious, the patron even had the legal ability to move against the deficient priest, removing and replacing him with another more obedient to the original charter. [47]

While reversion to founder or patron does not occur in these cases, there is here a clearly conceived notion that foundations and endowments are given conditionally. This attitude is, of course, feudal, yet it is not restricted to the lay condition, but is, in fact, found embracing all forms of ecclesiastical foundation. Property is given conditionally. And these conditions are the handles by which the founder and his heirs can direct the endowment toward its specific purpose of providing service. [48]

With the second Statute of Westminister lay patrons created an even more effective tool in their campaign to gain access to their own endowments. Now if the conditions of endowment were not met, there was the possibility of recovering property given to religious houses, chantries and other pious foundations in the event of alienation, neglect or misuse. [49] Repeatedly the conditionality of all clerical endowment was proclaimed. Again and again its companion notion was voiced: if conditions of endowment were unfulfilled, the endowing laity could and should resume their donations. The Statute of Westminister, therefore, was another response to clerical abuse; it was also one more legal remedy whereby secular lords, including the king, could continue to guard their original investment.

Armed with the legal weapons of Westminister, secular lords instituted any number of inquisitions designed to uncover misuse. It was a handy, if not calculated, devise. And, in fact, the king found this statute particularly useful in justifying his interference in the poorer monasteries, "since it empowered the benefactor of a monastery to take measures likely to ensure the performance of the established

---

[47] *Ibid.*, p. 84, fn. 2, where the large Register of the Prior and Convent of Durham, I, fo. 123v is quoted: "Sciturus quod si in premissis dicte cantarie serviciis seu ab eisdem sine causa racionabili indebite cessare repertus fueris vel minus honeste te habueris, ad amocionem tuam a dicta cantaria in forma ordinacionis eiusdem sine more dispendio nos cum consensu conventus predicti procedemus."

[48] Such conditions imply tenure for service. It is a very old notion that goes back at least as far as Bede. Pollock and Maitland, *History of English Law*, I, 242, relate the story in Bede of Oswy giving land to the church for prayers said on behalf of his entire people. Such land provided for the "militia caelestis" instead of the secular "militia terrestris."

[49] See *supra*, fn. 31.

works of piety." [50] In short, the statute, providing for intervention, established the principle in English law that all clerical endowment was conditional and that lay intervention in the affairs of religious institutions would become a fact of life. Neglect, alienation and misuse, and the inquiries they produced, created in England a body of legal records documenting not only the struggle of the laity to enforce ecclesiastical responsibility, but also its ability to recover property from spiritual institutions which had lost their ability to perform due services. [51] The nobility now had the opportunity of enforcing their conditional arrangements by resuming their documents. Lay patronage, an issue of the past, once again becomes a prominent tenet in the efforts of the secular noblity to direct, if not master, the English church.

It had been John Wyclif's contention that when the purpose of secular donations had been frustrated, those same donations ought to revert to their original owner. This seems, in fact, to have been true for a large segment of tenures. Wyclif had, of course, further asserted:

> if clerics occupying temporalities are wanting according to the form of the donation, temporal lords are held not only by fiscal law, but by the law of scripture to protect against the impoverishment of the land. [52]

This, too, is borne out in the legal remedies so consciously erected in the late thirteenth century. With the Statutes of Westminister, the writs of "cessavit" "per biennium," "de cantaria" and "Praecipe tali abbati," there is, indeed, legal and historical justification for Wyclif's position regarding the tenures of frankalmoign and divine service.

English law alone did not supply the attitudes that buttressed Wyclif's contention that all ecclesiastical property was given conditionally. The idea of confiscating church properties was a part of the English ambience in the fourteenth century. Even the literary output of the period persistently documents the view that patrons

---

[50] K. L. Wood-Legh, *Studies in Church Life in England under Edward III* (Cambridge, 1934), pp. 8-9. See *Rot. Parl.*, II, 333, for a petition requesting such an investigation.

[51] See especially *Year Books, 15 Edward III*, pp. 448-9, and *Year Books, 5 Edward II* (Seldon Society), pp. 128-9, both cited in Wood-Legh, *Perpetual Chantries*, p. 107.

[52] See footnote 25 above.

could resume their gifts when their pious intentions had been frustrated. Matthew of Paris in his *Chronica majora* is exceptionally rich in
examples of this kind. It includes, for example, a letter from the
English clerical community to Innocent IV then at the Council of
Lyons, protesting the extortions of the Roman curia. The gist of the
complaint is that they, the clergy, are injured when patrons are
defrauded of the rights of patronage and collation. They are injured
because it had been lay patrons who founded and endowed monasteries
with their own possessions in order that the religious might enjoy
security and the support so necessary for the fulfillment of their
religious duties. [53] Those duties, primarily prayer and good works,
were of extreme interest to the patron. Later in book four, Matthew
cites another letter lodging a complaint similar to the first. This one
it from the abbots, priors and brethren "in the provinces of Canterbury and York" and again it is addressed to Innocent IV.

> For the nobles and men of rank declare, that if the churches bestowed
> on the monasteries by them are conferred on Italian clerks, they will
> have a just right to recall those churches and other benefices into their
> possession, because the revenues proceeding from them ought by right
> to be applied to the benefit of poor and pilgrims, since this was the
> intention of the givers, and the cause of their being given. [54]

The threat registered here is multiplied during this period becoming
a most useful defense against extraordinary taxation, forced contributions, taxation and other infringements whether by king, mother-
house, or papacy. Repeatedly, when confronted with demands from
any of these quarters, monastic communities allude to the necessity
of consulting their patrons and to the horrible spector of founders
and patrons resuming their gifts because the ensuing poverty of the
house would cheat the patrons of their rights and intentions. [55] It was

---

[53] Matthew Paris, *Chronica majora*, ed. J. R. Luard (London, 1872-1883), IV,
442: "Quapropter non sine magna molestia nostra, et gravamine intolerabili nobis
valde, praefati religiosi possent patronatibus suis aut ecclesiarum collationibus ali-
quatenus defraudari."

[54] "Asserunt enim proceres et magnates, quod si ecclesiae collatae monasteriis ab
eisdem clericis Ytalicis conferantur, ipsas ecclesias et alia beneficia in proprietatem
suam juste poterunt revocare, quia ex eis fructus provenientes ad usus pauperum et
peregrinorum debent de jure deputari, cum haec fuisset intentio conferentium et
causa conferendi." *Ibid.*, p. 532. The translation is from *Matthew Paris's English
History*, trans. J. A. Giles (London, 1853), II, 153.

[55] Susan Wood, *English Monasteries and Their Patrons in the Thirteenth Century*
(London, 1955), p. 148f. For examples of mother-houses, see C. R. Cheney, *From
Becket to Langton* (Manchester, 1956), p. 158, and David Knowles, *The Monastic*

a persuasive argument. The Berkshire rectors used this defense in 1240 while answering papal demands for money to fight the emperor. Pinned between two responsibilities, they argued they could not agree to papal contributions without first consulting their patrons. Such consultation was necessary because if they were to obey the papal request, they would be unable to fulfill their spiritual obligations at home and "in this way the patrons will be cheated of their rights and intentions, for which they bestowed the benefice, and will resume their gifts ... [56] This is not an isolated case. Seven years later, Matthew of Paris records another instance of ecclesiastical alarm and fear:

> lest the laymen and secular princes and nobles, who or whose ancestors, had founded, endowed, and enriched the churches, for which purpose they had, in great measure, dilapidated their own possessions, and had given their charters thereof, being taught by example of the pope, would retake possession of the property of the churches 'notwithstanding' the tenor of such and such a privilege ... [57]

Ecclesiastical fears of confiscation were not unfounded, nor did they abate in the succeeding years. In 1295, the *Register of John de Pontissara*, the bishop of Winchester, illustrates the king's use of writ of "cessavit" and comments on the royal promises of correction and reform for the church. [58] And by the time the fourteenth century

---

Order in England (Cambridge, 1949), p. 156, where the limitation of Cluniac mother-houses by English founders and patrons is discussed.

[56] Matthew of Paris, *Chronica majora*, IV, 41ff. This is part of the famous reply of the Berkshire rectors to papal demands in 1240: "a quibus si procedat talis exactio, oportet cessare, et ita patroni suo jure et intentione hac causa donandi fraudati erunt; et sic donata repetere, vel saltem alia quaerent gravamina, nec iterum ecclesias de suis bonis fundabunt, vel conferent beneficia." The translation is from Giles, *Matthew Paris's English History*, I, 285. For the general background as well as a somewhat superficial treatment of the argumentation employed by the Berkshire rectors see A. L. Smith, *Church and State in the Middle Ages* (Oxford, 1913), pp. 25-29. Also William E. Lunt, *Financial Relations of the Papacy with England to 1327* (Cambridge, Mass., 1939), pp. 201-202.

[57] "Haec igitur cum ad multorum audientiam pervenerunt videlicet quod tam frequens extorsio pecuniae violenta per Papam et suos legatos sophisticos et transformatos facta est, nec praevaluerunt sanctorum privilegia vel indulgentiae patrum ipsos defendere; formidabant vehementer, ne principes et magnates laici et seculares, qui vel quorum praedecessores ecclesias fundaverunt, dotaverunt, et ditaverunt, et suas ob hoc possessiones pro magna parte mutilarunt, et inde cartas suas confecerunt, reacciperent ecclesiarum bona et possiones, exemplo papae edocti, non obstante talis vel talis cartae tenore." *Ibid.*, p. 619. Translation from Giles, *Matthew Paris's English History*, II, 223.

[58] *Registrum Johannis de Pontissara, Episcopi Wyntoniensis*, ed. Cecil Deeds, Canterbury and York Society (London, 1915-1924), II, 778.

began, the king and realm, acting with the Statute of Carlisle, assume responsibility for coercing the church to meet its obligations toward her founders and patrons. [59] Neither the king nor the realm were to be put off. Meeting at Stamford, 1309, Parliament reiterated its complaints lodged at Carlisle and the lords, acting in the name of the community of the realm, composed a letter to Pope Clement V strongly opposing the extent of papal provisions and annates. Not only did this letter define the negative results of papal policy, but it pointedly informed Clement that:

> According to the law of the land, possessions given to churches and religious places, should they be applied to a use contrary to the desire and intention of the founders and donors, can be most certainly recalled through their founders and donors or their heirs. [60]

These same lords, continuing, repeated the often heard charge that papal taxation would make it impossible for ecclesiastical foundations —the principal recipients of their endowments—to continue providing hospitality and alms and this was their original intention. [61] Finally in 1354, following the well-known first statutes of Provisors and Praemunire in 1351 and 1353, Henry Knighton reports of the magnates of the realm protesting papal reservations in England with the declaration that:

> Should the pope confer benefices of the church by means of provisors, whether on natives or aliens then these benefices, which their forefathers had given to religious men and ecclesiastics as alms in order that they should pray for their souls, should be resumed into their own hands. [62]

---

[59] See *Statutes of the Realm*, I, 150.

[60] This passage is only found in the Annales Londoniensis in *Chronicles of Edward I and Edward II*, ed. William Stubbs (London, 1882-1883), I, 164-165, and is cited by Haller, *Papsttum und Kirchenreform*, p. 397, and Buddensieg, p. 42. The text is: "... eapropter beatintudinem vestram omni qua possimus instantia filiali supplicamus humiliter, quatinus in praemissis, infra vestrae summae sanctitatis clementiam deductis et paterna meditatione pensatis, considerato etiam si placet attente quod secundum legem terrae, possessiones ecclesiis et locis religiosis collatae, si ad usum fundatorum et donatorum voluntati et intentioni contrarium applicentur, certissime per ipsos fundatores et donatores aut eorum haeredes poterint revocari ..." See also the discussion in John Tracy Ellis, *Anti-papal Legislation in Medieval England, 1066-1377* (Washington, D.C., 1930), pp. 93-95.

[61] See Brian Tierney, *Medieval Poor Law* (Berkeley, 1959), p. 158, fn. 55, where he quotes the Reg. Swinfield, p. 472, which relates this information. See also *Rot. Parl.* I, 219.

[62] *Chronicon Henrici Knighton, vel Cnitthon, Monachi Leyestrensis*, ed. Joseph Rawson Lumby (London, 1889-1895), II, as quoted by Loserth, "Studien zur Kir-

That abuse, fraud and failure to perform spiritual service existed is abundantly clear from the legal remedies forged in this period alone. This, in conjunction with parliamentary petitions and literary references to baronial threat of confiscation should the delinquency of the church continue, measure the concern of the laity in England and given definition to Wyclif's desire of removing all temporal possessions from the church.

Although John Wyclif draws upon Canon law and scripture, to effect ecclesiastical dispossession, [63] his primary weapon was the legal remedy provided for in the developing Common law as set down so explicitly in the statutes of the realm. Normally, temporalities given to the church were considered alms; held by various clerical corporations, these temporal endowments rested primarily on the tenures of frankalmoign and divine service. The distinction, described earlier, between these two tenures remained important. If specific and certain services were prescribed, if endowment or foundation came with certain conditions, then the tenure was that of divine service and was justicable in the secular courts under secular law. Should, however, foundation or endowment occur with no prescribed conditions, then that tenure was frankalmoign and could only be adjudicated by the ecclesiastical ordinary. [64] If the ordinary failed to act, no remedy could be had on the part of the patron.

Unlike the episcopacy who held the overwhelming portion of their tenancy "in capite" from the king on the basis of barony and knight service, monasteries held their major endowments by divine service or frankalmoign. Still, whatever the particular institution, the English church held its temporal property on the basis of these three tenures: barony and knight service, divine service and frankalmoign. The first two tenures were justicable, at least in terms of their temporalities,

---

chenpolitik Englands," I, 25, fn. 1: "Insuper magnates et proceres regni Anglia oblocuti sunt et minati, quod si papa conferret beneficia ecclesie talibus provisoribus, sive indigenis sive alienigenis, que quidem beneficia antecessores sui contulerant viris religiosis et ecclesiasticus in eleemosynam ut pro ipsis animabus suis orarent, ipsi ea beneficia in manus proprias repeterent sicuti antecessores habuerant, et de eis ad placitum disponerent."

[63] *VSS*, III, 22.

[64] For these distinctions and the following see Pollack and Maitland, *History of English Law*, I, 240ff. as well as Elizabeth Kimball, "Judicial Aspects of Frank Almoign Tenure," *English Historical Review*, XLVII (1932), 1-11, and her earlier article, "Tenure in Frank Almoign and Secular Services," *English Historical Review*, XLIII (1928), 341f.

in the royal courts while the last, frankalmoign, was a tenure outside the purview of the common law. [65]

Wyclif did not point out the technical differences between the tenures. Either he was ignorant of these differences or knowing them, he deliberately chose to confuse them in order to demonstrate that all ecclesiastical endowment proceeded under conditions which were justicable. Factually, of course, Wyclif was wrong. The entire endowment of the English church had not been given, as he asserted, in pure and perpetual alms. [66] Incorrect as he was though, he still punched through his basic argument in three propositions: all ecclesiastical property derives from the laity in the form of alms; those who first endowed the church did so with the intention of improving the spiritual welfare of the clergy; and, in case of those spiritual ends being frustrated, all secular endowment reverts to its origin. [67] That unfortunately, he concluded, was now the case. [68] Finally, after having worked up a legal structure, Wyclif applied it to his ecclesiology, reasoning that "neither God nor man has conceded anything of a sinful nature unless under condition, expressed or tacit." [69] Emphasizing this position, Wyclif asserted that if the property of the church were given to the clergy absolutely and without condition, this would not only destroy all law but would oppose biblical injunctions to the contrary. [70]

There is in all of this a constant emphasis upon the conditionality of endowment and alms. [71] From first to last Wyclif's concern with

---

[65] Glanvill, p. 106, where he notes there is no homage for frankalmoign. See also Coke upon Littleton, Sect. 136 (95a.966).

[66] VSS, III, 18: "relinquitur igitur ex quotlibet evidenciis, quod tota dotacio ecclesie sit ex elemosinis dominorum. Quod, ne tradatur in oblicionem, cavetur in cartis regni nostri Anglie, quomodo rex et alii fundatores in puram et perpetuam elemosinam donarunt talia dominia ecclesie." and 55: "carte enim regum Anglie habent, quomodo talia dona concedit in puram et perpetuam elemosinam ..."

[67] Ibid., p .21: "nam omnia bona, quibus dotatur ecclesia, sunt elemosine secularium dominorum ex supposicione prima, que donata sunt clericis, ut observant religionem primevum ex supposicione seconda. Cum igitur remanet penes eos capitale dominium, ex supposcione tercia, sequitur, quod frustrato per se fine dotaciones seculares debent ad bona propria resortiri."

[68] Ibid., p. 17.

[69] Ibid., p. 48: "... nec deus nec homo concedit quidquam nature peccabili nisi sub condicione expressa vel tacita."

[70] Ibid., p. 49: "Unde idem foret dicere, quod bona ecclesie erant tata clericis absolute sine condicione, et dicere, quod illi non possunt abuti illis bonis, quod blasfeme destrueret omnes leges."

[71] DOR, p. 178: "Item rex habet interesse cum suis elemosinariis racione dotacionis condicionate quam non licet pape infringere. Sed per talia privilegia infrin-

conditions has but a single purpose: to allow adjudication in the royal courts according to the law of the land. For with the conditionality of endowment established, tenure becomes that of divine right; and failure to adhere to conditions, to perform required services, either by abuse, fraud or simple curtailment, renders the church and its clergy accessible to correction or recovery of endowment. Moreover, such accessibility is found in the secular courts of the king; there remedies abound; there temporalities can be removed from the church justly, according to human laws. [72]

By the fourteenth century, the church needed reformation. And more and more concerned individuals, clerical and lay, saw redemption in the form of lay patronage. So did John Wyclif and he developed a program whose basic tenet was the dispossession of the contemporary church in cooperation with the lay patrons. He sought to accomplish this by legally removing temporalities under certain conditions. At this point the conditions themselves were unimportant, they could be worked out later; what was important was the principle that endowment was given conditionally. That was established. Parliamentary petitions, popular songs and literary sources called the magnates of the land to battle, encouraged them to act as the agents of God in reinstituting order, scattering God's enemies and restraining evil. [73] And there was always the ubiquitous threat of confiscation should the church continue its papal course. Nor was the threat of so many tongues an idle one. Wyclif's was certainly not. Confiscation was in the English air and as with so many other examples, Wyclif fed upon its spirit. [74] Legally there was precedent and remedy enough to make the revocation of ecclesiastical temporalities a very real possibility.

---

geretur, ergo rex debet in istis resistere. Condicio autem elemosine perpetue est ut elemosinarius serviat regi et regno spirituali servicie ad stabilimentum pacis regni ..." This conditionality is set down in detail and supported with all forms of human law including Roman law, Canon law and, most importantly for this study, examples from English law in the fifth chapter of *DCD*, II, 36-47. Not only is Magna Carta used extensively, but the Statutes of Westminster, Gloucester and others.

[72] *OM*, p. 424.

[73] *Rot. Parl.* I, 221: "Hec omnia ad extrahendum a regno pecuniam, ad exananitionem ecclesie manifestam et ad ditandum alienigenas spoliatis indigenis tendere dinoscuntur, nisi exurgat Deus et dissipentur inimici eius, ut per secularem principem ... tanta malicia reprimatur." Cited by J. Haller, *Papsttum und Kirchenreform*, p. 389.

[74] See Knowles, "Censured Opinions," p. 311, as well as Loserth, "Studien zur Kirchenpolitik Englands," I, 25.

CHAPTER SEVEN

THE LEGAL ARTIFICE

Although John Wyclif used many authorities, including English law, precedent and historical example, to support his contention that the laity was to correct its clergy, he began with the Bible and Canon law. Reworking Isidore of Seville, Wyclif asserted that:

> The temporal lords have power given to them by God, so that where the spiritual arm of the church does not suffice to convert the antichrists by evangelical preaching, ecclesiastical admonition, or the example of virtues, the secular arm may help its mother by severe coercion. [1]

And what applied to the secular lords in general was even more appropriate for the king. Wyclif's king, as the vicar of God, possessed "spiritual and evangelical power." Reincarnating the pontifical king with phrases such as "king and priest," Wyclif gave his king a definite mantle of sovereignty. The spiritual administration of the church would not be exempt from the supervisory role of the king. Above all, it belonged to the king's office to "defend vigorously the evangelical law"; the king was to be "priest and pontiff in his own realm." In processing this view that "the law of the church became the law of the king," Wyclif took the extra step of identifying God's law with English precedents. Seen then as the servant of Christ, the king held his kingdom as a trust, charged with "the perpetual salvation of himself and of the people, whose government God entrusted to him." [2] As such, the king's most basic functions were to rule, to judge and to correct; he was through these general tasks to defend not only Christ's law, but His institution, the Church—to do so he had to be sovereign, to be so he had to correct.

This corrective or regulatory rule of the secular power was perhaps the most important of Wyclif's ever-recurring themes for the reformation of the church. Not only did the Old Testament provide authorization "whereby the temporal lord held power for correcting the priesthood," especially under Solomon, but Isidore of Seville and

---

[1] *Supra*, chap. IV, p. 71, fn. 53.
[2] *Supra*, chap. IV, p. 76, fn. 80.

Gregory the Great were called upon to witness the correctness of Wyclif's position. [3] According to Pope Gregory:

> Righteousness elevates the people, sin makes them miserable. Then the realm is believed stable, since sin, when it is recognized, is emended. Thus, since the cause of the ruin of the people is evil priests, we ought to rise up to correct the priesthood, lest the crime of the few be the perdition of the many. [4]

Wyclif had reached this conclusion too. Prosperity and stability of the realm depended upon clerical righteousness. Of all those involved, it belonged primarily to the secular princes, the patrons, to help the clergy "assume righteousness" by appointing them, attending to them and correcting them. [5] Righteousness also meant for Wyclif that the clergy were to live "exproprietarily"—totally without coercive jurisdiction and without dominion. And while this did not mean that the church was to be without property, it did mean that only usufruct and not possession would be tolerated. Moreover, even usufruct could only be sanctioned conditionally. As long as the clergy recognized that their title was one of alms, that service was due, then they could enjoy their right to utilize those properties belonging to the laity. [6]

John Wyclif had already established the conditionality of the clerical tenures, of divine service and frankalmoign by blurring the distinction to allow adjudication in the king's court. Yet that did not suffice, for with this decision a supervisor was needed to arbitrate and, when necessary, to enforce the contractual arrangement. As an ecclesiastical tenure, divine service dealt with the problem in terms of religious foundations. That meant that a large part of the ecclesiastical endowment was held by "barony" and it lay beyond the corrective scope of the writ of "cessavit." Aware of this gap, Wyclif attempted to cast an even wider legal net.

---

[3] VSS, III, 235-236. Isidore's statement was incorporated into the Decretum and Wyclif's use of that canon can be found in DCD, I, 271; SS, I, 230, 234; Trialogus, p. 308; DE, p. 13; DOR, pp. 6, 22, 121, 186; DB, pp. 135-136, 56, 57. This is but a sampling; it by no means exhausts the list.

[4] "Istam sentenciam notat beatus Gregorius in Registro libri undecimi cap. vicesimo nono regine Francie ita scribens: 'cum scriptum sit: iusticia elevat gentem, miseros autem facit populos peccatum, tunc regnum stabile creditur, cum culpa, que cognoscitur, cicius emendatur. Ideo cum causa ruine populi sint sacerdotes mali, ad rectificandum sacerdocium debemus ardenter consurgere, ne per paucorum facinus sit multorum perdicio." VSS, III, 236.

[5] Ibid., pp. 235-236.

[6] DCD, III, 235; VSS, III, 1ff., and Dialogus, p. 79f.

John Wyclif, like so many of his contemporaries, quite naturally found a great need for correction in the fourteenth century church. The magnitude of this need, he felt, while often reflecting a general institutional failure was more specifically an episcopal one. Wyclif was not alone in rebuking episcopal sloth: "If corporal punishment were given, as it should be, to those who break the commandments of God, then there might be some hope of reform. But as this brings no enrichment to the bishop's or archdeacon's purse, it is neglected." [7] In his view the bishops had essentially only three functions—to flee worldly desires, to perfect their sacred office and to correct their subjects according to the law of Christ. [8] This last obligation was most important. Through it, all bishops, from the most insignificant to the pope himself, ministered to the people. Like the king's, their office was considered a trust, given by God and the people. Unfortunately, that trust was often spurned or neglected and nowhere was this more apparent than in the corrective role of the episcopacy. Wyclif registered his objection innumerable times, pointing out that not only did episcopal reluctance to correct weaken the church, but further contended that it would eventually destroy Christianity. [9]

In light of this situation, Wyclif postulated a remedy that became thematic in his reforming program: "If therefore bishops or other ecclesiastic[s] fail notably in their offices, it pertains to kings to correct them with discreet moderation." [10] Failure normally meant failure to correct. Again and again Wyclif returns to this principle: should prelates fail to correct and punish their delinquent clergy on the basis of the church's laws, then the laity must intervene under penalty of excommunication. [11] At the same time Wyclif repeatedly maintained that such action was extraordinary: "Laymen should not

---

[7] Owst, *Literature and Pulpit*, p. 252.

[8] "Debent enim omnes episcopi precipue desideria mundana aufugere, officium suum sancte perficere et omnino subditos suos secundum legem Cristi corripere ... Sed quantum ad correpcionem subditorum patet, quod eius omissio, licet non reputetur hodie propter consuetudinem peccatum, est tamen peccatum gravissimum et per consequens maxime detestandum. In ipsa igitur correpcione debent episcopi a domino papa usque ad infimum episcopum maxime populo ministrare. Ideo enim committitur regimen a domino et populo." *VSS*, III, 23.

[9] *Ibid.*

[10] "Si ergo episcopi et ceteri ecclesiastici desunt notabiliter in officiis istis, ad reges pertinet cum discreta moderacione ipsos corrigere." *DCD*, I, 291. Wyclif's interest in moderation is interesting. It is also repeated elsewhere, although in a different form. See *VSS*, III, 235-236: temporal lords do indeed have rights over priests, but they should not act without the advice and authority of the church.

[11] *OM*, p. 48; *DE*, p. 351; *VSS*, III, 76.

punish unless when ecclesiastical superiors default." [12] On one occasion he delineated situations when an ecclesiastic was to submit to secular correction, but usually this casual jurisdiction of the secular mandate rested in abeyance. Correction, whenever necessary, was simply carried out through the regular channels of the church's own bureaucracy. [13] When this system broke down, then Wyclif was more than willing to call in the secular powers "to defend the evangelical law by force!" He wished the civil power would impose its own legitimate, yet extraordinary, authority to correct clerical delinquency. [14] As with frankalmoign in the earlier cases and divine service, abuse and fraud of clerical endowment provided ample evidence for the failure of ecclesiastical responsibility as well as the growing need for correction. Having postulated a theoretical remedy to the problem of episcopal reticence, Wyclif proceeded to develop an articulated historical and legal justification for the action of the laity.

Wyclif began by thoroughly reviewing the rights and obligations of patronage. [15] Patrons endowed the church, he wrote, and were to assure that no priestly fraud occurred. This supervisory role, as with the bishop, was for them a major responsibility for which they were accountable.

> It pertains to the king or patron in default or spiritual superior to withdraw alms proportionately to the crime from the rector, curate, chaplain or cleric habitually abusing the goods of the church or patron. [16]

---

[12] "Unde ne darem scandalum secularibus, clero vel regno et specialiter saluti animarum specificavi tam verbis multiplicibus quam scripturis, quod 'domini temporales non debent hoc facere nisi auctoritate ecclesie in defectu spiritualis preposti et in casu quo sacerdos fuerit a fide devius." *OM*, p. 210. "Ideo supposuerunt leges ecclesie, sacerdotes Cristi esse pauperes et humiles instar sui et secundum eorum discrecionem esse iudicandos ad intra, non tradendos foro seculari, nisi ubi deficit prelatorum iudicium." *VSS*, III, 15. See also *DCD*, II, 4-5, 135 ff; *VSS*, III, 28-29 and 78: "Ideo sepe dixi, quod laici non debent punire nisi nudo nomine clericos et notorie anticristos in defectu spiritualis preposti, quod indubie non obviat ulli legi."

[13] *VSS*, III, 15.

[14] Wyclif redundantly accentuates his point: "Officium dominorum temporalium et regum precipue est legem evangelicam potestative defendere et ipsam in sua conversacione diligencius observare." *OM*, p. 71. *DOR*, pp. 78-79: "quod officium dominorum temporalium et regum precipue est legem ewangelicam potestative defendere et ipsam in sua conversacione diligencius observare." Or, "Unde quia seculares domini debent hanc legem Christi precipue potestative defendere ..." *SS*, II, 268.

[15] *DCD*, IV, 456, 463; *DOR*, pp. 74-75.

[16] "Quocunque rectore vel curato, capellano vel clerico elemosinario notorie et habitualiter abutente bonis ecclesie vel patroni, ad regem vel patronum pertinet in defectu spiritualis preposti collatum elemosynam subtrahere proporcionaliter ad delictum." *OM*, p. 45. See also *VSS*, III, 68; *DCD*, II, 131.

The king, moreover, as the "paramount and immediate patron of all the clergy" carried an even greater burden. [17] Not only was the king "patron paramount" but, because Wyclif had earlier identified the law of Christ with the law of the land, the king assumed in the reformer's scheme the responsibility for sin.

Sin became a civil crime to be tried in the king's courts according to his law. Again, while this problem was normally dealt with by the church, ultimately the king had jurisdiction in that he had to answer for the fulfillment of justice within his realm. Typically then, Wyclif has two arguments—a theological one and legal one—working for him. It is the legal one that bears the heavier burden here and it rested squarely on the institution of patronage as set down in church law.

Wyclif found little difficulty in supporting his contention of secular correction on the part of patrons in the Canon law. Moving from Isidore's "Principes" on through the pre-Hildebrandine tradition, Wyclif writes: "Behold how plainly the pope conceded to seculars, when prelates failed to correct, that temporal lords should coerce even the so-called priests of the church." [18] Then, quoting a canon from the Council of Toledo, he continues:

> To sons or nephews and their more respectable relatives, who have constructed or have endowed a church, it is permitted to have this care so that if they should discern that a priest defrauding any of the contributed things, they should either restrain him by a proper fine or denounce him for correction to a bishop or judge. But if a bishop should try to do such things, they ought to report this to his metropolitan. If, however, the metropolitan should do such, they should not fail to bring this to the ears of the king. [19]

---

[17] The prologue to the Parliament of 1351 describes the king as the "paramount and immediate patron of all the holy Church." ("des genz de seinte Esglise, dont le roi est avowe paramount immediat").

[18] Wyclif began this statement with a papal quote (*Decretum*, XXIII, q. V, c. 43): "forte timidus es, ne persequi videaris. De patrum autoritate hec breviter nobis dirigenda curavi, cum mille alia exempla et constituciones sunt, quibus evidenter agnoscitur, quod facientes scisma in sancta matre ecclesia non solum ex illis, sed eciam proscripcione rerum et dura custodia per publicas potestates debeant coherceri." He then continues: "Ecce, quam plane papa concedit secularibus, ubi deest prelati coreccio, quod domini temporales coherceant eciam vocatos prelatos ecclesie." *VSS*, III, 68.

[19] "Filiis vel nepotibus ac honestioribus propinquis eius, qui construxit vel dotavit ecclesiam, licitum sit, hanc habere solerciam, ut, si sacerdotem aliquid de collatis rebus defraudare previderint, aut honesta convencione compescant aut episcopo vel iudici corrigenda denuncient, quod, si episcopus talia agere temptet, metropolitano eius hoc insinuare procurent. Si autem metropolitanus talia gerat, regis hoc auribus

On another occasion, Wyclif proposed that the whole community under the bishop should seek fulfillment of justice from the metropolitan in the event of the bishop failing to provide properly for correction. Yet in continuing Wyclif subtly altered the appellate procedure; bringing it up to date, he allowed the pope and his curia a position in the judicial hierarchy.

> ... but if the metropolitan should fail, the realm can send nuncios to the Roman curia in that cause at the expense of the failing prelate; but if the pope should fail, the realm ought wholly to subtract the goods of the church from there. 20

The pope, accustomed to exercising final arbitrament, had now in Wyclif's scheme been relegated to a distinctly subordinate juridical position. He constituted a court of appeal, but not the final court. That final authority was reserved for the king and the realm.

In the tract *De Ecclesia*, Wyclif had his opponent admitting the propriety of lay correction in the event of ecclesiastical failure. That opponent also agreed that Wyclif's conception of the appellant system, progressing from diocesan through metropolitan to pope was correct. But "it should not be presumed," he writes, "that in these three signs the church of Christ should fail." 21 Wyclif could not have disagreed more strongly. He pointed out in his rebuttal that bishops did in fact fail as was patently clear with the contemporary clergy. Nor was the pope himself exempt from sloth or error; for the king to expect correction from him would be, because of various reasons, both practical and jurisdictional, the height of folly. 22 If correction was to take place when all else had failed, it would have to be done by

---

intimare non different." *VSS*, III, 68-69. Wyclif's use of this canon can also be found in *DCD*, II, 131, and *DCD*, IV, 459.

20 "Laici enim tenentur, prelato prodere clericum taliter criminosum, quod cum sit precipuum opus ecclesie, potest legitime capere de decimis ecclesie pro expensis, quod, si prelatus a debita correpcione deficiat, tota sua parochia vel comunitas iurisdiccioni sue subiecta debet a metropolitano complementum iuris expetere: quod, si ipse defuerit, potest regnum nuncios in causa illa sub expensis prelati desidis ad romanam curiam destinare; quod, si papa defuerit, debet regnum omnino bona ecclesie ab eo subtrahere ..." *VSS*, III, 27. Then Wyclif proves this from the law of the Church.

21 Wyclif's opponent writes: "... clerus nunquam debet castigari per laicum nisi in defectu spiritualis prepositi, et per consequens nunquam antequam papa defecerit, oportet ergo subditum corripi per diocesanum, secundo per metropolitanum, et si illi defecerint, tunc per papam. Et non est presumendum quod in hiis tribus signis ecclesia Christi deficiet." *DE*, p. 351.

22 *DE*, pp. 351-353.

the secular lord. Justice would have to be fulfilled for "according to Common law, such fulfillment belonged to the office of the king, from which the king is not to bar his almsmen." [23]

It was difficult, however, for Wyclif to find a great deal of support in English law. Technically, English law knew of no such elaborately defined and graduated appellate system as described by Wyclif. [24] Only Canon law possessed such a system. What English law recognized was a series of subtle processes whereby actions could be either removed from one court to another before judgment or when the plea of *falsum judicium* questioned the method of judgment. [25] *Falsum judicium* was a royal plea stemming from the time of the *Leges Henrici* and could accomplish what amounted to an appeal. But it was used charily as an appellate process. The idea, as Maitland expressed it, "of a complaint against a judgement which is not an accusation against a judge is not easily formed." [26] Gradually though, under the influence of the Canon law model, appellate action came to be accepted. The Constitutions of Clarendon, for example, demonstrated the process of appeal from archdeacon to bishop, and from bishop to archbishop with the further stipulation that "if the archbishop should fail to do justice, the case must come at last to the lord king, in order that by his command the dispute may be determined in the archbishop's court ..." [27] By 1258 and the Petition of the Barons, the idea of a hierarchically arranged system of courts was

---

[23] After reviewing the appelate system in which the "king's ears" followed the court of the archbishop, Wyclif wrote: "Nec dubium legiste, quin ad hoc debet finaliter intimari regi provincie, ut ipse faciat in suo regno iusticie complementum. Hoc enim est de comuni iure regis officium, a quo non licet elemosinariis suis eum precludere." *VSS*, III, 69. Wyclif refers to the fulfillment of justice in a number of places. See especially *DE*, p. 40: "... rex debet in casu subtrahere suas elemosinas a nominetenus clericis et restituere eas sancte matri ecclesie. Nam hoc foret complementum iusticie ...; cum ergo ad regem maxime pertinet facere iusticiam in rebus subiectis suo domino, sequitur quod ad regem pertinentissime spectat complementum talis iusticie."

[24] Pollock and Maitland, *History of English Law*, II, 664.

[25] *Ibid.*

[26] *Ibid.*, p. 668.

[27] "De appellationibus si emerserint, ab archidiacono debent procedere ad episcopum ab episcopo ad archiepiscopum. Et si archiepiscopus defuerit in justitia exhibenda ad dominum regem perveniendum est postremo, ut praecepto ipsius in curia archiepiscopi controversia terminetur, ita quod non debeat ulterius procedere absque assensu domini regis." William Stubbs (ed.), *Select Charters* (9th ed. rev.; Oxford, 1921), p. 165, cap. viii. This was later confirmed by the Statute of Praemunire which forfeited to the crown all lands, goods, chattels of anyone appealing to courts of law outside England.

common enough to allow the removal of a plea or action from a lower court to a series of higher courts on the grounds of default, that is, refusal or inability to act. [28]

Clearly then, there was ample authority, if not a pattern, in Canon and Roman law for Wyclif's assertions concerning the appellate action on the basis of default. English authority for the action of the king is more dubious. Certainly the appellate jurisdiction of the crown was recognized and used, but not in the way specified by Wyclif and certainly not with respect to the church: the king could not reverse the findings of the ecclesiastical courts. He could, nonetheless, limit them in terms of their interference and when they acted upon the authority of royal writ, he could prevent appeals outside England. [29] But that was not Wyclif's assertion. Whether he consciously misconstrued the provisions in the Constitutions of Clarendon or simply misunderstood them, the result was the same: He thought he had adequate authority in English law for royal correction in default of justice. [30] And the point of this exercise for Wyclif was to render the clergy of the realm accountable to the political authorities on the basis of standardized legal precedents.

Appellant correction was by no means the only legal device used by Wyclif in his drive to construct a legal machine capable of rendering the clergy accessible to secular control. If patrons were responsible for correction, that responsibility was often forced upon them by clerical fraud or abuse of ecclesiastical endowment. This was particularly true of bishops.

> In case of any bishop having habitually and notoriously abused the goods of the church, the secular lords ought to, in that case, withdraw them for his correction as well as for the restitution of the property of the poor. [31]

---

[28] Plucknett, *Legislation of Edward I*, p. 25.

[29] Pollock and Maitland, *History of English Law*, II, 665f.

[30] It is impossible to determine which of the three laws was most instrumental in Wyclif's thought. Wyclif, for instance, specifies that bishops remiss in correction are to have three admonitions before action is to be taken against them. (*VSS*, III, 19-22, 100.) The magical number three, however, is simply too common to pin down. Both legists and canonists, relying on the *Digest* speak of the necessity of three summonses as does Glanvill and the writ of Novel Disseisin. See Gaines Post, *Studies in Legal Political Thought*, p. 176, as well as Pollock and Maitland, *History of English Law*, II, 592, and Plucknett, *Legislation of Edward I*, p. 89.

[31] "Quocunque episcopo habitualiter et notorie abutente bonis ecclesie principes seculi debent in casu ipsa ad sui correpcionem et bonorum pauperum restitucionem subtrahere." *OM*, p. 41.

Nor was Wyclif willing to stop here; what applied to bishops was also applicable to cardinals and even the pope himself. [32] Originally material wealth had been given to the church and its officials conditionally for the spiritual welfare of the realm as well as the individual. If used improperly, if abused, such wealth lost its spiritual aspect and became a burden whose weight pushed one into criminal acts. Falling away from righteousness, becoming a criminal, the abusing cleric should face withdrawal of endowment or benefice. [33] Abuse or fraud was sufficiently heinous, but if in addition it was habitual, it went beyond the normal pale of civil crime, and became the equivalent of apostasy and heresy. [34] Jeremiah lent his support to good effect: "Cursed is he who does the work of God fraudulently." [35]

Wyclif repeatedly equated fraud, misuse and abuse of endowment with heresy. [36] Individuals, he wrote, unjustly occupying the goods of the church or misusing them were heretics. [37] Although seldom explicit, Wyclif's working definition is clear enough: whoever keeps

---

[32] "Licet mundi principibus tam subtrahere quam auferre temporalia a Romano pontifice in casu quo eis habitualiter abutatur ... Cum ergo debent regere seculariter temporalia bona ecclesie, eo quod illud regimen non convenit pape, patet quod domini seculares debent regere temporalia pape, si de possibili sint abusi." *Ibid.*, p. 37. For inclusion of the cardinals in this form of correction, see p. 39: "Si cardinalis aliquis vel cetus plurium per abusum temporalium fuerit ad onus et periculum subversionis ecclesie, domini temporales et laici eis subditi tenentur ipsum fraterne corripere et post continuacionem oblaciones vel elemosinas ecclesie constanter subtrahere."

[33] *DCD*, I, 345; *DCD*, IV, 463; *OM*, pp. 42-45, 413.

[34] Wyclif's terms—abuse, habitual and removal—are defined in *DCD*, II, 130-131: "... eo ipso quo homo quitquam occupat de bonis Domini, dum est in mortali peccato, abutitur isto bono ... Patet ex hoc quod omnia dicta dona sunt data homini, ut serviat caritative Deo suo et sic serviendo mereatur finaliter beatitudinem. Quem ordinem homo pervertit, dum est in mortali peccato; ideo usum verum vertit in abusum, ..." From abuse, Wyclif hurries on to a definition of "habitual": "... sicut una irundo non facit ver, sic nec opera mala unum opus malum vel bonum per se inducit habitum vicii vel virtutis. Sed dum homo radicatur ad tantum in peccato mortali quod post triplicem correpcionem evangelicam permanet inobediens legi Christi; et tunc suppono ipsum notorie habituatum in malo et resipiscentum infra correpcionem evangelicam suppono dispositum." For habitual abuse being equated with heresy, see *DE*, p. 297; *VSS*, III, 11-12, 25-29. After defining habitual abuse, Wyclif then instructs the secular lords to take no punitive action until the guilty have been warned three times: "Nec videtur michi ante talem correpcionem triplicem licere dominis temporalibus procedere clericum puniendo: sed post triplicem correpcionem, cum sit obstinatus, excommunicatus et hereticus, debet a quocunque potente secundem modum castigari." *DCD*, II, 131.

[35] Jeremiah 48:10, as quoted in *DE*, p. 297.

[36] "Quicunque clericus habitualiter vel pertinaciter proprietarie abutitur bonis ecclesie, debet redargui tanquam hereticus." *DCD*, III, 261.

[37] "... patet ex hoc quod omnis sic pertinaciter abutens bonis ecclesie est hereticus ..." *DE*, p. 340. See also *VSS*, III, 28-29, 48-49, 237, and *DCD*, III, 261.

God's law is a Catholic, whoever does not is a heretic. [38] Avarice is another indication: if one desired endowment contrary to Christ's estate, then one was a heretic. [39] Endowment, in fact, led inexorably to heresy; as an enticement to sin, endowment disrupted and disrupting endowment becomes heretical. [40] Bishops, as the clerical ordinaries, should control this greed, correct the abuses and generally direct the church through the dangers of endowment. But they were supervisory failures, and "failing to punish offending priests," Wyclif wrote, "they must themselves be deprived." [41]

There is design in Wyclif's insistence upon the heretical nature of these failures. He views them basically as crimes and although he does not term them civil crime, that is the implication. [42] English law, while not entirely lacking experience with heresy before the Lollards, was not sure how to deal with heretics. [43] It was convinced, however, that suppression of heresy was a royal matter, for it excited people "to the great peril of all the realm." [44] A more compelling reason for royal control and for royal intervention in heretical matters can be found in the *Close Rolls* and the *Calendar of Liberate Rolls:* confiscation by the king. In 1236, a wine merchant named Ernald of Periqueux, was convicted of heresy and his goods seized by the king who claimed that "all condemned heretics, wheresoever found within the realm and the king's dominions, were forfeit to the crown." [45]

Another case involved William Lyn and David Browery. When the bishop of Ely condemned them in 1373 on a charge of heresy, he adjudged their goods and chattels to be confiscated by the king *secundum iura ecclesiastica.* [46] Nor did one need to be convicted of heresy in any formal fashion. Accusation alone was enough for the

---

[38] *DB*, p. 72.

[39] *DA*, p. 91.

[40] See *VSS*, III, 237, and *SS*, IV, 8-10.

[41] *VSS*, III, 13, 24f., and 28.

[42] "Unde hereticus dicitur ab heros, quod est incisio, quia divisionem et perturbacionem facit in populo. Sicut ergo tota pacificacio ecclesie vel regni stat in purgacione eius a crimine, sic tota sua perturbacio stat in non purgacione eius a foventibus tale crimen." *SS*, IV, 8.

[43] See Pollock and Maitland, *History of English Law*, II, 547ff.

[44] *Statutes of the Realm*, III, 25-26.

[45] This example is to be found in H. G. Richardson, "Heresy and the Lay Power," *English Historical Review*, LI (1936), 2, who quotes from the *Close Rolls*, 1234-1237, 293, 359, 485.

[46] *Ibid.*, p. 4.

king to lay his hands upon the defendant's property. [47] Seemingly this practice was common enough for Wyclif to have been aware of it. The last provisions of the Statute of Gloucester call for all benefices held by apostate cardinals, that is cardinals not obeying Urban in the schism, to be confiscated by the king. And what Gloucester called for, Rymer's *Foedera* documented in precise, legal cases. [48] Confiscation for heresy or apostasy, however, was but a half-way measure. It did not remove the clergy from the jurisdiction of the ecclesiastical courts, but it did encourage the king to be alert and forceful when dealing with heresy. Recognizing this, Wyclif utilized the possibility of royal confiscation for his own reforming ends. [49]

To label abuse, failure and fraud heretical was but a first step. The next was to assert these acts to be not only heretical, but treasonous as well. [50] Bishops, therefore, failing to correct their sheep were heretics and, more importantly, traiters to God, king and realm. [51] Papal provisors, *ipso facto*, fell from God's law and took up the property of the poor—that too was treasonous. [52] Nor was Wyclif's identification of heresy with treason completely unique or arbitrary; there was some precedent. Already in 1199, a decretal of Innocent III compared heresy with treason. [53] In the case of both heresy and treason, the issue was betrayal. And Wyclif, by equating the two, sought to implement his goal of clerical correction through confisca-

---

[47] *Ibid.*, who cites the *Close Rolls*, 1237-1242, 368.

[48] See Gwynn, *Austin Friars*, p. 244. Cf. also Rymer's *Foedera*, VII, 208, 284.

[49] See *DS*, p. 7, where Wyclif points out the advantages of heresy for himself: "Quoad tercium patet, quod aliqua bona hereticorum mobilia confiscarentur principibus, qui heresim eorum destruerent, et omnia bona eorum immobilia, ut redditus et predia quibus dotati sunt, redirent ad manus secularium ..."

[50] "Nec valet dicere quod ad regem non pertinet cognoscere super heretica pravitate; quia ad regem pertinet cognoscere quod elemosinarius suus vivat clericaliter, tum quia sub illa condicione sunt elemosine sibi date, tum eciam quia degenerando ab ista vita foret monstrum maxime proditorie faciens ad destruccionem regni, et per consequens incurrens contemptum regis gravissimum." *DE*, pp. 340-341.

[51] Speaking of bishops, Wyclif wrote: "Et indubie viso quod in hoc deficit habitualiter propter suum defectum in Deum et hominem, debent intimide omnia sua temporalia confiscari, cum sit proditor Dei, regis, et regni ..." *OM*, p. 86. See also *VSS*, III, 64.

[52] *SS*, II, 406-408.

[53] Pollock and Maitland, *History of English Law*, II, 549. Cf. also Ernst Kantorowicz, *Frederick the Second, 1194-1250*, trans. E. O. Lorimer (New York, 1931), pp. 264ff. Here Kantorowicz points out in detail how Frederick II equated heresy with treason on the basis of Roman law. The intent of this identification was to focus on Frederick's conception of Catholicism as a "State religion"; in this respect there are similarities with Wyclif's thought.

tion. He again pointed to English law. Treason was first adequately defined in 1352 by statute. It was non-clergyable; that is, it was a crime over which the ecclesiastical courts had absolutely no jurisdiction. Instead, treason was dealt with directly by the king. Treason, as opposed to felony, also provided for all lands and chattels to be forfeit to the king. [54]

Custom, of course, had long preceded statutory law. In 1204, King John had seized alien priories, not because they were the property of aliens, but rather because they were the property of traitorous Normans. [55] A second major confiscation of these priories took place under Edward I. Again the justification was treason. They constituted, it was claimed, a grave and serious danger to the safety of the realm. [56] Clearly treasonous actions delineated a very fertile and profitable field within which the king's best interests could be served.

Naturally, royal lawyers were anxious to extend treason's field of action. Wyclif knew this and used it. He also knew the advantages of treasonous action brought: non-clergyable, direct jurisdiction of the king, full forfeiture to the crown. He was positive—traitorous clerks fell under the law of England. [57]

Wyclif returned to the rights of patronage provided for in English law to establish the regulatory power of the king. They provided his most cogent argument. Beginning with the proposition that all endowment stemmed from the laity and that only secular powers had coercive jurisdiction, he reasoned that it belonged to them to supervise the clergy, and correct it whenever they felt it necessary.

> ... it pertains to the king to take cognizance of whether his almsman is living clerically; for one thing because the alms were given under that condition, for another because if the almsman degenerated from a clerical life, he would be a monster, working treacherously and most effectively to the destruction of the realm .... [58]

---

[54] See T. F. T. Plucknett, *A Concise History of the Common Law* (2nd ed.; Rochester, 1936), pp. 393ff.; Holdsworth, *History of English Law*, III, 249ff.; Pollock and Maitland, *History of English Law*, II, 165f. and 46ff. Imperial law too, as set forth by the glossators and post-glossators, emphasized that lands belonging to traitors were to escheat to the crown. See M. H. Keen, "The Political Thought of the Fourteenth-Century Civilians," *Trends*, p. 116.

[55] Ellis, *Anti-Papal Legislation*, pp. 43, 85.

[56] New, *Alien Priories in England*, pp. 53-55.

[57] Commenting upon the biblical text, "a fructibus eorum cognoscetis eos," Wyclif wrote: "Ista autem pars patet ex lege triplici: primo ex lege Anglie, que iudicat tales clericos proditores ad mortem in casu lese regie maiestatis." *OM*, p. 406.

[58] *DE*, p. 341: "Nec valet dicere quod ad regem non pertinet cognoscere super heretica pravitate; quia ad regem pertinet cognoscere quod elemosinarius suus vivat

Later in the same tract, Wyclif clarified this position in a more pragmatic fashion. "Our king," he wrote, "rules over his liege clergy with respect to the goods of nature and fortune according to civil lordship." Continuing, he maintained:

> If ... they had lived a wholly propertyless life ... they would not be thus subject. Hence, by reason of goods of fortune and goods of nature in a case in which abuse or notable contempt should be brought against them, it is permitted to the king to coerce them civilly, not in their capacity as priests, but in their capacity as almsmen of the king or as his liegemen who are in contempt. And so they are subject to their king in body and properties in many ways. [59]

The conclusion was programmatic. Departing from the thrust of his earlier arguments that had been a mixture of theological and legal elements, Wyclif tried a new tack. Now he would deal solely with the realities of the English king's actual power. He would base the power of the monarch to correct and to confiscate on the tenurial nature of the clergy's holdings in English land law and their responsibility to him as their feudal lord. The spiritual power of the "pontifical king" could only be extrapolated from the Bible and pre-Gregorian tradition, and both remained subjective. The extant English law, however, was tangible, and through its precedents, Wyclif was determined to render the clergy, and especially, its episcopacy, accessible to the king. What he had earlier established canonically, or eclectically from English practice, he now substantiated according to a specific reading of English feudal law.

The English episcopacy held most of its immense temporalities from the king on the basis of tenure by barony and knight service. As such, English law had long maintained that through their baronies, the king had coercive jurisdiction over them. [60] Wyclif was more than aware of this situation:

---

clericaliter, tum quia sub illa condicione sunt elemosine sibi date, tum eciam quia degenerando ab ista vita foret monstrum maxime proditorie faciens ad destruccionem regni ..." See also *DDD*, III, 202.

[59] "Servus autem civilis est omnino expers libertatis civilis, et sic serviunt clerici regi libere, qui tenent de illo in capite; et sic videtur mihi quod rex noster habet super clerum suum legium quoad bona nature et bona fortune secundum quid civile dominium. Si autem viverent vitam omnino exproprietariam ... non forent sic subiecti, et sic racione bonorum fortune et bonorum nature in casu quo contingat in eis abusus vel contemptus notabilis licet regi eos civiliter cohercere, non in quantum sacerdotes, sed in quantum regis elemosinarii vel homines eius legii contempnentes. Et sic regi suo in corpore et bonis multipliciter sunt subiecti." *Ibid.*, pp. 350-351.

[60] Bracton, *De Legibus*, VI, 371, 493.

With respect to the laws of England, it is clear that from rational and approved custom, the king of England can remove temporalities, movable or immovable, from clerics who are guilty of contempt, treason, or other crime incurring forfeit. 61

Such action on the part of the king was justifiable, he argued, because ecclesiastics have voluntarily accepted their temporalities as feudal holdings with all attendant responsibilities. And then to dispel all lingering doubts as to the legitimacy of this position, Wyclif quoted the Magna Carta: "no ecclesiastical person," it stated, "shall be amerced according to the size of his ecclesiastical benefice, but according to his feudal holding." 62 Citing the Statute of Westminister, Wyclif clinched his argument: not only have clerics voluntarily assumed their temporalities, they have even sworn homage or fealty and paid the price of a palfrey. 63 The grants were therefore conditional, the tenures feudal and the clerics came under the coercive measures of civil law when the conditions of tenure were disregarded. This was, of course, precisely what Wyclif had meant when he asserted above that the clergy could be coerced civilly "in their capacity as almsmen of the king or as his liegeman who are in contempt." 64

Pushing for correction and confiscation, Wyclif emphasized the feudal responsibilities of the clergy. They were legally accountable to the king and the major avenue to this end was the principle of contempt. Underpinning this principle was not difficult. In the *De Ecclesia*, he devoted an entire chapter to this topic, pointing out that all of the English kings, from William the Conqueror to Richard II, had defended their ability to confiscate temporal holdings of the

---

61 "Quoad iura Anglie constat quod ex racionali ac approbata consuetudine, quod propter contemptum cleri, prodicionem vel aliam forisfacturam potest rex Anglie ab eis anferre temporalia tam mobilia quam eciam immobilia; et hoc ex voluntaria eorum obligacione propria." *DCD*, II, 39.

62 "Nam in Magna Carta, cui rex et magnates Anglie ex iuramento obligantur, capitulo XXII, sic habetur: 'Nulla ecclesiastica persona amercietur secundum quantitatem beneficii ecclesiastici sui sed secundum laycum tenementum suum.'" *Ibid.* As Edith Tatnall has pointed out in her recent article, "John Wyclif and Ecclesia Anglicana," *Journal of Ecclesiastical History*, XX (1969), 30, Wyclif's version of Magna Carta does not correspond verbatim with the standard text which reads: "Nullus clericus amercietur de laico tenemento suo, nisi secundum modum aliorum predictorum, et non secundum quantitatem beneficii sui ecclesiastici." For this text and lengthy discussion, see William Sharp McKechnie, *Magna Carta: a Commentary on the Great Charter of King John with an Historical Introduction* (2nd ed.; Glasgow, 1914), pp. 298ff.

63 *Statutes of the Realm*, I, 92.

64 *Supra*, fn. 59.

clergy in both word and deed. Moreover, he asserted, "this power pertained directly to the crown." [65] Nor was Wyclif willing to rest his case here. He laboriously illustrated his stand with trenchant examples from the historical testimony of Ralph Higden's *Polychronicon*. Some of these were well known—like the action of the French king, Phillip, against the Templars and William the Conqueror's high-handed treatment of the Anglo-Saxon monasteries. [66] Other examples were not so familiar and included the confiscation of temporalities from such English bishops as William Bateman of Norwich, John Grandisson of Exeter and the friar bishop, Thomas of Lyle at Ely. [67] Earlier, Wyclif had also found it expedient to give his version of the historical record with respect to William Rufus, Simon de Montfort, Henry III and others. [68] But then as he said himself (with no apparent embarrassment), "it is not fitting to multiply examples by which the kings of England have taken property from the church for avarice, contempt and just wrong." [69]

Contempt, of course, was the justification for these and numerous other examples of confiscation. It was the means by which the king

---

[65] *DE*, pp. 331-332.

[66] For William the Conqueror, see *DCD*, II, 47, 51ff.; *DE*, p. 332: "... patet legenti cronicas regni nostri quomodo Willelmus conquestor multas elemosinas regum saxonum de abbatiis, de episcopatibus et aliis dotacionibus sub nomine perpetue elemosine pro perpetuo variavit, nunc subtrahendo, nunc transferendo et nunc loco cleri prioris extraneos inducendo ... Et sic de sompnio quo fingitur ipsum post restituere omnes ablatarios clericos, sicut nec restituit heredes Saxonum rebellantes." For the Templars, see *DCD*, II, 4, 34, 113f., and 253, where Wyclif maintained that pontiffs too were corrected through confiscations.

[67] "Infectiva dico, quia hereticaret reges clerum et populum interim succedentes; sed dimissis destruccionibus Templariorum et ablacionibus privatis que interim contigerunt, recolamus de ablacionibus talibus que diebus nostris per illustrem regem Edwardum tercium erant facte. Nam temporalia domini Willelmi Bathman Norwycensis capta sunt in manus regis et tenta duodecim annis continuis pro contemptu. Et idem contigit de domino Johanne Gransoni Exoniensi, de fratre Thoma de Lyle, episcopo Heliensi, et sic de multis ablacionibus quas diebus nostris cognovimus. Ymmo Ricardus II. rex noster sicut avus suus practizat hoc annuatim in religiosis possessionates de Francia; nec super isto consulunt curiam Romanam, quia ut constanter defendunt ista potestas directe pertinet ad coronam." *Ibid.* For confirmation of this information see Tatnall's citations from Walsingham in her article, "John Wyclif and Ecclesia Anglicana," p. 33.

[68] *DCD*, II, 52.

[69] "Nec oportet multiplicare exempla quibus reges Anglie pro avariciantibus, pro contemptibus et forisfacturis iustis ceperunt ab ecclesia tam bona mobilia, cum ex legibus humanis superius allegatis illud sit licitum peccato supposito, et posicionem peccati experiencia memoralis satis docet. Et nemo dubitat quin consequatur rex iuste temporalia ab ecclesiastico abutente auferendo." *Ibid.*, p. 49.

punished in order to correct. [70] It represented, among the regalian rights of English kings, a privilege consonant in Wyclif's opinion, with catholic truth. [71] It was a position to be constantly reiterated. [72] Sometimes the reason for confiscation was stated, as when the bishop deposed a curate from the king's service or when a treasonous act occurred. [73] Perhaps, again, the bishop summoned a liegeman of the king into his court without the king's license. [74] More often, however, the nature of the contempt charge was not noted by Wyclif as he was simply arguing the principle. [75] In any event, Wyclif concluded that the historical endowment of the English church had, from its genesis, carried with it conditions which allowed for confiscation in the event of royal contempt. These had been maintained through custom and practice and codified in the statutes of the realm.

Wyclif's conclusion was basically correct. In the *Calendar of Close Rolls* for 1276, the sheriff of Oxford was informed that the king had caused the abbey of Osney, of which he was patron, "to be taken into his hands with all its temporalities by reason of a certain contempt ..." [76] A few years later, Robert Winchelsy, the archbishop of Canterbury, had his temporalities confiscated, [77] and under Edward III this practice was included, although negatively, into the statutory law: "Item because the temporalities of archbishops and bishops have oftentimes been taken into the king's hands for contempt done to him upon writs of Quare non admisit and likewise for divers other causes ..." [78] English law defined contempt broadly. According to the Register of Wykeham and Rymer's *Foedera*, sixteen bishops had their persons seized in July of 1372 for alleged detention of the sub-

---

[70] *DE*, p. 332.

[71] "Tercio suppono facta regum Anglie superius memorata et perseveranciam regis et regni ad defendendum hanc potestatem tamquam legitimam et regis Anglie Precipuam regaliam. Ex quo sequitur quod ipsi supponunt hoc regis privilegium non esse catholice veritati dissonum sed consonum, cum (ut dicunt) sit fundabile in scriptura in qua omnis veritas et non nisi veritas catholica est contenta." *Ibid.*, p. 334.

[72] "Nam rex ex notato suo contemptu confiscat redditus episcoporum ac aliorum religiosorum, quanto magis ex maiori contemptu Dei ..." *SS*, II, 84. See also *DE*, pp. 49, 372, and *DCD*, I, 345.

[73] *SS*, III, 212; *OM*, p. 97.

[74] *OM*, p. 162.

[75] *DCD*, II, 73-79.

[76] *Close Rolls*, 1272-1279, 273.

[77] Loserth, "Studien zur Kirchenpolitik Englands," I, 12.

[78] "Item p' ce q les temporaltees des ercevesques & Evesqes ount este sovent foitz pris en la main le Roi, p' contempt fait a lui s' le brief Ouare non admisit, & ensement p plusures aut's causes ..." *Statutes of the Realm*, I, 326.

sidy to the king. [79] The *Rotuli Parliamentorum* also contains a wealth of documentation attesting to loss of temporalities for clerical contempt of the king. [80] Thus, adequate precedent existed in English law to substantiate Wyclif's contention "that it belonged to the king for contempt or another forfeiture of his homage to punish even bishops by removal of temporalities proportionate to the crime." [81]

The legal prohibitions against clerical alienation provided Wyclif with another expedient avenue to the English clergy. By the thirteenth century alienation of property had become a serious problem for the feudal lord. [82] With alienation the lord often lost services due from the alienated land. Consequently, restraints preventing alienation were constructed or resuscitated, reflecting the numerous grievances of the feudality whose interests were damaged. [83] Sometimes kings cried loudest. Henry II, for instance, used the older *Leges Edwardi Confessoris*, to justify his revocation of rights, dignities and land that had formerly belonged to the king. In the process not only did he find authoritative precedents, he inserted the whole question of inalienability into English land-law. Later that question was further inflated when, under canonistic influence, English kings adopted a concept of the crown as an impersonal institution, possessing rights of its own that were themselves inalienable. [84]

While alienation of land with all its attendant rights and services was a general feudal problem, it was particularly acute with those lands migrating into the hands of the church. Almost inevitably once there, obligations were sloughed off, feudal incidents lost and legal redress impaired. [85] It was therefore in the interest of all feudal

[79] Rymer, *Foedera*, III, 958; *Wykeham's Register*, T. F. Kirby (ed.) (2 vols.; Hampshire, 1896, 1899), II, 577-580. Both citations are given in Workman, *John Wyclif*, I, 212.

[80] *Rotuli Parliamentorum*, I, 94a, 102a, 152b, 245a, 153a.

[81] "Numquid non licet regi ex contemptu vel alia forisfactura omagiarii sui, eciam episcopi, punire, per ablacionem temporalium proporcionalem ad delictum?" *DCD*, II, 75.

[82] A short survey of inalienability in thirteenth century England can be found in F. M. Powicke's, *The Thirteenth Century* (Oxford, 1953), pp. 5-7. A more detailed introduction is Peter Riesenberg's, *Inalienability of Sovereignty in Medieval Political Thought* (New York, 1956). See also Hartmut Hoffmann, "Die Unveräusserlichkeit der Kronrechte im Mittelalter," *Deutsches Archiv*, XX (1964), 389-474, as well as Ernst Kantorowicz, "Inalienability. A Note on Canonical Practice and the English Coronation Oath in the Thirteenth Century," *Speculum*, XXIX (1954), 488-502.

[83] *Monumenta Germaniae Historica*, Leges, II, 38, and *Libri Feudorum*, I, xiii; II, ix; III, xxxiv.

[84] Kantorowicz, *King's Two Bodies*, p. 355f.

[85] J. M. W. Bean, *The Decline of English Feudalism, 1215-1540* (Manchester, 1968), pp. 49ff.

lords, including the king, to either limit or prohibit the alienation of feudal lands into mortmain. By 1217 and the reissue of Magna Carta during Henry III's minority, a beginning was made.

> It shall not be lawful for anyone henceforward to give his land to any religious house in such a way that he resume it again to hold it of the house .... If anyone for the future shall give his land in this way to any religious house and be convicted thereof, the gift shall be quashed and the land forfeited to the lord of the fee. [86]

This, however, was only a beginning. Something more was needed to protect the beleaguered interests of the feudality. In 1258, the barons in desperation petitioned the king that "men of religion should not enter into the fee of earls and barons and others against their will, whereby they lose forever wardship, marriages, reliefs and escheats." [87] This part of the petition was later translated into one of the Provisions of Westminister of 1259: "it is not lawful for men of religion to enter the fee of anyone without the licence of the chief-lord of whom it is immediately held." [88] And finally, in 1279, the ultimate restriction was incorporated in the Statute of Mortmain:

> We therefore, intending to provide convenient remedy to the profit of our realm, by the advice of our prelates, earls, barons, and our other subjects who are of our council, have provided, laid down and ordained, that no religious person or other whoever he may be, may buy or sell any lands or tenements, or under the colour of gift or lease, or by reason of any other title, whatever it may be, may receive lands or tenements, or by any other craft or device may presume to appropriate to himself under pain of forfeiture of the same, whereby such lands or tenements may in any way come into mortmain. [89]

---

[86] "Non liceat alicui de cetero dare terram suam alicui domui religiosae ita quod illam resumat tenendam de eadem domo ... Si quis autem de cetero terram suam alicui domui religiosae sic dederit et super hoc convincatur, donum suum penitus cassetur et terra illa domino suo illius feodi incurratur." Stubbs, *Select Charters*, p. 343. The translation is that of Bean, *Decline*, p. 50.

[87] Item ten of the Petition of the Barons: "Item petutnt remedium, quod religiosi non intrent in feodum comitum et baronum et aliorum sine voluntate eorum, per quod amittunt in perpetuum custodias, maritagia, relevia et eschaetas." *Ibid.*, p. 375, again as quoted by Bean, *Decline*, p. 51.

[88] Chapter fourteen reads: "Viris autem religiosis non liceat ingredi feodum alicujus sine licentia capitalis domini, de quo scilicet res ipsa immediate tenetur." *Ibid.*, p. 393.

[89] "... nos super hoc pro utilitate regni congruum remedium provideri volentes, de consilio praelatorum, comitum et aliorum fidelium regni nostri de consilio nostro

This was hardly revolutionary. The crown had long been protecting its interests. As early as 1228 Henry III had issued writs to all the sheriffs of the land demanding that:

> ... no one who holds of us in chief ... as he values his body and tenement may grant or sell or in any way alienate anything of his tenement to any religious house or any ecclesiastical persons without our licence. 90

But there is novelty with Westminister and the Statute of Mortmain. The prohibition has breadth; what had applied, only to the crown, now applied to the other feudal lords as well. The church was not to extend its landed holdings in the future. Forbidding all acquisitions of land by the church, except with the licence of the lord of the fee, the crown itself undertook the responsibility of protecting feudal interests through intervention and forfeiture.

There was, however, another side to the problem. If all ecclesiastical temporalities were originally the conditional gift of the laity, then it was only reasonable to prevent alienation out of clerical hands and service as well. This kind of clerical alienation had long concerned canonists. By the late twelfth century, English lawyers such as Glanvill also dealt with the topic, noting that: "... neither a bishop nor an abbot can alienate in perpetuity any part of his demesne without the lord king's consent and confirmation ..." 91 Later this civil prohibition was spelled out with greater precision in the Statute of Westminster and as with alienation into the church, the king undertook the responsibility of preventing the reverse, alienation out of the church.

> Our lord the King hath ordained, that if abbots, priors, keepers of hospitals, and other religious houses founded by him or by his progenitors, do from henceforth aliene the lands given to their houses by him or by his progenitors; the land shall be taken into the King's hands, and holden at his will, and the purchaser shall lose his recovery as well as of the lands as of the money that he paid. 92

---

existentium providimus, statuimus et ordinavimus, quod nullus religiosus aut alius quicunque terras aut tenementa aliqua emere vel vendere, aut sub colore donationis aut termini vel alterius tituli cujuscunque, ab aliquo recipere, aut alio quovis modo, arte vel ingenio, sibi appropriare praesumat, sub forisfactura eorundum, per quod ad manum mortuam terrae et tenementa hujusmodi deveniant quoquo modo." *Ibid.*, p. 451, as quoted and translated by Bean, *Decline*, p. 52.

90 See Bean, *Decline*, pp. 58ff. ,who quotes from the *Close Rolls*, 1227-1231, 88, and discusses the implication of these writs with respect to the Statute of Mortmain.

91 Glanvill, *Tractatus de legibus, ed. Hall*, p. 74.

92 *Statutes of the Realm*, I, 91.

Nor was the king only concerned with his own foundations; choosing not to stand alone, he included the foundations of "an Earl, Baron, or other Persons" in the provisions of the statute. All lay foundations were to be protected from alienations away. [93] If any doubt existed as to the seriousness of the intent, it was quickly dispelled when legal actions providing for recovery, such as the writs of "contra forma collationis" and "cessavit" were developed and appended.

John Wyclif was not unaware of the multiple problems encircling the question of alienation, either into the church or out of it. He knew that loss of service was a frequent companion to alienation and that recovery was difficult.

> Without the consent and licence of the chief-lord, no one can alienate lordship; for service due according to the law would then be removed. Consequently, he should be injured by the withdrawal of lordship which is his. [94]

Alienation could only take place with the licence of the king. [95] Wyclif knew his law. His paraphrasing of the legal proscriptions found in the Statute of Mortmain were surprisingly accurate even when detailing the appropriate action to be taken when the inferior or mediate lords failed to enter possession of estranged lands. [96] On occasion Wyclif could even paraphrase the actual form of the licence to alienate as used by Edward I. [97]

> ... revenue should not be permitted to devolve into the hands of the religious unless having first diligently noted that injury should not fall to the king and to the realm from revenues so entering mortmain, in order that compensation shall be given to king or realm before a licence for doing so is issued. [98]

---

93 *Ibid.*

94 "Prima pars patet eo quod nemini licet alienare dominium sine consensu et licencia capitalis domini; cum exinde tolleretur servicium capitali domino de iure debitum, et per consequens sibi iniuriavetur subtrahendo domino quod est suum." *DDD*, pp. 206-207.

95 *PW*, I, 42; *SS*, II, 50; *DCD*, I, 7; *DCD*, III, 236, 252; *DDD*, pp. 201-203, 224-225; *OM*, p. 413; *DA*, p. 243.

96 "Sicut ergo statutum est quod religiosis perquirentibus terras aut tenementa sine speciali regis licencia emcione, dotacione vel appropriacione dominus immediatus debet infra annum ingredi et domini mediati gradatim infra medietatem anni, quo inferiores domini in hoc desunt et demum dominus rex in quadrivio vel citra aliis deficientibus in hac parte." *DCD*, II, 45-46.

97 *Year Book, 32-33 Edward I*, A. J. Horwood (ed.) (London, 1864), p. 489. See also Plucknett, *Legislation Edward I*, p. 100.

98 "... quod non permitteretur redditus devolvi in manus religiosorum nisi prius diligenter notato quod dampnum cederet regi et regno ex reditibus sic mortificatis, ut vel sic fiat regi vel regno ante licenciam recompensa." *DCD*, IV, 483-484.

Again Wyclif knew his law and used it. He knew that the Statute of Mortmain had not only prohibited all acquisitions of land by the church, but that the crown itself had assumed responsibility for enforcing it. [99] Yet he also knew that it was primarily a threat and that in fact, under Edward I, alienations were possible with the issuance of a royal licence. Repeatedly, he returned to this theme: "According to the just laws of England, the king inquires, through the people, into clerical alienation as to what injury acquisition of this kind brings to the realm." [100] The king, he continued, should inquire into such disruptive action and see whether the witnesses were deceived when determining what injury would come to king, lords, and realm. Wyclif was convinced that should this inquiry occur the inspector of the king would recognize that by definition *all* clerical acquisition was injurious and should therefore be confiscated. [101]

The inquest referred to here by Wyclif had to take place before a licence to alienate lands into the church was granted by the king. The writ "ad quod dampnum" initiated the action. Its purpose was to disclose "the anticipated loss to the king and others" in terms of the tenement's value, both feudal and fiscal. [102] Wyclif's use of the writ and the inquisitional procedure it initiated to supplement his own, very different argument was noteworthy. English law gave him two opportunities to contain the growth of clerical wealth. On the one hand stood the Statute of Mortmain, and Wyclif saw its enforcement as legally dissolving the wealth of the church. [103] But he also knew that its prohibitions were being circumvented through the issuance of royal licences to alienate land into mortmain. He would have preferred the enforcement of mortmain, but that was not now possible, so

---

[99] *Supra*, fn. 96.

[100] "Si ergo secundum iustas leges Anglie rex in cleri mortificacione facit inquiri populo ad quod dampnum huiusmodi perquisicio cedit regno?" *DCD*, III, 313-314. Given the context, the beginning "Si" should probably be read as "Sic."

[101] "Et item cum semper sit infra etatem ad faciendum complementum iusticie, quanta diligencia mandaret et remandaret ad inquirendum redditus huiusmodi perquisicionem enormem reipublice turbativam, nedum si testes decepti sunt de valore rei quoad regem, dominos et regnum pro cunctis futuris temporalibus, sed quanta circumvencio facta est undique; et credo quod politici non taxarent dampnum faciliter, precipue pensato quod clericorum proditoria irreligiositas sit regno infinitum dampnabilior quam prodicio cuiuscunque temporalis possibilis. Et tunc credo quod scrutator regis descerneret omnia clericorum suorum perquisita temporalia confiscanda; et si Deo placeret, hoc esset frenum clericis, ne tam dampnabiliter populum taxarent." *Ibid.*, p. 314.

[102] Plucknett, *Legislation of Edward I*, p. 100.

[103] *DCD*, IV, 484.

instead he opted for the prevailing legal practice. Legally, it would carry greater weight with his contemporaries; practically, he could not imagine an inquest that would fail to describe clerical alienation as injurious. Consequently, when Wyclif protested that without special licence all donations were invalid, and that the common law itself demanded confiscation in the event of nonprocurement, he did so with the law at his finger tips. [104]

Wyclif's strategy in all of this was to see English law as a mass of authoritative technicalities which he could ingeniously combine to secure his goal of rendering the clergy accessible to secular correction and reform. The king, in the process, would become, like the pope, a "universal ordinary." [105] Such clerical coercion was no "unheard novelty," he wrote, but "the law and custom of our realm." [106]

The "law and custom of the realm" was another way of saying statute and case made English law. Wyclif said that too. [107] And there were many laws in the realm of England concerning confiscation and forfeiture. Often enough they revolved around the regulatory power of the laity. Magna Carta itself, Wyclif held, forced the lords to swear to defend "not only the laws of the realm, but the immunities and liberties of the church." Wyclif's litany was simple: the realm rests primarily on its priesthood. Unflinchingly he drew the conclusion: when the temporal lords assume responsibility for the correction of the clergy, they are fulfilling by word and deed their obligations under Magna Carta. [108]

Working in an English tradition of custom and law, Wyclif set out

---

[104] *PW*, I, 249.

[105] Wyclif himself does not use this phrase, but Bracton did and Wyclif would have agreed. See Bracton, *De Legibus*, IV, 248.

[106] "Et nemo dubitat quin consequatur rex iuste temporalia ab ecclesiastico abutente auferendo. Et patet quod dicta conclusio de possibili non est novitas inaudita." *DCD*, II, 49, 133ff. "... huiusmodi est lex et consuetudo regni nostri quoad clericos cohercendos, ergo conclusio." *DCD*, II, 75.

[107] Having granted a particular assumption to his opponent, Wyclif continues: "Unde non est possibile legem rectam statui et casum contingere, quin secundum regulam sacre scripture tolli potest inconveniens peccati..." *DE*, p. 258.

[108] "Item, domini temporalies in Anglia astringuntur solempniter iuramento (ut patet in Magna Carta) defendere nedum regni iura sed immunitates et libertates ecclesie. Cum ergo ius et profectus regni precipuo stat in virtutum observancia quoad clerum, videtur quod ius debet esse precipue executum. Et ex parte libertatis ecclesie patet idem. Nam iuxta primam partem XXXIX. capitulo edificacio, libertas et profectus ecclesie non stat in accumulacione bonorum fortune sed in viciorum destruccione et virtutum ministracione. Sed reges et domini temporales iurant ad observandum et non ad destruendum libertates ecclesie, ergo tenentur de huiusmodi prepositis providere; ..." *DCD*, II, 45.

the customary ability of the temporal power to enforce correction of its clergy through confiscation, coercion and punishment.

> For every custom from a time which is beyond human memory, and which has been continued without repugnance to scripture, ought to be continued as if just law; the law and custom of our realm is of this kind with respect to coercing the clergy. [109]

All that was authoritative, canon law, popes, canonized kings, holymen, recognized and approved the laws of England which enforced the principle of customary interference and punishment of priests. [110] To assert otherwise would restrict the sovereignty of the king and realm, would vitiate the regalian rights, and make heretical the customs of English law concerning patronage and feudal tenure. [111] That could not be.

---

[109] "Nam omnis consuetudo a tempore quo non est humana memoria, continuata sine repugnancia eiusdem consuetudinis ad scripturam est tamquam lex iusta continuanda; huiusmodi est lex et consuetudo regni nostri quoad clericos cohercendos, ergo conclusio." *Ibid.*, p. 75. This type of phraseology was very common. For "secundum legem et consuetudinem regni," see Glanvill, *Tractatus de legibus*, ed. Hall, index; *Bracton's Notebook*, ed. F. W. Maitland (Cambridge, 1887), III, 310; Bracton, *On the Laws and Customs of England*, trans. and ed. Samuel E. Thorne (Cambridge, 1968), II, 19ff. Custom is precedent and that can be enough, as the author of the *Dialogus de Scaccario*, Richard Ely, pointed out. "There are cases where the causes of events and the reasons for decisions are obscure, and in these it is enough to cite precedents, particularly those derived from men of sense, whose actions are cautious, and founded upon reason." *Dialogus de Scaccario*, ed. A. Hughes, C. G. Crump and A. Johnson (Oxford, 1902), pp. xvii-xviii.

[110] "Patet ergo quod non est intencionis Romane ecclesie leges infringere regnorum, set statuta sua, que videntur legibus regum contraria, cum excepcione consuetudinis loci concordare, ut patet ... Minor autem ex hoc evidet, quod multi sancti pape saltem tacendo, multi sancti reges Anglie ab ecclesia canonizati, confessores et martyres, approbando in dictas leges Anglie usque ad mortem consenserant ..." *Ibid.*, p. 76.

[111] "Secundo dico quod non est de intencione huius doctoris nec alicuius sani capitis asserere, quod in nullo casu quitquid clericus vel religiosus fecerit debet puniri per iudicem secularem. Hoc enim foret tollere iura regnorum, ut patet specialiter de Francia et Anglia, ac hereticare consuetudines eorum de layco feodo, de iure patronatus et similibus, de causis civilibus que consequuntur forum rei eciam in clerico, et (quod maximum est), dare clericis audaciam ad spoliandum" *Ibid.*, p. 133.

CHAPTER EIGHT

NECESSITY KNOWS NO LAW

While John Wyclif preferred the technicalities found in the English land law to authorize clerical correction by the laity, he was not insensitive to the many opportunities available in the theoretical arguments concerning the "State" and its public authority. The revival of Roman law in the twelfth century and the inception of Aristotle in the 1260's had long given political theorists an ample field of play to deal with such classical abstractions as the "State." [1] By the fourteenth century, both canonists and legists had not only developed a body of ideas dealing with the corporate state as a fictive person, but these ideas, often so respectful of political reality, had percolated through society, permeating it with justifying theorems. At the heart of this development was a galaxy of ideas that revolved around "reason of state," and that which must be done "to preserve the health and strength of the State." [2] These ideas originated with the presumption that there existed a general welfare that was to take precedence over all private interests and that its defense was not only legitimate, and morally proper, but necessary.

The general welfare, often expressed with the word *utilitas*, was a classical concept commonly found in the Roman law. Conceptually it survived Rome and lived through the decline of public law associated with Germanic Europe by the expedient strategem of ecclesiastical adoption. [3] From Isidore of Seville to Gratian and then to St. Thomas

---

[1] Post, *Studies*, p. 112. Here and in the following paragraphs I have relied heavily upon these very able and fundamental studies whose subject and excellence of treatment have made Post an authority in his own right and a point of departure for the now burgeoning topic of the medieval state. The concentration of this work is on the legal thought that permeated political society as it sought to square theory with reality.

[2] See Friedrich Meinecke's work on the *Idée der Staatsräson* as it appears in the English translation under the title, *Machiavellism. The Doctrine of Raison d'Etat and Its Place in Modern History*, trans. Douglas Scott (London, 1957), pp. 25-27, as cited by Post, *Studies*, p. 242.

[3] Post, *Studies*, pp. 8-9, maintains that the concept of public utility and its allied themes of necessity and emergency originated in the Roman law. He also, however, acknowledges some scholarly opposition from Walter Ullmann, who, in his *Principles of Government and Politics in the Middle Ages* (London, 1961), p. 133, holds that the "principle of *publica utilitas*" probably stemmed from a Germanic conception.

Aquinas, the commonwealth (*utilitas*) was accepted as the final basis for all legitimate public authority. 4 Under the auspices of the church, and in the general exchange of ecclesiastical and feudal principles, the laity too subscribed to the goal of *utilitas*. Consequently, whatever the existing law, be it customary, consentient or arbitrary, it has as its object the general welfare of society. 5

The English statutes took full cognizance of the instrumentality of law. Evolving in this thoughtful, if not heady, atmosphere, they made it plain indeed that the idea of the common good was not limited to the church, the Roman law nor the feudal states of the continent. As early as 1236, the Statute of Merton emerged after a "discussion about the common utility of the realm" by prelates and nobles. 6 Later statutes continued this discussion. Westminister I, for example, came to fruition "for the common profit of Church and State." 7 Finally, the controversial Statute of Mortmain, reflecting the disenchantment of the many in mid-fourteenth century England, had but a single purpose: to defend "the utility of the realm." 8

On the basis of the conviction that the common good (*utilitas*) superseded all other considerations of state, whatever the activity, whatever the authority, political theorists had long posited, and believed in, a doctrine of necessity. Like so much else, this too came to Western Europe first in Roman dress and then under the guise of clerical garb. 9 It was a tool so useful that it became a standard doctrine acceptable to jurists of every hue. 10 Although its ramifications were

---

Whatever the origin, Post seems on sure ground when he asserts that "the terms and concepts used in the barbarian kingdoms, *publica utilitas* and *status regni*, were a survival of the tradition of the imperial authority in the Roman Empire." See especially Floyd S. Lear, "The Literature on Public Law in Germanic Custom," *Rice Institute Pamphlet*, XXXVII (1950), 1-20.

4 Charles C. Bayley, "Pivotal Concepts in the Political Philosophy of William of Ockham," *Journal of the History of Ideas*, X (1949), 201-202. See also, Plucknett, *Legislation of Edward I*, 5, fn. 1, who gives the appropriate citations for Aquinas' use of the theory of *utilitas* as well as the passages in Gratian and Isidore.

5 *Ibid.*, and Post, *Studies, passim*.

6 *Statutes of the Realm*, I, 1: "cum tractatum esset de coi utilitate regni ..." as quoted by Plucknett, *Legislation of Edward I*, p. 5ff.

7 *Ibid.*, p. 26: "... pur ceo ke nostre Seygnur le Rey ad graunt volente & desir del Estat de son Reaume [adrescer], en les choses ou mestier est del amendement, a ceo pur le cōmun profit de Seint Eglise e del reaume; ..."

8 *Statutes of the Realm*, I, 51: "nos super hoc pro utilitate regni congruum remedium provideri volentes ..."

9 *Supra*, fn. 3 and 4.

10 Otto Gierke, *Political Theories of the Middle Age*, trans. Frederic William Maitland (Cambridge, 1900), pp. 79-80, was among the first to note a medieval

not, the doctrine of necessity was exceedingly straighforward, deceptively simple: necessity knows no law. When the general welfare is threatened by exigency or endangered by lapses in the aggregate of existing, positive law, then acts of an extra-ordinary nature are allowed by the natural law to preserve the integrity of the self. [11] The king of the realm decided when such a crisis existed for it was he who adjudged and administered the common good. [12] Normally (*regulariter*) the king acted with the definition of existing law, the law that regulated societal relationships according to private rights and privileges. Only casually (*casualiter*) did he step out of bounds and then only for the welfare of the whole. [13] Allowing the king this freedom of action, the doctrine of necessity assured him the means of defending his charge of preserving the realm and its *utilitas*. It did so by not letting any private privilege or right prevail. [14] St. Bernard put it as well as any: "Whenever necessity is urgent, dispensation is excusable; whenever utility demands it, dispensation is praiseworthy. The common utility, I say, not one's own." [15]

Often the urgency of necessity had to do with the defense of the common welfare that stood superior to all of the private rights of king and subjects. Medieval practice termed this public utility, the *status regni*. [16] Defense of the common welfare was paramount and since it was also identified with the realm, to defend the *patria* or fatherland was the greatest virtue. [17] The king, to accomplish this task, had to meet expenditures that went far beyond his own personal

doctrine of appropriation based on "just cause" and necessity. This topic was of particular concern to C. H. McIlwain, *Constitutionalism Ancient and Modern* (Ithaca, 1947), pp. 67-95. For more recent treatments, see Wilks, *Problem of Sovereignty*, pp. 208ff., 217ff., 449f., with extensive bibliographic references, and Post, *Studies, passim*.

[11] Bayley, "Pivotal Concepts," pp. 201-202.

[12] Post, *Studies*, p. 15.

[13] Wilks, *Problem of Sovereignty*, pp. 210f., 316.

[14] Post, *Studies*, pp. 21, 243, 253, 559.

[15] As quoted by Post, *Studies*, p. 267.

[16] *Ibid.*, p. 453. See also, F. M. Powicke, "Reflections on the Medieval State," *Transactions Royal Historical Society*, XIX (1936), 9f.

[17] Cf. Kantorowicz, *King's Two Bodies*, pp. 232-272, as well as his paper, "Pro patria mori," *American Historical Review*, LVI (1951), 472-492. See also Gaines Post's work, now available in *Studies*, pp. 434-493, which is an extension of an earlier study, "Two Notes on Nationalism in the Middle Ages: 1. Pugna pro patria," *Traditio*, IX (1953), 281ff.; Helene Wieruszowski, *Vom Imperium zum nationalen Königtum* (Munich and Berlin, 1933), pp. 168ff. and *passim*; Joseph R. Strayer, "Defense of the Realm and Royal Power in France," *Studi in Onore di Gino Luzzatto* (Milan, 1949), pp. 289ff.

means. In such times he could not "live of his own," and it was precisely here that the king claimed "necessity." [18] Since it was for the common welfare of all, he had a recognized right to levy an extraordinary tax for the defense of the realm. [19] For the public utility, the king stood at the head of an emergency above the normal processes of law: "For the common utility, the Lord King, by means of his prerogative, is in many cases above the laws and customs used in his realm." [20] Moreover, defense of the realm was a plea that excused others besides the king from the normal procedures of legal activity. Bracton, the Crown lawyer, writing of those failing to appear in court, thought it quite appropriate that those serving in the king's army "for the defense of the realm" in a necessary and useful cause, should be excused. [21]

Theories of necessity and defense marked a growing interest in the notion of the public good; they also reflected a willingness on the part of both ruler and ruled to use this symbiotic set of ideas to express legally their drive for sovereignty. [22] Nowhere was this set discussed with greater intensity than in the tense relationships between emerging national states and the wide, general interests of the universal church.

More often than not, the context of such discussion was the issue of clerical taxation by the laity. [23] The issue was an old one. Even the canonists agreed, however, that in times of necessity, independent kingdoms—and Italian cities—had the right to extract extraordinary taxes from the clergy. [24] The speculative mystic, Hugh of St. Victor, was of the same opinion. If reason and necessity demanded it, he declared, churches and their property owed a civil obedience to the royal power. [25] But by the time of the Third Lateran Council in 1179,

---

18 Strayer, "Defense of the Realm," p. 292.

19 Post, *Studies*, pp. 112-113.

20 *Rot. Parl.*, I, 71: "Dominus Rex ... pro communi utilitate per prerogativam suam in multis casibus est supra leges et consuetudines in regno suo usitatas."

21 Bracton, fol. 336b, Woodbine, IV, 71, as quoted by Kantorowicz, *King's Two Bodies*, p. 237, fn. 134.

22 Post, *Studies*, p. 114.

23 See Joseph R. Strayer, "Consent to Taxation under Phillip the Fair," in Strayer and C. H. Taylor, eds., *Studies in Early French Taxation* (Cambridge, 1939), pp. 6ff., as well as Powicke, "Reflections," p. 15f., and Post, *Studies*, pp. 114, 123n.; Kantorowicz, *King's Two Bodies*, pp. 257, 268; Wilks, *Problem of Sovereignty*, pp. 182-183.

24 Post, *Studies*, p. 284.

25 *Ibid.*, p. 258. In addition, consult fn. 33 for further citations of interest.

the church forbade lay rulers to demand subsidies from the clerical estate. There was one exception: should the bishop and his clergy feel that the need was sufficiently great, that a crisis existed, then they could decide to grant a subsidy. [26] The Fourth Lateran Council met in 1215. By then it was abundantly clear that a stronger position had to be taken on the part of the church; clerical subsidies were still being demanded illegally by the laity and it was the laity who were determining the state of emergency. Accordingly the Council decided that bishops and their clergy could grant aids to the king but only in time of need and only under two conditions. First, the demands of the crisis had to exceed the means of the laity and second, the lord pope had to approve each and every grant. [27] This position could not be maintained in the push of thirteenth century politics. It began as a goal and although Boniface VIII struggled to maintain this stance of the church with his bull *Clericis Laicos*, he eventually had to give way when challenged by the French king and a rebellion of cardinals. [28] In his capitulation, the pope conceded that if the danger to the realm was so great and so immediate that there was no time for approval, the king could tax his clergy without papal authorization. Furthermore, the bull *Etsi de Statu* explicitly stated the principle that the king alone would determine when such a state of emergency existed and whether time was of an essence. [29] Long before this political solution, Aegidius Romanus had said much the same thing: when both reason and necessity concurred, the king did not have to await papal approval to tax the clergy of his realm. [30]

Later the legists Accursius, Baldus and Bartolus turned their attention to the state-creating themes of necessity and public authority. Concerned with sovereignty of one kind or another, they agreed that in a time of necessity, when war or famine or catastrophe created a crisis situation, "the public authority could ignore *pro bono publico* the ordinary law of the land." [31] Then necessity knew no law—or as it was also put in the Canon law—"that which is not licit by law,

---

[26] *Corpus iuris canonici*, Decretales, III, xlix, 4, ed. Emil Friedberg (2 vols.; Leipzig, 1879, 1881), II, 654-655.

[27] See Post, *Studies*, pp. 18, 234.

[28] Brian Tierney, *The Crisis of Church and State, 1050-1300* (Englewood Cliffs, 1964), pp. 172-175.

[29] *Ibid.*, p. 178.

[30] See Post, *Studies*, p. 258, where the full quotation is given.

[31] Bayley, "Pivotal Concepts," p. 201.

necessity makes licit." [32] But it was the Englishman and theologian, William of Ockham, more than any other, who fully developed the idea that the ruler had an emergency right to go outside the existing law if the general welfare of the community required it. That was the king's prerogative, and in Ockham's view, its extension was large enough to allow the king to intervene in the affairs of the church, to resume alms and revoke privileges. [33] Necessity would recognize no privilege. [34]

Theologians, philosophers, jurists had all contributed in the production of a body of political thought that centered on the *status regni* and the maintenance of its integrity. They were developing a concept of national sovereignty that accorded with existing political realities. In an emergency, the interests of the realm were to be all embracing, irrespective of any internal division. The realm was a corporate whole possessing a *status* which acknowledged no superior right or privilege, either of individuals or corporations. [35] There existed appropriate maxims in the civil law supporting this view. King Edward I, William of Ockham and many others eagerly applied these legalisms of state to national ends. *Quod omnes tangit*, for example, was a realistic formula: what touches all must be approved by all, clergy and laity alike. [36]

If John Wyclif was to employ this kind of argumentation in his drive to confiscate ecclesiastical temporalities in England, he had to have an entity capable of possessing a common welfare. England, considered as a national, territorial unit possessed such a welfare that could be appealed to and defended. Such a conception was not unusual in the fourteenth century. Territorial views of sovereignty had long replaced notions of personal sovereignty throughout Europe to the extent that papal decrees embodied territorial conceptions as a measure of recognized sovereignty *vis a vis* the emperor. [37] Taking advantage then of contemporary political theory, John Wyclif, the theologian,

---

[32] *Corpus iuris canonici*, Decretales V, xli, 4, ed. Friedberg, II, 927: "Quod non est licitum lege, necessitas facit licitum."

[33] Ewart Lewis, "Natural Law and Expediency," *Ethics*, L (1939-1940), p. 156f.

[34] See Wilks, *Problem of Sovereignty*, p. 212; Bayley, "Pivotal Concepts," p. 205.

[35] Post, *Studies*, pp. 6-24 *passim*, 114, 147, 187, 248f., 310-311 *passim*, as well as Powicke, "Reflections," pp. 8-11.

[36] *Ibid.*, pp. 163-238 *passim* and 284, 451.

[37] See F. H. Hinsley, *Sovereignty* (London, 1966), p. 126ff., and especially Walter Ullmann's discussion of territorial sovereignty in his *A History of Political Thought: The Middle Ages* (Baltimore, 1965), p. 195ff. under Pope Clement V.

defined England as a territorial entity and a sociological body composed of groups or estates. [38] However defined, fourteenth century England was a community of estates with common interests. This notion of the realm as a community was still relatively new, having only recently replaced the older feudal concept of personalized lordship over individuals. Now not only those tenants who held in-chief had a slice in the affairs of the realm, but all men with an "interest." [39] And England became "the body of the whole realm"—a community recognizing that it held a shared responsibility with the king for the preservation of its interest, for the continuance of its existence. [40] For Wyclif too, the realm was a single, integrated unit: "the whole realm," he wrote, "is one body" made up from all its inhabitants. [41] That body was, in Wyclif's opinion, a territorial whole, ruled by the king, and possessing definite boundaries. That too was new; twelfth century Europe did not think in terms of definite boundaries, but rather spheres of influence. Proximity to the king was everything. By the fourteenth century, the body of the realm had "natural" boundaries and the king's power extended "undiminished, to a precise frontier." [42] And what royal government claimed, Wyclif supported: "it is clear concerning the terrestrial king," he said, that he "is virtually and powerfully at many points of his imperium." [43]

---

[38] For the community of England, see *PW*, I, 332; for England as a community of estates, see *OM*, p. 428; *PW*, II, 421; for Wyclif's view that the realm was composed of provinces, see *PW*, I, 103. This is a very short sampling; for a much larger selection, see Fürstenau, *Wiclif's Lehren*, pp. 68-73 and especially 70, fn. 92.

[39] G. R. Elton, *The Body of the Whole Realm. Parliament and Representation in Medieval and Tudor England*, Jamestown Essays on Representation (Charlottesville, Va., 1969), p. 3.

[40] F. M. Powicke, "England and Europe in the Thirteenth Century," *Harvard Tercentenary Publications: Independence, Convergence and Borrowing* (Cambridge, 1937), p. 142.

[41] "... ista materia suppono quod ecclesia sive regnum sit unum corpus omnium incolarum inhabitancium ipsum regnum ..." *SS*, IV, 7; "totum enim regnum est unum corpus ..." *DPP*, p. 377; "Nam corpus regni tunc constat in sanitate politica quando cor eius, quod est regia potestas, influit tam superioribus clericis quam infereioribus wlgaribus quod est iustum." *DOR*, p. 96. See also *VSS*, III, 98, and *FZ*, p. 258.

[42] For this important discussion, see Joseph R. Strayer, "The Laicization of French and English Society in the Thirteenth Century," *Speculum*, XV (1940), as reprinted in *Change in Medieval Society*, ed. Sylvia L. Thrupp (New York, 1964), p. 109.

[43] "... sicut patet de rege terreno qui est virtualiter et potencialiter ad multa puncta sui imperii;" *OE*, II, 167. Wyclif's use of the word "many," implying exceptions to the king's authority might at first glance appear contradictory, but a close reading of his other work and an important passage in *DOR*, confirms the omni-

England's wholeness was constantly and consistently accentuated through the use of such phrases as "the whole body of the realm," [44] "the whole land," [45] or more commonly, "the whole realm" [46] and "the whole realm of England." [47] In addition to these terms, Wyclif spoke very openly about the "community of our realm," [48] the "community of England," [49] and the "community of the people of our realm." [50] Clearly, Wyclif saw England as an organized, autonomous corporation possessing a *persona*, capable of speaking (in parliament) and acting. [51] His realm then was a fictive person, who bore a multitude of rights and obligations. [52] It could, for instance, initiate action, [53] approve or disapprove of royal activity on the basis of its consent, [54] possess a treasury [55] or even occasionally sin. [56] As a person

---

potence of the king, everywhere in his realm. "Et propter hoc dicunt doctores quod rex ad similitudinem dei habet triplex esse in regno; sciliet esse individuale, esse presenciale, et virtuale vel potenciale. Esse individuale habet in situ per quem extenditur, sicut et alie substancie quarum individuacio ex loco et tempore a nobis cognoscitur. Esse presenciale habet extensius per tantum situm per quantum est presens, et hoc est presens presto sensum in sua specie, sicut per locum per quem est sensibilis. Sed esse virtuale habet supra secundum esse extensius per totum regnum suum ubi virtute eius civiliter dominabile regulatur." *DOR*, p. 93.

[44] *DOR*, p. 67: "... in quo precipue stat regni prosperitas, quia tunc totum corpus regni foret ..."

[45] *OM*, p. 17: "Et postquam iste quatuor bestie totam terram infecerunt ..." See also *SS*, II, 253, where Wyclif speaks of "terra nostra."

[46] *DB*, p. 197: "Et eo, quia expectari debet tocius regni exhortacio sive consilium." Or *ibid.*, p. 269: "... quomodo non liceret toti regno, secundum mandatum dei, in parliamento publico ad tocius regni subsidium se iuvare?" See also *Dialogus*, p. 36; *DA*, p. 6; as well as an almost infinite number of other passages strewn throughout Wyclif's work.

[47] *VSS*, III, 87.

[48] *PW*, II, 421: "Et hinc communitas regni nostri ..."

[49] *PW*, I, 332: "... quis dubitat, quin committeret ydolatriam cum cum illo ordine et scelus nequissimum pro communitate Anglie, ..."

[50] *DA*, p. 88.

[51] *Tractatus de Eucharistia*, pp. 319-320; *DE*, p. 255: "... sed totum regnum est virtualiter congregatum in parliamento, ..."

[52] For Wyclif's awareness of the concept of a fictive person, see *SS*, II, 328: "Tercius gradus et periculossissimus consuetudinis erronee est consuetudo ficta persone ex pluribus aggregate." For the realm considered as a fictive person with particular rights, see *DPP*, p. 244.

[53] *VSS*, III, 98: "ideo totum regnum debet arguere segnes prepositos ..."

[54] See especially the rejection of England's feudal tribute to the papacy in the speech of the seventh lord. *OM*, p. 429: "Constat ibidem quod improvida regis paccio ex peccato suo ingruens non debet vigere sine consensu regni legittimo ad perpetuum eius detrimentum." The speaker continues, saying that King John "illegitime sine communi consensu regni obligavit se curie, ut notatur." The tribute was illicit, it was argued, since as a general tax, it required the consent of all those "interested," and that had not been given. "Oportet igitur iuxta consuetudinem regni

who could be virtually represented in the parliament of the land, [57] the realm clearly had a body with a head, its king. [58] Together, king and realm comprised an act of creation: a fictive person. [59] Operating, therefore, under the fundamental assumption that the realm of England was a corporate and juridical personality, Wyclif gave his organological creation a welfare common to all. [60]

Wyclif was not always explicit in dealing with the welfare of the realm. Nonetheless, it was always there in the reservoir of assumptions he worked with and, when the occasion called for it, he found it to be a useful argument. In attacking the privilege of sanctuary conceded to Westminister, for instance, he continually employed the concept of the general welfare to buttress his shaky position. "It is not in the power of the prince," he declared, "to concede that which should turn to the injury of God, the destruction of the realm or the enervation of the regalian rights and laws through which he should rule his realm." [61] The motif was drawn: to harm the realm is to harm its welfare, an intolerable notion. [62] Nor was the king the only one limited by the demands of what was good for the realm. Temporal lords received their instruction as well: "the Church had not been endowed," he wrote, "unless to the honor of God and the welfare (*utilitatem*) of the Commonwealth." [63] Whatever the situation, whoever the participants, the general welfare of the community had to be supported. [64] But if anything raised Wyclif's ire and forced him into his "common welfare" argument, it was the claim of the church

---

ad tale commune pedagium quamlibet personam regni in se vel suo capitaneo consentire."

[55] "Si, inquam, totus thesaurus regni ..." *DB*, p. 274.

[56] *DE*, p. 427; *DCD*, II, 412.

[57] *DE*, p. 255. For full quotation, *supra* fn. 51.

[58] *DOR*, p. 67.

[59] "Totum regnum cum rege est una persona, ut hic supponitur, cuius caput vel cor est rex influens criminis conservacionem sensum et motum." *Ibid.*, p. 91. Another indication of this creation in Wyclif's work is the ubiquity of Wyclif's double-jointed phrase: "rex et regnum."

[60] *DB*, p. 274.

[61] "Cum ergo non sit in potestate principis concedere quod vergeret ad Dei iniuriam, ad destruccionem regni sui, ad enervacionem regalie et legum per quas regeret regnum suum, ..." *DE*, p. 148. Later, *DE*, p. 218, this assertion of royal limitation is repeated. "Item, rex non potest quicquam rite concedere quod vergeret ad enervacionem regni sui vel iniuriam sui populi, ..." and finally, p. 260.

[62] *DE*, pp. 218, 260, 336-338.

[63] "Pono secundo quod domini temporales considerent quod ecclesia non fuit dotata nisi ad honorem Dei et utilitatem reipublice ..." *DCD*, II, 108.

[64] See, *OE*, II, 196; *DB*, pp. 6, 188-189, 192, 201.

and especially the friars to special privilege and independence. Complaining of them as often as he did, he had ample opportunity to preach of the need for everyone to submit to the general welfare. But preaching accomplished little. They still refused to pay taxes, ignored the public good and in general destroyed or weakened the unity of the realm. They were in a word, "parasites." [65] Such a situation was, in Wyclif's eyes, indefensible and intolerable. The clergy, both regular and secular, were citizens of a realm that possessed a clear and defensible welfare. That welfare required the support of all, clergy and laity alike. In shirking that responsibility, in promoting their own interests to the detriment of England, the friars asserted a principle of private good that was anathema to him. Precisely because the friars and the church undertook a stand of privacy, he argued, they denied the general good of Christianity as a whole. [66]

Nor did Wyclif subscribe to the seductive idea that the pursuit of self-interest could ultimately benefit the common welfare. Quite the contrary: "every common good," he decided, "is better than any private one." [67] Willingly he applied that argument to the Canon law injunction concerning the right of the patron to appropriate his endowment in time of need: "the reason of greater need for the public good, as of the realm of England, is better than the reason saying that those revenues ought to be returned for the good of a private family." [68] The idea of a "common welfare" served Wyclif admirably; it provided him with a compelling argument that most people within the realm of England would accept. Clearly, Wyclif thought of the realm as a corporate body, a fictive personality, with a welfare of its own that took precedence over the private rights of all others, be they kings, nobility or clergy.

In "reason of state," Wyclif discovered a limitation of privilege and an affirmation of social consciousness that accorded nicely with his own conception of what was best for the English Church Militant

---

[65] See especially, *DB*, pp. 188-189, 214-217.

[66] *DA*, p. 42.

[67] "Consequencia patet ex hoc: omne bonum commune bono privato generis sui prestancius. Et argumentum patet ex hoc quod repugnat reipublice omnes homines esse monachos, sed omnes homines debent esse christiani; ..." *DCD*, III, 31.

[68] "... racio autem maioris indigencie pro bono publico ut regni Anglie est prestancior quam racio dictans reddendos redditus pro bono utili private familie. Si igitur sanctus episcopus non habuit potestatem de aliquo bono iure detinendi redditus ad eam privata familia, multo magis indigni clerici non habent de iure aliquo potestatem detinendi tam multos et magnos redditus ad iniuriam tocius populi Anglicani." *DCD*, IV, 485.

and through its identification with the realm, the state of England. Because it was normally the king, supported by advice and consent, who determined what was in the best interests of the realm, the *status regni* could serve as a useful device to either initiate or abet clerical reform through disendowment. Wyclif explored this tactic in his treatise *On the Office of the King*. In his explication of the royal function, he noted that the king should guide his subjects with prudence and circumspection to the "honor of God and the welfare of the realm and of himself." [69] Wyclif thought this "commonweal" might be best accomplished if the king were whole-hearted in the defense of his subjects' rights while circumscribed as far as his own. To put it positively, the king was to remain within the confines of his own law, limiting his private interests to benefit the whole. [70]

Self-limitation on the part of the king was a common theme in the law books of the thirteenth century as attested, for instance, in the *Sachsenspiegel*, the *Assizes of Jerusalem* and England's own Bracton. [71] Along with others, Wyclif himself relied on the influential pseudo-Aristotelian *Secreta Secretorum* to justify his contention that the supreme wisdom for any king was to obey his own law. [72] Consistently Wyclif maintained that restrained by his own sense of responsibility, [73] directed by his own law, the king should voluntarily bind himself, as Christ did, to his own law. [74] This royal submissiveness to the law, however normal or compelling, in no way conflicted with the king's prerogative to act *casualiter*. Although Wyclif felt the king was "to submit to the existing legal institutions," not in the sham of legal fiction, but in the reality of process, still this in no way abrogated his undeniable right to dispense with the law. He was superior to the law. When reason required it, he could dispense with the law. [75] Or as Wyclif wrote elsewhere: as "lord of the law," the

---

[69] "... oportet enim prudenter domare subditos ad honorem dei et utilitatem regni ac sui." *DOR*, p. 97.

[70] For the limitation of the king, see the pertinent passages in *DOR*, p. 93ff.

[71] See Wilks, *Problem of Sovereignty*, p. 215; F. M. Maitland, *Bracton and Azo*, Selden Society, VII (London, 1895), 65; G. L. Haskins, "Executive Justice and the Rule of Law," *Speculum*, XXX (1955), 530f.; G. J. T. Miller, "The Position of the King in Bracton and Beaumanoir," *Speculum*, XXX (1956), 272-273.

[72] *DOR*, p. 57.

[73] *DCD*, I, 198.

[74] *DOR*, p. 93f.

[75] "Quamvis autem rex dispensare potest in casu cum execucione legis tamquam superior lege sua tamen numquam nisi quando dispensabilitatis racio hoc requirit ..." *Ibid.*, p. 57.

king could subtract from it in time of necessity. [76] With brevity and clarity, Wyclif delineated the privilege "that the king, in time of necessity for himself or the realm, can take with discretion the temporalities of the laity and the clergy as his own." [77] The anatomical analogy he drew, though technically incorrect, was both cogent and graphic: "the heart," he said, "draws for its necessity warmth and moisture from all of its external members." [78]

The general doctrine Wyclif was evoking was that of necessity knowing no law; or better, the common welfare was antecedent and superior to any positive law insuring individual rights. Because the king was the recognized steward of that public welfare, "every Englishman ought to obey his king, especially in those things necessary to the governance of his realm." [79] Wyclif, phrasing this idea somewhat differently, claimed that if it turns "to the necessity of the governance of his realm" and is consonant with the law of God, then "the obligation to the king is greater, the care of the governance of the realm more necessary" than any conceivable consideration of private interest. [80]

Argumentative constructs that depended upon the notion of *utilitas* or welfare possessed considerable potency when coupled with the urgent necessity of defending the realm. Often they simply rendered impudent any and all opposition and for this reason alone, they were a favorite instrument of the crown. When Edward I, for example, incorporated the Roman law maxim of "what touches all shall be approved by all" into his legislative voice and spoke of "common dangers" being met "by measures proved in common," his object was not so much approval as the securing of cooperative action. [81]

---

[76] "... dominus autem legis et subtrahere potest de lege quod propter necessitatem temporis iussit ..." *DCD*, III, 118.

[77] "Nec obest istis, sed consonat, quod rex in tempore necessitatis sui aut regni capiat tam a laicis quam a sacerdotibus suis, cum discrecione tamen, temporalia tamquam sua." *DOR*, p. 97.

[78] "Sic enim cor trahit pro sua necessitate calidum et humidum a membris exteris quibuscumque." *Ibid*.

[79] "... ergo multo magis ad tantum obedienciam tenetur quilibet Anglicus suo regi specialiter in necessariis regimini regni sui." *DE*, p. 146.

[80] "... ergo cum mandatum hoc vergit ad necessitatem regiminis regni sui, non obvians sed consonans legi Dei, sequitur quod dicti subditi tenentur in hoc parere monitis regis sui. Assumptum patet ex hoc quod obligacio regi est maior, cura regiminis regni est necessarior et pena delinquencium in regem est ex scriptura fundabilior." *Ibid*.

[81] "Rex venerabili in Christo patri Roberto eadem gratia Cantuariensi archiepiscopo, totius Angliae primati, salutem. Sicut lex iustissma, provida circumspectione sacrorum

Common interests meant common obligations. In 1297, Edward I enjoined all men to defend the realm against the advances of France because, as he wrote to his sheriffs: "the matter is so great and thus touches all and each of our said realm, so that we can defer to no one." [82] And that statement of obligation applied as much to the English clergy as anyone else. It was a difficult argument to oppose. Constantly the clergy were reminded of their responsibilities to the king and realm, repeatedly they were accosted with the argument of necessity. Naturally if that necessity involved the actual defense of the realm their role was circumscribed; they could not fight. Yet they could do what they did best, namely, pay and pray. Here they found consistent encouragement. [83] The church was not to be allowed to remain aloof.

These admonishments became one of John Wyclif's most persuasive weapons in the arsenal he used to revoke the temporalities of the English church. When addressed with the problem of general danger and the independence of the church, the king was unequivocal. Wyclif was as well: "it is permitted for a time of necessity to remove the goods of the religious and give these into the hands of the knights,"

---

principum stabilita, hortatur et statuit ut quod omnes tangit ab omnibus approbetur, sic et nimis evidenter ut communibus periculis per remedia provisa communiter obvietur." Stubbs, *Select Charters*, p. 480, as cited by Barnaby C. Keeney, "Military Service and the Development of Nationalism in England, 1272-1327," *Speculum*, XXII (1947), 541, fn. 44.

[82] In letters from Edward I to the sheriffs dated May 5, 1297, he wrote: "Quia nobis adhuc non constat quando fidelibus nostris de regno nostro indigebimus occasione presentis guerre inter nos et regem Francie existentis, et aliquid per inimicorum nostrorum insidias emergere subito posset, quod nobis et ipsis fidelibus nostris, ac eciam toti regno nostro dampnosum et periculosum forsitan esse posset, nisi nos et ipsi essemus melius et cicius premuniti et ad hoc apponeremus consilium quod possemus, volentes hujusmodi dampnis et periculis caucius obviare, perpendentesque quod istud negocium est tam gzande et ita communiter omnes et singulos de dicto regno nostro tangit quod in hoc nemini deferri potest ..." F. Palgrave, *Parliamentary Writs and Writs of Military Summons* (London, 1827-1834), I, 281, no. 4 as quoted by Keeney, "Military Service," p. 541. Generally the English government insisted upon the principle that all property could be taxed for the defense of the realm. Bartholomaeus Cotton, for example, reports that Hugh le Despenser said following papal disapproval of a clerical grant: "Ego ex parte domini regis, comitum baronum, militum et aliorum domini regis fidelium vobis dico, quod de tali subsidio per quod terra defendatur de bonis ecclesiae provideatis, ne dominus rex, comites et barones de rebus vestris ecclesiasticis ordinent et disponant pro suae libito voluntatis." This passage is quoted in Strayer, "Laicization," p. 114, fn. 18, who also cites *Parliamentary Writs*, I, 393, where the clergy were outlawed until they paid.

[83] *Parliamentary Writs*, II, part ii, 122, no. 75, as cited by Keeney, "Military Service," p. 546, fn. 78.

he said. [84] His decision had fallen; in a time of ultimate necessity, anything can be used, even that which had been consecrated. [85] Time after time Wyclif returned to this fundamental principle: the church should not be exceptional. "All goods," he proclaimed, "either of the secular clergy or of their religious orders, appropriated in a time of necessity without regard of persons, ought to be common to all." [86] Clearly the king can exact from everyone in a time of necessity including the church; and just as clearly, it was the king who determined the nature of that necessity and its applicability in terms of the law.

On the authority of St. Ambrose and a number of decretists, Wyclif asserted that "it was permitted to the king, in a time of necessity, to remove not only many of the superfluous precious objects of the clergy, but also the chalices, expensive tomb-shrines and ornaments of the Church." [87] The purposes Wyclif enumerated that would in some way justify such action on the part of the king stem from the *Decretum* and included liberating captives, granting alms to the poor and repairing churches. [88] Later these were carefully altered. The

---

[84] "... quod licet auferre pro tempore necessitatis bona religiosorum et dare in manus militum, ..." *DCD*, IV, 482.

[85] "... ergo cum in tempore necessitatis omnia debent esse cuicunque christiano communia, sequitur quod in casu pro communitate vel principe racionabiliter sunt exponenda ... Ex qua sentencia patet quod licet in tempore necessitatis uti quamtumlibet consecratis. Unde in tempore ultimate necessitatis talia Deo dedicata non sunt ad usus prophanos exposita sed ad redimendum maliciam ..." *DCD*, II, 28. See also *DA*, p. 88: "Unde, ut alias declaravi, regnum nostrum instaret in parliamentis quod de bonis temporalibus cleri magis vacantibus rex et regnum ad eius subsidium releventur; omnis enim ista sunt bona pauperum, de quibus propter superfluitatem et ocium regnum debet pro tempore necessitatis citissime relevari; ..."

[86] "Ex multis similibus dictis doctorum ecclesie possumus patenter colligere quod omnia bona clericis sive secularibus sive religiosis per laicos appropriata debent in tempore necessitatis sine personarum accepcione esse cunctis communia." *Ibid.*, p. 101.

[87] "Ex istis verbis huius doctoris sanctissimi et decreti videtur, primo quod regi licet in tempore necessitatis multiplicis auferre nedum iocalia cleri sui superflua sed et calices et preciosa tumbarum et ecclesie ornamenta ..." *DE*, p. 376. The principle is set forth in *DCD*, II, 27-28: "Ecclesie vero, sanctuaria et vasa facta racionabiliter vocari possunt sacra, quia sanctis vel sacramentalibus sunt ad specialem usum divine officii limitata. Ymmo videtur probabile multis doctoribus quod pro tempore necessitatis liceat exponere vasa sancta." Then, after quoting the appropriate biblical passages from the book of Kings, Wyclif concludes that: "ergo cum in tempore necessitatis omnia debent esse cuicunque christiano comunia, sequitur quod in casu pro communitate vel principe racionabiliter sunt exponenda."

[88] "*DCD*, II, 98, begins a discussion of clerical alienation by the laity with the statement that according to the *Decretum* "this is not permitted unless in form and in cases delineated in the law." Then it is licit. These cases are three in number and are described by Wyclif. "Sunt autem tres casus in quibus hoc est licitum: primo pro captivis ecclesie redimendis, ut XII, questione II sic dicitur: 'Sacrorum

king should alienate ecclesiastical land to redeem captives who have fought in the defense of the realm and who will be necessary for its renewed defense. Secondly, the king could confiscate ecclesiastical possessions when normal solvency was lacking for the defense of the realm; and finally the king could act to avoid oppressive taxation of the common people. [89] Elsewhere Wyclif remarked that:

> In a case in which necessity should be imminent, it is permitted for the defense of a city to tear down a cathedral and construct there a tower, to sell or melt down the chalices and give the money to soldiers. [90]

This was not rhetorical hyperbole; it was not the contrived construction of the reformer, but rather the hard, practical, legalized fact of life that both history and custom supported. In a case of absolute necessity, "when possible danger is imminent, our princes," wrote Wyclif, "have been able to withdraw their alms and so it follows that they can do likewise in the future." [91]

Wyclif equated in his own mind ecclesiastical treasure with endowment. That which had been granted by the founders was a fundamental part of the treasury of the church and when necessity abridged the positive law, that treasury could be claimed in its entirety. [92] To

---

canonum statuta et legalis permittit auctoritas licite res ecclesiasticas in redempcionem captivorum inpendere.'" Continuing, Wyclif applied this law to England, saying: "Unde et illud practisatum est in Anglia, ut narrat Cestrensis libro VII, capiutlo XXIII. Nam pro redempcione regis Richardi 'capta est tota lana monachorum alborum et canonicorum, et prelatorum anuli, vasa, cruces, calices cum auro de sanctorum feretris abraso sunt conflata; et pro certo ego nescio concludere quod iniuste." Then Wyclif gave the two other instances found in this canon of the law; for the relief of the poor, for supplying the wants of the church, ecclesiastical property can be alienated.

[89] "... quod regi licet in tempore necessitatis multiplicis auferre nedum iocalia cleri sui superflua sed et calices et preciosa tumbarum et ecclesie ornamenta, ut puta, si aliunde vel oportunius regnum non sufficit redimere captivos qui in defensione regni legitime militarunt; et pro iterata defensione regni necessarii sunt. Secundo, si regnum pro sua defensione necessaria non habeat aliunde vel congruencius unde militantibus pro defensione regni ministraret stipendia. Et tercio, si vulgus per taxas gubernacioni regni necessarias ad nimiam pauperiem sit reductus." DE, pp. 376-377.

[90] Licet enim in casu quo immineat necessitas ad defensionem civitatis basilicam prosternere et ibi turrim construere; calices vendere vel conflare et precium militibus ministrare; ..." DOR, p. 185.

[91] "... patet (ut sepe dixi) quod principes nostri absolute necessario potuerunt suas elemosinas subtrahere, periculo possibili imminente. Et per idem sequitur quod potuerunt cum possibilibus paribus subtrahere in futurum ..." DE, p. 337.

[92] "Preterea debent fundatores considerare quod bona collata ecclesie sunt quasi thesaurus depositus quem licet eis in tempore necessitatis repetere, quod probatur lege triplici ..." which Wyclif then does from the Canon law. DCD, IV, 455-456.

support this view, Wyclif devoted an entire chapter in the *Tractatus de Civili Dominio*, calling upon numerous examples from Canon law which dealt with the rights of the ecclesiastical patron. Usually these examples had to do with a type of reserve clause found in the endowments that reserved the right of the founder or his family to draw upon the wealth of his foundation should he or his family ever fall upon hard times. [93] This reservation had long been recognized as binding in the *Decretum* and canonical practice. The conclusion Wyclif drew was a superb bit of specious reasoning: beginning with the prerogative of the individual founder to have a prior right to his endowment in case of need, Wyclif progressed to the claim that the founders in general have the right and authority to use, in times of necessity, the common wealth of their churches before all others. [94] His final conclusion, found at the end of the chapter, was even more drastic. After again giving a general synopsis of the rights of the patron or his heirs to draw on their foundations in time of need, Wyclif zeroed in on English practice. At the same time, he modernized private need into a notion of general welfare. [95]

> The reason, moreover, of greater need for the public good, as of the realm of England, is better than the reason saying that those revenues ought to be returned for the good of a private family. If therefore the holy bishop [Aurelius] did not have the authority to detain revenue to the said private family on the basis of some other good law, much less do unworthy priests have the authority to detain more and greater revenue to the injury of all the Anglican people. [96]

The implication was that the king, as both the Advowee Paramount,

---

[93] *Ibid.* The Canon law passages quoted are XVI. q. vii, c. 29 (Friedberg, I, 808); XVI. q. vii, c. 30 (Friedberg, I, 808-809): XVII. q. iv, c. 43 (Friedberg, I, 827-828).

[94] *Ibid.*, p. 457.

[95] *Ibid.*, pp. 484-485: "Notemus igitur legem XVII questione ultima "Quicunque," in principio huius capituli allegatam et pensemus si ex decreto sanctissimi et subtilissim Augustini sanctus Aurelius Cartaginensis episcopus non habuit iure divino potestutem reddendi collatum ecclesie propter indigenciam filiorum; et ex porrecto animo cogitemus qua lege nos clerici Anglicani petulantes et superhabundanter possessionati habemus potestatem attinendi temporalia a genere fundatoris, quod ex defecta temporalium necessitatur furari vel atteri tirpitudini implicari ..."

[96] *Ibid.*, p. 485: "Racio autem maioris indigencie pro bono publico ut regni Anglie est prestancior quam racio dictans reddendos redditus pro bono utili private familie. Si igitur sanctus episcopus non habuit potestatem de aliquo bono iure detinendi redditus ad eam privata familia, multo magis indigni clerici non habent de iure aliquo potestatem detinendi tam multos et magnos redditus ad iniuriam tocius populi Anglicani."

the patron of bishoprics, and steward of the realm's welfare, had first crack at the wealth of the church whenever the *status regni* required it. [97] What had been the private right of the individual patron, now became the public right of the king. What had been established to provide insurance for the possible need of the individual family, now became a bank account accessible to the realm.

The greatest necessity for the realm was, of course, self-defense. Not only were laymen obliged to make sacrifices for the defense of the realm in the form of taxation and direct service, but the church as well. Defense of the realm had long been thought a proper cause for clerical taxation, and Wyclif thought so too. [98] He was again adamant: according to the law of nature, the properties of the church were an integral part of the realm, and as such he was sure they could be used "for the defense of the fatherland." [99] Defense was a common obligation benefiting both clergy and laity. Lords repay clerical tribute, "now by fighting for the fatherland, now by giving judgments, now by inciting to greater rewards." The clergy are freed from the burdens of temporalities, secular intercourse and the need to fight. [100] In time of necessity, this reciprocity demands that all clerical alms cease. The clergy has received its temporalities from the king. These properties, so eagerly sought, subject the clergy to the jurisdiction of the king. Otherwise, Wyclif argued, the clergy would injure the secular branch in the "goods of nature and fortune" and,

---

[97] For Wyclif's notions on royal patronage, see *DS*, pp. 34-35. Here, among other things, Wyclif points out that all patronage was originally lay and then goes on to note: "Ecce quod domus religiosa stat in iusto arbitrio fundatoris et multo magis in iusto iudicio regni et regis ..." The king, as patron paramount, stands above all. For an excellent study of royal patronage in England and the role of the king as Advowee Paramount, see Howell, *Regalian Right in Medieval England*, p. 186ff.

[98] *DE*, pp. 376-377; *FZ*, pp. 258-271 *passim*; *SS*, IV, 10; *DOR*, p. 52.

[99] "Et patet quomodo inconsonanter et avare nostri ecclesiastici murmuraverant contra principes seculares colectas vel decimas pro regni tuicionibus exigentes ... Confirmatur ex hoc quod de lege nature pro defensione patrie sunt bona eiusdem, usibus necessariis incolarum minus occupata, primitus exponenda; huiusmodi sunt temporalia prepositorum ecclesie ut videtur, ergo conclusio." *DCD*, I, 200.

[100] "Et patet secunda conclusio apostoli, quod a subditis regibus et specialiter a clero per eos elemosinato tributum voluntarie est prestandum. Et signanter dicit apostolus quod prestatis, quia secundum glossam ipsi reddunt, nunc pugnando pro patria, nunc agendo iudicia et nunc excitando ad premia ampliora." Continuing, Wyclif concludes: "Magna igitur securitas in prestante, ubi servando bonum animum non oportet timere quin exclusus erit ab onere temporalium, exemptus a pungnis et intricacionibus illatis per seculum, et demum premiatus mercede saciante totaliter appetitum." *DOR*, pp. 9-10.

secondly, their properties would not be subject to the consideration that must be overriding—the defense of the realm. [101]

Wyclif, always repetitive, never tired of writing that the church had already acquired more than one-third of the realm. That, in his view, was contrary to the law of Christ. Almost as important, that acquisition disregarded the "great necessity" for resisting the "imminent" enemies that threatened England. [102] Wyclif was not content to let the matter rest here. Concluding his argument with an appeal to the "public good," he repeated a parable he had reportedly heard from two "possessing monks" at the Parliament of London in 1371, concerning the possible disendowment of the monastic orders. [103] That parable described a meeting of a number of birds, including an owl who had lost its feathers. Pretending to suffer from the cold, the owl shiveringly sought feathers from the other birds. Moved by the sight of the miserable wretch, they responded with so many feathers that the owl took on a grotesque, misshapen form. Suddenly a hawk threatened in the distance; the birds naked and unable to fly to avoid the danger, asked for the return of their own feathers. When these were not voluntarily returned, the birds snatched them away violently and the owl was left featherless and alone. Obviously, the story had a pungent moral and the speaker was quick to draw it: should war break out, it was justifiable to confiscate from the "possessing clergy" temporalities that had been given as alms. National emergency, self-preservation and the public good, all allowed that temporalities common to the whole kingdom should be used for its defense. [104]

Wyclif's inclusion of the owl parable as presented to Parliament indicated his willingness to use and comment upon contemporary issues of moment. The doctrine of necessity was one of those. Such

---

[101] "Sed tales curati per abusum temporalium nedum iniuriant regi et regno sed pauperibus quos spoliant bonis suis. Ergo rex debet eos in hoc defendere et non restat defensio nisi secuta fuerit restitucio. Ergo rex debet secundum leges suas facere restitucionem fieri laicis suis iniuriatis. Et patet quod eo ipso quo rex dotat clericos regni sui subiecit eos sue iuridiccioni, quia aliter possint quantumcumque iniuriari seculari branchio in bonis fortune et nature sine hoc quod pateret regi defensio contra illos, nec bona sua subicerentur defensioni regni ..." *Ibid.*, pp. 69-70.

[102] "... ergo per idem temporales in regno Anglie non debent in aliquo casu de sacerdotibus possessionatis quicquam exigere, licet appropriarunt plus quam terciam partem regni, quantumcunque adversati fuerint legi Christi et quantumcunque magna necessitas immineat hostibus resistendi." *DCD*, II, 6.

[103] *DCD*, II, 7.

[104] See also Walsingham, *Historia Anglicana*, I, 314. For the secondary literature see Daly, *Political Theory of John Wyclif*, p. 56f.; Tatnall, "John Wyclif and Ecclesia Anglicana," p. 25; McFarland, *Origins*, p. 52f.

action as advocated by the parable was neither unusual nor illegal in England during the 1370's.

Two Austin friars had presented to the Parliament of 1371 arguments similar to Wyclif's. [105] Pleading for partial confiscation of the church's temporal wealth at a time of national need when many members of the higher clergy were refusing to contribute a grant without a formal vote in convocation, the articles adamantly asserted that all property was really common. Private property, they reasoned, was simply a human invention sanctioned by custom and human law. When a common need arose, private property had to yield to the general welfare. They then quoted St. Ambrose to the effect that should any subject of the realm be captured, the temporalities of the church, including chalices and vestments, ought to be used to effect his release. Clearly, if such a principle applied to the defense of individuals, it did so too for the defense of the realm. Finally, the decretals were again reinserted to show that Constantine's donation was a gift to be demanded back in the event of a national need. Time and again, the friars met any and all objections with the principle that national necessity required total commitment.

There were examples, too, of clerical taxation. The *Rolls of Parliament* speak of "the lands and possessions of the Holy Church of the realm" being taxed by the king in that same year, 1371. [106] The previous year, Edward II had been charged to dispose of all the "prebends, dignities, churches and chapels of all the enemies of the realm" and employ the profit to the defense of the realm. [107] The church was not exceptional; if anything, tradition and practice supported its actual involvement. Nor were the church's temporalities

---

[105] The actual articles have been edited and discussed by V. H. Galbraith, "Articles Laid Before the Parliament of 1371," *English Historical Review*, XXXIV (1919), 579ff. Gwynn, *Austin Friars*, pp. 213-216, 250, also spends some time on the articles, as has Daly, *Political Theory of John Wyclif*, p. 55ff. who argues that the similarity of Wyclif's argumentation with the articles "does not itself prove Wyclif's actual dependence. I would concur with this judgment; the ideas expressed were simply too common by the fourteenth century to warrant an assertion of reliance.

[106] "Forspris en ceste Grant la Counte de Cestre, & les Terres & Possessions de Seinte Eglise de Roialme amortizez devant l'an le Roi l'aiel, & taxez ove la Clergie a la Disme." *Rot. Parl.*, II, 304, no. 11.

[107] "Qe nre Seignr le Roi peusse doner touz les Prebendes, Dignitees, Esglises & Chapelles de touz Enemys du Roialme, du Roialme, dumurrantz es pties de l'enemistee nre Seign' le Roi, q' ont tieux Benefices deinz le poair nre dit Seign' le Roi. Et q les profitz ent endementiers soient seifiz en les mayns nre Seign' le Roi, & tournez a defens de la terre & de Seinte Esglise d'ycelle." *Ibid.*, II, 154, no. 36. Also *ibid.*, p. 172, and Haller, *Papsttum*, p. 416.

to be locked forever in mortmain. Wyclif contended that not only was the land held in mortmain accessible, but that land held in this fashion would alone suffice for any defense of the realm. The king and his council, he concluded, should not hesitate to take it. [108]

The fugitive scraps of the doctrine that all ecclesiastical temporalities can be removed or confiscated for the defense of the realm were strewn throughout John Wyclif's work. [109] The buttresses of that doctrine, the welfare of the realm and necessity, were capable of an almost infinite growth, for in tandem with defense, and extended to their logical limitations, these ideas meant that one had to protect the realm against division, heresy, impoverishment or anything that in some way disturbed the order of the realm. These doctrines were inflatable and Wyclif did in fact extend his argument into these promising fields. [110]

The *Fasciculi Zizaniorum Magistri Johannis Wyclif*, a compilation of documents commonly ascribed to Thomas Netter of Walden, incorporated a tract called "Responsio Magistri Johannis Wyccliff, Ad Dubium Infra Scriptum, Quaesitum Ad Eo Per Dominum Regem Angliae Ricardum Secundum, Et Magnum Suum Consilium" that closely mirrored the Articles of the friars on clerical obligation. [111] In that document, Wyclif was faced with a query from the king's council as to whether "the kingdom of England may lawfully, under the urgent necessity of her defense, withhold the treasure of the realm from being carried abroad, even though the Lord Pope require this on pain of censure ..." [112] Wyclif began his reply with a disclaimer.

---

[108] *SS*, IV, 143; *OM*, p. 174. Also Loserth, "Wiclif's Sendschreiben," p. 54: "Sufficeret enim pars regni, que est iam toxice in manu mortua, per se debellare vel in iusta causa resistere cuicunque populo barbarico invadenti, sicut ex chronicis temporum, quibus fuerint multi reges in Anglia ..."

[109] *DE*, p. 144; *SS*, II, 49; *VSS*, III, 58, 64; *PW*, I, 253. See also the numerous passages in *DB* which deal with the injury brought on England by the friars as well as *SS*, III, 101ff.; *DCD*, III, 352; *DCD*, IV, 456.

[110] For notions and use of disruption see, *DB*, p. 194; *DCD*, II, 15, 75, 79, 84, 135; *DPP*, p. 379; *SS*, IV, 8ff. For impoverishment of the realm see, *VSS*, III, 84; *PW*, I, 253, 192ff.; *SS*, II, 337, 406ff., 435; *SS*, III, 112.

[111] *FZ*, 258 pp. Although James Crompton, "Fasciculi Zizaniorum II," *Journal of Ecclesiastical History*, XII (1961), 155ff. has recently called the authorship of Thomas Netter of Walden into question, pointing out that Netter's responsibility rests solely with the authority of John Bale writing some eighty years after the actual composition, the Wyclif tract and its authenticity remains unimpaired. For a discussion of this piece see, Gwynn, *Austin Friars*, p. 250; Workman, *John Wyclif*, I, 303f. The translation I have used is that of A. R. Myers, who included this tract in his edition of *English Historical Documents, 1327-1485* (New York, 1969), p. 656f.

[112] *Ibid*. See also Robson, *Wyclif and the Oxford Schools*, p. 232, and Daly,

He would leave the legal issues to others more experienced in the law than himself. He was a theologian and would only deal with the problem according to the law of Christ. Theologically, though, he substantiated in detail the arguments then current in the English law. "Every natural body," he declared, "is given power from God of resisting what is hostile to it, and of duly preserving itself." [113] Moving on to the tangibility of English experience, he drew his conclusion:

> Since therefore the realm of England ought, in the language of Scripture, to be one body, and the clerks, lords, and community of its members, it seems that it has such power given from God. [114]

England, therefore, as a natural body must preserve itself and that meant in Wyclif's view that it should hoard its own treasure for defense should necessity require it. Not only did the law of nature require such action, but the law of conscience, he said, supported it as well. Kings and lords were conscience-bound "to defend the prosperity and state of their realms." This defense of the general welfare of corporate England could not be accomplished in the event the pope were allowed to remove clerical wealth. That wealth had been given "not to any church whatever, but to the English churches" to provide for pious living which could not be achieved without foundation. [115] Moreover, since there would be no prosperity without a pious priesthood, withdrawal of alms would threaten the ruin of the realm. [116]

Working in the legal environment of the fourteenth century that reflected the new order of Church and State devised by the political theorists of the thirteenth century, Wyclif emphasized the public responsibilities of both king and realm. He did so for a variety of reasons, not the least of which was to emancipate the secular element from unwarranted and undesirable ecclesiastical interference. To accomplish this, Wyclif first adopted and then altered the secular arguments of utility, necessity and defense that had proven to be so

---

Political Theory of John Wyclif, p. 43f. For an assessment of Wyclif's relationship to the Crown in general, cf. Joseph Dahmus, "John Wyclif and the English Government," *Speculum*, XXXV (1960), 51-68.

[113] *Ibid.*

[114] *Ibid.*

[115] *Ibid.*

[116] For much the same argument as above, see *PW*, I, 244.

effective in earlier struggles for national sovereignty. To a large degree these ideas had developed as a result of altered notions concerning the king and the realm. Within the old feudal framework of lord and vassal, questions of public utility and defense of the realm could have had little influence. But once the realm was seen as a corporational territory, possessing rights and obligations, then that same entity was capable of authorizing a public authority to define and protect a territorialized interest. It was a new conception of *regnum* and its *status* could only be fully provided for if that realm, including its head, were in fact sovereign.

English political practice had been shaped by the push and pull of these arguments. Wyclif, capitalizing on theory and practice, preached no radical doctrine, but one made common by frequent use. The English king had the right, for the sake of the public welfare, to subject all the "interested," the clergy as well as the laity, to his jurisdiction. It was a break with the clerical past, but the needs of the public welfare had to be met, whatever the cost to individuals or corporations. Utility must prevail over tradition.

Wyclif was particularly interested in applying this principle of utility to the traditional church. No longer could ecclesiastical privilege, immunity or liberty stand in the way of the realm's general welfare. Both the church and its clergy had to face up to their political obligation, as a part of the realm, to aid in the defense of its general welfare. No longer an exempt body, free to grant voluntary gifts at its discretion, the church was drawn into the realm where it would exist as an integral part of the realm, subject to the sovereignty of its welfare as determined by the public authority.

It was an effective argument on Wyclif's part. Once he had established it, he extended it to include any danger whatever, be that physical or spiritual. Identifying the political realm with the English Church Militant, its welfare and defense enabled Wyclif's king to use, in imminent danger, clerical temporalities to correct the clergy and, when others failed, to confiscate ecclesiastical possessions to initiate reform.

CONCLUSION

Unfortunately the integrity and coherence of Wyclif's thought has been generally neglected in favor of specialized studies which, while important in themselves, have done little to promote an understanding of Wyclif's program of reform as a whole. Usually this direction has resulted in a pronounced bias to understand Wyclif only as "the scholar, the daring theoretician, the master of abstraction," [1] while avoiding the more practical political aspects of Wyclif's work with the excuse that they were "devoid of immediacy" or characterized by a "lack of worldly wisdom." [2] The reasons for this emphasis have been varied: Workman, for example, Wyclif's best biographer, was a Victorian, who obviously disliked what he called the "squalid byways of the political world." [3] His man of religion should be above mundane secular concerns, being "an idealist ... who had his gaze so fixed on his ideal that often times he lost the sense of proportion in the means." [4] Others, seeing only Wyclif's personal failures in the realm of political activity, transferred that failure to his reforming ideas, calling him "in politics little better than a child" and his ideas "purely theoretical." [5] Success for them was the sole criterion of political viability. Clearly, they reasoned, John Wyclif was important, but just as clearly that importance had little to do with a feasible program of reform. Consequently, his importance rested only on his ability as a theoretician. His stridently unrealistic, antipapal theories in an age of universal Christendom gave him historical stature. The result, with few exceptions, has been a general refusal to deal with the totality of Wyclif's thought and especially those aspects which deal with the actual implementation of his projected reform. [6]

---

[1] Gustav Benrath, "Wyclif und Hus," *Zeitschrift für Theologie und Kirche*, LXII (1965), 205.

[2] Cf. Leff, *Heresy*, II, 207, and John Stacy, *John Wyclif and Reform* (Philadelphia, 1964), p. 160. Elsewhere Stacy terms Wyclif impractical and "devoid of worldly wisdom." See John Stacy, "The Character of John Wyclif," *London Quarterly and Holborn Review*, CLXXXIV (1959), 135.

[3] Workman, I, 276.

[4] *Ibid.*

[5] Cf. McFarlane, *John Wycliffe*, p. 99, as well as Matthew Spinka, *John Hus' Concept of the Awards* (Princeton, 1966), p. 126.

[6] Cf. Kaminsky, Wyclifism," p. 58.

Again, that is unfortunate for, far from being an intellectual monist, Wyclif's thought reveals a breadth of interest and complexity that is intimidating in its range. That range is nowhere more conspicuous than in the argumentation he was willing to use to effect his reform.

Obviously, John Wyclif did not emerge into this world a mature reformer; he became one. And just as obviously he did not limit his reforming drives to the elucidation of an abstraction whose sole merit was an intellectual exercise in political futility. John Wyclif wanted reform. Presupposing the correctness of his apostolic ideal and the necessity of lay correction to effect a return to the evangelical church, John Wyclif concentrated on removing the contemporary church from its entanglement in debilitating secular affairs. This, in turn, initiated an adventure in ecclesiastical criticism that ended with his total rejection of the prevailing Roman church. In the process, he formulated a reformatory ideology in which biblical precept ordered contemporary English society into a recrudescent Apostolic Church. John Wyclif's reformation, then, began with a doctrinal system whose motivation was an overwhelming desire to reconstruct the institution of Christ's Church.

Such theorizing, if ever to be effective, necessitated the development of an ecclesiology which had, particularly in the fourteenth century, disturbing political implications. John Wyclif's problem was, therefore, one of devising a theoretical structure that would both conform to his conception of the evangelical church and contain sufficient political recommendations for its implementation in the real world of secular power. Otherwise it would be simply a child of abstraction, still-born in the lively world of political activity. Phrased another way, Wyclif had to offer an alternative to the contemporary church that would be at once highly original in its conceptualization of reformation as well as politically viable in the context of English realities.

Wyclif faced the problem squarely. Instead of simply denying the arguments of the papal monarchists, who had subsumed the political community into the church, he turned the papal argument on its head, integrating the church into the actual political construction of England. Every secular element, whether that of political office or social class, was given a religious function and an evangelical definition on the basis of its imitation of Christ. It was an artful arrangement for now the realm could be defined as a religious polity, a mutually supportive system in which the imitation of Christ was shifted from its traditional subject, the atomistic individual, to the participating classes of the new Christian community.

To accomplish this communal goal Wyclif relied on two basic elements: The sufficiency of Christ's law for governing all human activity, which he later identified with the law of England, and a revalued conception of Christian kingship. Christ's law would serve as the guide for the daily practice of government as well as an exemplar for life. In effect, Christian doctrine was now applied to the problems of secular government in the hope that once this law influenced and structured human society, it would make inevitable a return to the pristine liberties of the Apostolic Church; it would force the imitation of Christ within all the orders of Christian society. The executor of this testament was the Christian king. As the vicar of God, Wyclif's king possessed "spiritual and evangelical power"; he was in other words "priest and pontiff in his own realm," the "head" of a religious polity. Seen then as the servant of Christ, the king held his polity as a trust, charged with "the perpetual salvation of himself and of the people, whose government God entrusted him." The king, then, was to defend vigorously the evangelical law; to do that, he not only had to judge and correct (he had to defend the institution of that law, the church, as well).

One of the most important precepts voiced in that law was the evangelical poverty of Christ's life and institution. Following Christ's example, His clergy was exhorted to live as He had. As an integral part of God's scheme, this evangelical poverty became a part of Wyclif's order the minute biblical precept became his principle of political organization. Wyclif was adamant: The ruin of the church stemmed from the avarice of the clergy, forever grasping, in the hope of secular power. "Instead of shepherds," he said, "they want to be lords."

The source of this greed, Wyclif reasoned, was the endowment of the church. As a result of Constantine's endowment and its subsequent expansion, the Church Militant had declined and it would continue to do so until such time as the clergy's greed could be eradicated and poverty and humility reestablished. The agency for this reform was primarily the secular lords, under the leadership of the king. The means was the radical dispossession of ecclesiastical temporalities, thereby forcing the church to return to its spiritual essence. In theory and in practice, rulers had to relieve the church of its endowment, not in order to despoil it, but to revive it.

The theoretical creation of a religious polity whose goal was the societal imitation of Christ was a stroke of genius for it not only met the problem of developing a reforming ideology that would conform to Wyclif's conception of the evangelical church of Christ, but it incorporated a creative selection of English elements so as to correspond nicely to many of the actual conditions found in contemporary England. This construct has been correctly termed by Kaminsky an ideology of revolution divesting as it did the "status quo of the objective sanctity that earlier religious thought ... had not begrudged it," while allowing the political order to participate in "all the forces of reform that were built into Western Christianity."

Still, as ingenious as this solution was, it introduced attendant problems that have plagued historians in their treatment of Wyclif, for the solution tended to divide much of his reforming thought into aspects which were practical or theoretic. Practically he made specific political recommendations concerning the implementation of his reform in terms of tenurial obligations, advowsons, statutory law and obligations of state. Theoretically he dealt with the nature of the church and the role of the political community in God's order. There was then in Wyclif both the theoretical idealogue, convinced of the correctness of his model, and the practical reformer, recognizing the need to be politically relevant.

Wyclif managed to reconcile the two in a system of reform that was extremely pragmatic. The principled position remained, but at no time did Wyclif polarize the practical fulfillment of his goals. His methods for achieving reform were flexible and attuned to English political realities. In his drive for a reforming ideology he rested his case on the Bible, while England, on the other hand, provided the institutions of reform and his own experience the tactical sense. It was only after his theological principles were energized through the English experience that his involvement in political affairs began. It may be that his political thought found its necessary impetus from political necessity rather than speculation, but the one was unthinkable without the other. One gave shape to the other and the alliance created a system. However revolutionary his ideology may have been in scope and willingness to overturn the present, his own reforming goals were not. If John Wyclif's reformation did not begin with an attempt to build the future on the present, at least it ended with that in mind. The result was a religious reformer who devoted a great deal of attention to the practical problems of eradicating abuse, influencing public opinion and effecting reformation—that meant, as it does now, a devotion to political concerns.

This interesting combination of stark idealism and political expediency, however, had to be implemented. To do so Wyclif turned to those elements in England most capable of concentrated political action—the king and the secular nobility and brought them to bear on the issue of ecclesiological reform. Given the correctness of his ecclesiology and its religious polity, his methodology of reform was simple and direct. Legalize ecclesiastical reform around the fundamental responsibility of the laity, especially in the form of the king as God's "captain and interpreter," to regulate the English church To accomplish this Wyclif drew together a variety of legal sources, both canonical and lay, which focused upon the legal obligations of the king. In doing so, he constructed a legal artifice that would subject the whole of the English clergy to lay regulation and ultimately ecclesiastical reform through the dispossession of the clergy's temporality.

The significant feature of this artifice, and a mark of Wyclif's creativity, was its ability to provide a legal-historical justification for the responsibility of the secular power to eradicate abuse within the church. It did so at two very different levels: theologically, based on the Fathers and the Canon law and legally within the framework of English feudal law and practice. Interested in actualizing his reforming ideals, Wyclif departed entirely from the theological arguments he had earlier used to establish the regulatory role of his Christian king in the affairs of the English church. Now, instead, he based his argument and the power of the king to correct the English clergy on the tenurial nature of their landed holdings and upon their responsibility to him as a feudal lord. In this latter argument there was a conscious decision to deal solely with the realities of the king's actual power rather than that kind of political theology so common among Wyclif's contemporaries. They were willing to work far removed from the facts of political life. Wyclif was not. The spiritual power of the king could only be extrapolated from the Bible and that remained subjective, but the law of the king was tangible and definite. Theological ideas had to be translated into juristic modes of reform.

His strategy in this was to see English law as the instrument of reform, to see English law as a mass of authoritative technicalities which he could ingeniously combine with theological principles to secure his goal of rendering the church accessible to secular correction and finally reform. Instead of functioning as a series of discouraging hurdles to be overcome, the law would be a welcome and responsive instrument to effect wide-sweeping change. The means were at hand, all that was required was their enforcement.

This was possible for two basic reasons. First, the struggle for legal sovereignty between the emerging national state and the international church had already established the principle of secular responsibility over the affairs of the clergy. Secondly, the legal remedies that emerged from that struggle rendered the church both accountable and justicable to the king. Taking full advantage of the growing ideology of the national state, and capitalizing on the intensity of English anti-clericalism in the 1370's, John Wyclif decided to implement his reforming program on the basis of existing English law. An appeal to that law could hardly be considered radical even to an entrenched nobility; it was but a conservative weapon in the reform of the church, the agent of his intended reform.

Time and again, in work after work, Wyclif spoke of proceeding against the endowment of the church or the correction of its clergy with "discretion" and "moderation." [7] Wyclif also spoke of it as "medicinal" reform; [8] and though it was a bitter pill, he would force dispossession upon the church, for however bitter, it was necessary for its salvation. He approached his reformation, in other words, with a gentle legalism that belied the steely radicalism of his ideology as well as the hardness of his convictions. What needed to be done, the restoration of the evangelical church through ecclesiastical dispossession, could be done with mercy and circumspection; [9] and it could be done conservatively by utilizing the existing English law. As revolutionary as Wyclif's ideology undoubtedly was, his methodology of reform was not; it was to be accomplished legally and responsibly. [10] Wyclif wanted to take away the temporalities of the church in order to repristinate Christ's Church. Having already established the historical conditionality of all ecclesiastical endowment, he therefore drew

---

[7] DOR, p. 97.

[8] VSS, III, 236.

[9] DCD, IV, 462.

[10] DOR, p. 56: "Et per idem sic est de quolibet eius vicario, qui non solum ex persona propria sed vi communitatis totius regni sui mandat ut sic legaliter procedatur." Writing of disendowment, Wyclif says, "Et quoad decretum dico quod intelligit quod hoc non licet nisi in forma et casibus limitatis in iure." DCD, II, 98; cf. also VSS, III, 87-88.

the legal ramifications of that contractual arrangement. Legal provision already existed in England to do just that.

Here again, as with so many other elements, the dualistic character
of Wyclif's work comes into focus. Now idealogue, now reforming
tactician, Wyclif harmonized the discordant positions into a reforming
system. Now "pathologically obdurate and inflexible," [11] now moderate, he combined a theological extremism on doctrinal questions
with a practical reformer's willingness to experiment. The result for
historians has been bafflement when considering the viability of his
reforming program. Theoretically his concept of dominion based on
the tenets of grace has been well understood. At the level of practical
politics, however, that same theory of dominion has been dismissed
as unrealistic even though Wyclif wrote that it "is at the root of many
of the laws of England, in regard to forfeiture, the prerogative rights
of the lord in chief, and the reservation of service due to the lord in
chief." [12] Once more Wyclif has two arguments going for him—a
theological one and a historical-legal one. That which he grounds
theologically, he also founds upon the actual political dominion,
which in turn rests upon the law of the land. The theoretical justified
the structural context for the actual, political work of reformation.

John Wyclif's originality, his creativity, did not rest so much on
his theoretical constructs, but on his ability and willingness not to
look back to a golden age, nor forward to a utopian future, but to
work within the constricting framework of England. At the same time
he met the problem of offering an alternative to the Roman church
that conformed to his evangelical church and one that was politically
feasible in England. Foregoing elaborate theoretical justifications based
on a theological tradition, he relied instead primarily on the ability
of the English law to effect his desired reform. Human law would
decide the issues, not theological argument. Origin, nature of tenure,
method of clerical acquisition—these were the questions he asked
and they were strikingly atypical for a realistic theologian. It was
especially unorthodox for a clerical reformer interested in the spiritual
revival of the evangelical church. Nonetheless, by employing this kind
of argumentation to justify his reforming ideas, Wyclif made his
approach all the more persuasive to those interested in, and capable
of, effecting his reformation. Wyclif's contribution then was not only
an ideology that "opened up the secular order to all of the forces of

---

[11] David Knowles, *Saints and Scholars* (Cambridge, 1962), p. 245.
[12] *DCD*, I, 37, as quoted in Kaminsky, "Wyclifism," p. 67.

reform that were built into Western Christianity," [13] but a method of reform as well. That method rested on the vehicle of the law of the land; it rested on acceptance of the double-truth in politics as well as in philosophy. Distinctions had to be made between the theoretic and the practical, between principles and expedients, with the greatest attention paid to the realism of political circumstance.

It is highly erroneous therefore to include Wyclif among the opponents of papal claims who failed "to adjust their schemes to the political or legal framework of their own country." [14] Nor was Wyclif's reforming program based on "the most ideal scheme of polity conceived in the middle ages, and the furthest removed from practical possibility." [15] Quite the contrary, far from exhibiting an "irritating refusal to adjust theories to practice," [16] of a "lack of worldly wisdom," this man, who has been characterized as "being in politics little better than a child," [17] was a master adjuster, moving only after legal, if not political, consensus had been reached. In fact, his reforming methodology was pegged down at any number of points and rested upon a clear-headed appraisal of elements that were essentially legal if not political. To term his program "unrealistic" or "purely theoretical" is to misunderstand not only the integral character of his work, but the practical techniques he so effectively employed. Wyclif was aware of and willing to use existing English institutions to deal with the problem of ecclesiastical reform. That reform had to do with property; therefore, his proposals were couched in a plethora of political and legal terms that were fundamentally consonant with English political realities. He was not an air-brained Oxford don caught up in the wheel-spinnings of his own mind. His head was not dizzied nor was he a caricature of academic dithering. He was a political pragmatist capitalizing on general fourteenth century thought to encourage his reforming ideology. Wyclif was neither limited to the insularity of his own mind nor immune from practical considerations. Reform, if it were to be accomplished, had to be done within the confines of the Common law and supported by

---

[13] Kaminsky, "Wyclifism," p. 69.

[14] Reginald Lane Poole, *Illustrations of the History of Medieval Thought and Learning* (2nd ed.; London, 1920), p. 247.

[15] *Ibid*.

[16] B. L. Manning, "Wyclif," *Cambridge Medieval History* (Cambridge, 1952), VII, 498.

[17] McFarlane, *John Wycliffe*, p. 99.

both historical tradition and utility. Reform, in other words, had to conform to the conditions expressed within the framework of his own English institutions. And for this reason, ideological constructs had to be applied; his methodology of reform, the deprivation of clerical temporalities, had to be grounded in that English tradition and not left simply to the utopian musings of an Oxford reformer.

EPILOGUE

The political influence of John Wyclif's legal reform has been adjudged negligible. This failure to effect policy, it has been argued, is *prima facie* evidence of a willful disregard of political realities. In fact, most historians have dismissed Wyclif's attempts at institutional reform precisely because they were so ineffectual, so unsuccessful. This should not be the case. Instead of looking to the immediate usefulness of his ideas, instead of seeking a successful legacy, the question of Wyclif's political realism ought to be assessed by investigating the intent with which he drafted his reforming steps. John Wyclif's attitude ought to be the measure for establishing the realism of his legal reform. Seen in this fashion, Wyclif's political reform is both demonstrative and defensible.

Such an assessment, however, provides little insight as to why Wyclif's influence was so limited and his followers so few. Accomplishment should not be the major criterion for delineating political realism. Yet considering Wyclif's attempts to devise a viable reform on the basis of English law and precedent, the questions raised by his failure to influence policy remain nagging ones.

Wyclif's doctrine of kingship offers a convenient example of this failure. He spent an immense amount of effort documenting the existing power of the monarchy as well as its potential. And although he exalted the English king at every opportunity, his reforming program elicited scarcely any support from that sensitive quarter. Wyclif had returned the king to an earlier context; he had restored a spiritual dimension to the king that had been lost in the Investiture Conflict and its aftermath. Moreover, Wyclif had worked up a legal argument based on the usage of royal rights that appeared eminently feasible in initiating reform. In tract after tract, Wyclif set out historical precedent and trenchant example. Constructing a religious polity out of the English patterns he found, Wyclif saw the English realm transformed into a theocracy headed by a spiritual king and a pontifical monarch.

Royal authority ballooned in this vision of extended activity and intensified responsibility. It not only commissioned unusual avenues of supervision over the laity, but, radically extended to include the clergy, it provided the king a corrective purchase on an otherwise elusive adversary. No where was this of greater benefit to the royal estate than when dealing with the higher clergy. The spiritual nimbus surrounding the Wycliffian king, combined with the legal authority given the English king by a parliament concerned with the community of the realm made for an official whose ability to command was little short of awesome.

Wyclif added other elements to boost the king's authority. He empowered his king, for example, to inaugurate new paradigms of confiscation in order to correct erring bishops or a recalcitrant church. Royal confiscation of ecclesiastical property became for Wyclif a fundamental principle reform. For countless others it was already a practice sanctioned by long usage. Wyclif, as with so much else, made this practice his own while wedding to it theories of "public good" and "necessity" or "defense" of the realm. In tandem these theoretical arguments for the political supremacy of the "state" pinched the "liberties" of the church and were a welcome addition to the developing arsenal that English kings were using against pope and bishop alike. Given this situation one might think it remarkable that kings did not gather about Wyclif's reforming standard.

The difficulty here is that Wyclif was both a theoretical ideologue, deriving his model from a biblical past, and a practical reformer who had to be politically relevant if his program was to have any chance of success. His program for reform, as legal and historical as it was, reflected this dychotomy. And that hybrid contained too many elements that were essentially hostile to the goal of royal and secular sovereignty sought by so many disparate elements in English society. Certainly reform was desirable, but the cost would be counted. That cost included the fact that while the king was to rule in accordance with God's law, exacting obedience by virtue of His appointment, he was also to be selected because of his own "super-excellence" and the acceptance of his own people. Nor was that all. In fact, so many theological restrictions were placed on the exercise of power that any temptation to accept the mantel of grace, Wyclif was so willing to bestow, was easily resisted by kings conscious of their promising future. Finally, the theological baggage accompanying Wyclif's template for reform was simply too debilitating. Moreover, what the king received from Wyclif in terms of argument, procedure and precedent, he already had.

Nonetheless, Wyclif's legal-historical justification for church reform was potentially useful. It did fit nicely with a contemporary sensibility which saw in a resusitated royal theocracy an alternative to papal monarchy. It did offer a case for royal sovereignty that was compatible with the prevailing view that political authority was fundamentally divine. Still, when Wyclif put together his legal-historical construct, he did so on the basis of what the English king already had and he inflated the cost of the product by working in theological demands that rendered the program far too expensive for the practical tastes of English kings. Ecclesiastical accountability was desirable, confiscation of church property was encouraging, and Wyclif's use of the law a welcome and responsive instrument. The cost, however, was too great.

Within a few decades Wyclif's theological solution, already rejected by the secular authorities, underwent further declination, becoming if not anachronistic, at least no longer current. Other possibilities of secular sovereignty became fashionable. These often drew upon a purely secular tradition of political authority and they emerged to haunt an interested laity. A new constellation of political ideas attempted to provide a secular basis for the exercise of power. In a sense, Wyclif who himself had overturned an archaic conception in favor of an approach that was modern enough to elicit not only support but divine approbation, found the tables turned. Once that had occurred, Wyclif's programmatic attack through the instrumentality of a legal reform became little more than an obscure feature of a notorious English heresiarch.

The object of Wyclif's attention had always been the reformation of the Church. God's law had to be returned to a position of authority and direction. Somehow correction had to occur through the agency of the English legal structure. In the attempt to capture for himself and his program existing English institutions and laws, Wyclif transvalued them, giving them configurations that fit his exacting requirements. Herein lay the problem. Transvaluing was a dangerous business. Not only did it lead to general confusion and semantic devaluation, but it blurred every effort to identify source. That was fine when Wyclif sought political action, when he desired to establish coalitions and advocates, but it was absolutely fatal to the corpus of reforming ideas when it sought to find a successor.

This approach was particularly hazardous for Wyclif. His goals remained vividly clear—he wanted to revive the Primitive Church—but his methodology was so in tune with reality, with English tradition that when his ideas and methodology were used in succeeding years, there was no way to recognize the father. Anyone and everyone could claim the common and inherited tradition in the same way Wyclif had and many did so claim it. When legal solutions similar to Wyclif's tack were actually used, such as with the Lollards and later, no one felt compelled to credit Wyclif. The reason was clear: These notions belonged to a shared tradition and a recognized pattern of activity that seemed altogether commonplace to the English populace. That was the reason Wyclif had originally employed them and, in fact, sought them out. At the same time that is the reason for their demise and burial deep within the body of Wyclif's thought. When people, therefore, tried to define what was characteristically Wyclif, they concentrated on those peculiar theological constructs such as "dominion" through grace and the late eucharistic heresies, leaving unrecognized his attempts at political realism.

A third reason for the failure of Wyclif's legal reform to find worthy successors was the official and public condemnation of his teachings in 1382. Condemnation was a critical blow. His presentation had been directed consciously and with motive at those most capable of concerted political action—the secular nobility. His pitch had included matters likely to conjure up sympathetic support: use of ecclesiastical property to reduce taxes of laity, prohibition of all payments to Rome, and the like. After 1382 and the condemnation, this sector of society found it extremely difficult to continue supporting Wyclif's suggestions. Either they acquiesced to authority, salving their convictions with less heretical programs, or they carried on in a Wyclif-inspired movement that forced them underground. In either case, theological excesses and doctrinal tinkering discredited Wyclif's legal reform and alienated so many of those in positions of influence.

If this were not enough, the associations between Wyclif's disciples and the leaders of the Peasant's Revolt of 1382 made it impossible for large groups of the secular nobility to champion his cause. And while Wyclif shouldered none of the responsibility for the uprising in England, still the general populace remembered earlier views that smacked of egalitarian conflict, if not of actual revolt. That impression was strengthened with the rumor that John Ball, the conspicuous leader of the revolt, had once studied with Wyclif at Oxford. Collusion was only a rumor, but the landed nobility did not like what they heard. It was quite one thing to be evangelical, anti-sacerdotal, and in sympathy with Wyclif's reforming desires. It was quite another to support a condemned heretic whose followers violated the principle of private property, the foundation of the established order, in paroxysm's of self-righteous revenge. Destruction went beyond the actual physical damage they were able to inflict for they ruined with their outrage any further hope of reform, clerical or otherwise. Wyclif was attacking privilege—all privilege, secular and ecclesiastical and however much the nobility might appreciate his assaults on the clergy, they could hardly endorse that same zeal when it was directed toward them.

The coalescence of first heresy, then of revolt and finally the treasonous activity of the Lollards, as Wyclif's supporters were called, all made an appeal to a Wyclif formula for reform anathema to the governing class. And as a consequence of having once inspired sedition and unsuccessful revolt, the heresiarch's works were eventually condemned, his body exhumed and burned and his program of reform reduced to the doctrinal fumings of a heretical quack. Certainly one sees this. Certainly the Wyclifian program reverberated through the succeeding decades of the fourteenth and fifteenth centuries, certainly the secular law came to be used as a tool for ecclesiastical reform. But just as certainly, no credit was given John Wyclif.

BIBLIOGRAPHY

A. WYCLIF WORKS

Fasciculi Zizaniorum Magistri Johannis Wyclif cum Tritico. Ascribed to Thomas Netter of Walden. Ed. W. W. Shirley. London: Rolls Series, H.M.S.O., 1858.

Wyclif, Johannes. *De Ente Predicamentali.* Ed. R. Beer. London: The Wyclif Society, 1891.

Wyclif, Johannes. *De Veritate Sacrae Scripturae.* Ed. Rudolf Buddensieg. London: The Wyclif Society, 1905-1907.

Wyclif, Johannes. *Dialogus sive Speculum Ecclesie Militantis.* Ed. Alfred W. Pollard. London: The Wyclif Society, 1886.

Wyclif, Johannes. *The English Works of Wyclif Hitherto Unprinted.* Ed. F. D. Matthew. London: The Early English Text Society. Original Series 74, 1880. Revised, 1902.

Wyclif, Johannes. *Johannis Wyclif Summa de Ente: Libri Primi Tractatus Primus et Secundus.* Ed. S. Harrison Thomson. Oxford: The Clarendon Press, 1930.

Wyclif, Johannes. *Miscellanea Philosophica.* 2 vols. Ed. M. H. Dziewicki. London: The Wyclif Society, 1902-1905.

Wyclif, Johannes. *Opera Minora.* Ed. Johann Loserth. London: The Wyclif Society, 1913.

Wyclif, Johannes. *Opus Evangelicum.* 2 vols. Ed. Johann Loserth. London: The Wyclif Society, 1895-1896.

Wyclif, Johannes. *Polemical Works.* English edition. 2 vols. Ed. Rudolf Buddensieg. London: The Wyclif Society, 1883.

Wyclif, John. *Select English Works of John Wyclif.* 3 vols. Ed. Thomas Arnold. Oxford: The Clarendon Press, 1869-1871.

Wyclif, Johannes. *Sermones.* 4 vols. Ed. Johann Loserth. London: The Wyclif Society, 1886-1889.

Wyclif, Johannes. *Tractatus de Apostasia.* Ed. M. H. Dziewicki. London: The Wyclif Society, 1889.

Wyclif, Johannes. *Tractatus de Blasphemia.* Ed. Michael Henry Dziewicki. London: The Wyclif Society, 1893.

Wyclif. Johannes. *Tractatus de Civili Dominio.* Vol. I, ed. Reginald Lane Poole. London: The Wyclif Society, 1885. Vols. II, III, and IV, ed. Johann Loserth. London: The Wyclif Society, 1900-1904.

Wyclif, Johannes. *Tractatus de Dominio Divino, Libri Tres.* Ed. Reginald Lane Poole. London: The Wyclif Society, 1890.

Wyclif, Johannes. *Tractatus de Ecclesia.* Ed. Johann Loserth. London: The Wyclif Society, 1886.

Wyclif, Johannes. *Tractatus de Mandatis Divinis, accedit Tractatus de Statu Innocencie,* Ed. Johann Loserth and F. D. Matthew. London: The Wyclif Society, 1922.

Wyclif, Johannes. *Tractatus de Officio Pastorali.* Ed. G. V. Lechler. Leipsic: 1863.

Wyclif, Johannes. *Tractatus de Officio Regis.* Ed. A. W. Pollard and C. Sayle. London: The Wyclif Society, 1887.

Wyclif, Johannes. *Tractatus de Potestate Pape.* Ed. Johann Loserth. London: The Wyclif Society, 1907.

Wyclif, Johannes. *Tractatus de Simonia.* Ed. Herzberg-Frankel and M. H. Dziewicki. London: The Wyclif Society, 1898.

Wyclif, Johannes. *Trialogus cum Supplemento Trialogi.* Ed. Gotthard Lechler. Oxford: The Clarendon Press, 1869.

B. OTHER SOURCES

Bailey, C. C. "Pivotal Concepts in the Political Philosophy of William of Ockham," *Journal of the History of Ideas,* X (1949), 199-218.

Barraclough, Geoffrey. *Papal Provisions.* Oxford: Oxford University Press, 1935.

Bean, J. M. W. *The Decline of English Feudalism, 1215-1540.* Manchester: Manchester University Press, 1968.

Benrath, Gustav Adolf. *Wyclifs Bibelkommentar.* Berlin: Walter De Gruyter & Co., 1966.

Bracton, Henrici de. *De Legibus et Consuetudinibus Angliae.* Ed. Travers Twiss. 6 vols. London: Rolls Series, H.M.S.O., 1878-1883.

Bracton. *De Legibus et Consuetudinibus Angliae.* Ed. George E. Woodbine and trans. with rev. Samuel E. Thorne. 2 vols. Cambridge, Mass.: Harvard University Press, 1968.

Bracton's Notebook. Ed. F. W. Maitland. 3 vols. Cambridge: Cambridge University Press, 1887.

Buddensieg, Rudolf. *Johann Wiclif und seine Zeit.* Halle: Verein für Reformationsgeschichte, 1885.

Cantor, Norman F. "The Crisis of Western Monasticism, 1050-1130," *The American Historical Review,* LXVI (1960), 47-67.

Cheney, C. R. *From Becket to Langton: English Church Government, 1170-1213.* Ford Lectures, 1955. Manchester: Manchester University Press, 1956.

Chronicles of Edward I and Edward II. Ed. William Stubbs. London: Rolls Series, H.M.S.O., 1882-1883.

Coke, Edward. *The Institutes of the Laws of England.* 3 vols. 1st American edition. Philadelphia: 1812.

Copleston, F. C. *Medieval Philosophy.* New York: Harper and Brothers, 1961.

Corpus Iuris Canonici. 2 vols., ed. Emil Friedberg. Leipzig: B. Tauchnitz, 1879.

Coulton, G. G. *Five Centuries of Religion.* 4 vols. Cambridge: Cambridge University Press, 1923-1950.

Courtney, F. *Cardinal Robert Pullen: An English Theologian of the Twelfth Century.* Romae: Apud Aedes Universitatis Gregorianae, 1954.

Crompton, James. "Fasciculi Zizaniorum II," *Journal of Ecclesiastical History,* XII (1961), 155-166.

Daly, L. J. *The Political Theory of John Wyclif.* Chicago: Loyola University Press, 1962.

Dialogus de Scaccario. Richard fitz Nigel, ed. A. Hughes, C. G. Crump and A. Johnson. Oxford: 1902.

Döllinger, Johannes Jos. Ign. von. *Die Papstfabeln des Mittelalters.* Munich: J. G. Cotta'chen Buchhandlung, 1863.

Dunbabin, Jean. "Aristotle in the Schools," in *Trends in Medieval Political Thought.* Ed. Beryl Smalley. New York: Barnes and Noble, 1965.

Durig, Wilhelm. "Der Theologische Ausgangspunkt der mittelalterlichen liturgischen Auffassung vom Herrscher als Vicarius Dei," *Historisches Jahrbuch,* LXXVII (1958).

Ellis, John Tracy. *Anti-papal Legislation in Medieval England, 1066-1377.* Washington, D. C.: Catholic University of America, 1930.

Elton, G. R. *The Body of the Whole Realm. Parliament and Representation in Medieval and Tudor England.* Jamestown Essays on Representation. Charlottesville, Va.: 1969.

Emden, A. B. *A Bibliographical Register of the University of Oxford to A.D. 1500.* 3 vols. Oxford: The Clarendon Press, 1957-1959.

Eulogium Historiarum sive Temporis: Chronicon ab Orbe Condito usque ad Annum

Domini MCCLXVI, a Monacho Quodam Malmesburiensi Exartum. Accedunt Continuationes duae, quarum una ad annum MCCCCXIII. Vol. III. Ed. Frank Scott Haydon. London: Rolls Series, H.M.S.O., 1963.

Fesefeldt, Wiebke. *Englische Staatstheorie des 13. Jahrhunderts. Henry Bracton und sein Werk.* Göttingen: Musterschmidt, 1963.

Fürstenau, Hermann. *Johann von Wiclifs Lehren von der Einteilung der Kirche und von der Stellung der weltlichen Gewalt.* Berlin: R. Gartners Verlagsbuchhandlung, 1900.

Galbraith, V. H. "Articles Laid Before the Parliament of 1371," *English Historical Review*, XXXIV (1919), 579-582.

Gierke, Otto. *Political Theories of the Middle Ages.* Trans. F. W. Maitland. Cambridge: 1900.

Gilson, Etienne. *History of Christian Philosophy in the Middle Ages.* New York: Random House, 1955.

Glanvilla. *Tractatus de legibus et consuetudinibus regni Anglie qui Glanvilla vocatur.* Ed. G. D. G. Hall. London: Thomas Nelson and Sons, 1965.

Grabmann, Martin: "Die Erörterung der Frage, ob die Kirche besser durch einen guten Juristen oder durch einen guten Theologen regiert werde bei Gottfried von Fontaines und Augustinus Triumphus von Ancona," in *Eduard Eichmann Festschrift.* Paderborn: F. Schonigh, 1940, pp. 1-19.

Graus, Frantisek. "Social Utopias in the Middle Ages," *Past and Present*, XXXVIII (1967), 3-19.

Gwynn, A. *The English Austin Friars.* Oxford: Oxford University Press, 1940.

Haller, Johannes. *Das Papsttum, Idee und Wirklichkeit.* Esslingen am Neckar: Port Verlag, 1962.

Haller, Johannes. *Papsttum und Kirchenreform. Die vier Kapitel zur Geschichte ausgehenden Mittelalters.* Berlin: Weidmannsche Buchhandlung, 1903.

Harnack, Adolf von. "Christus Praesens—Vicarius Christi," *Sitzungsberichte der Preussischen Akademie der Wissenschaften*, phil.-hist. Klasse, XXXIV (1927).

Haskins, G. L. "Executive Justice and the Rule of Law," *Speculum*, XXX (1955), 529-538.

Hay, Denys. "The Church of England in the Later Middle Ages," *History*, LIII (1968), 35-50.

Hinsley, F. H. *Sovereignty.* London: 1966.

Hoffmann, Hartmut. "Die Unveräusserlichkeit der Kronrechte in Mittelalter." *Deutsches Archiv*, XX (1964), 389-474.

Holdsworth, W. S. *A History of English Law.* 13 vols. London: Methuen, 1922-1952.

Howell, Margaret. *Regalian Right in Medieval England.* London: University of London Press, 1962.

Jacob, E. F. *Essays in the Conciliar Epoch.* Manchester: Manchester University Press, 1953.

Kaempf, H. *Pierre Dubois und die Geistigen Grundlagen des Französischen Nationalbewusstseins um 1300.* Leipzig und Berlin: B. G. Teubner, 1935.

Kaminsky, Howard. *A History of the Hussite Revolution.* Berkeley and Los Angeles: California University Press, 1967.

Kaminsky, Howard. "Wyclifism as Ideology of Revolution," *Church History*, XXXII (1963), 57-74.

Kantorowicz, Ernst. "Inalienability. A Note on Canonical Practice and the English Coronation Oath in the Thirteenth Century," *Speculum*, XXIX (1954), 488-502.

Kantorowicz, Ernst. *The King's Two Bodies. A Study in Mediaeval Political Theology.* Princeton: Princeton University Press, 1957.

Kantorowicz, Ernst. "Pro Patria Mori," *American Historical Review*, LVI (1951), 472-492.

Kantorowicz, Ernst. *Selected Studies*. Locust Valley: J. J. Augustin, 1965.

Keen, M. H. "The Political Thought of the Fourteenth-Century Civilians," in *Trends in Medieval Political Thought*. Ed. Beryl Smalley. New York: Barnes and Noble, 1965, pp. 105-126.

Keeney, Barnaby C. "Military Service and the Development of Nationalism in England," *Speculum*, XXII (1947), 534-549.

Kempf, Friedrich. "Die päpstliche Gewalt in der mittelalterlichen Welt," *Miscellanea Historiae Pontificiae*, XXI (1959), 135-153.

Kern, Fritz. *Kingship, Law and Constitution in the Middle Ages*. Trans. S. B. Chrimes. Oxford: Blackwell, 1948.

Kimball, Elizabeth. "Judicial Aspects of Frank Almoign Tenure," *English Historical Review*, XLVII (1932), 1-11.

Knowles, David. *The Monastic Order in England: A History of Its Development from the Times of St. Dunstan to the Fourth Lateran Council, 943-1216*. Cambridge: Cambridge University Press, 1940.

Knowles, M. David, O.S.B. "The Censured Opinions of Uthred of Bolden," *Proceedings of the British Academy*, XXXVII (1951), 305-342.

Knowles, M. David, O.S.B. "A Characteristic of the Mental Climate of the Fourteenth Century," in *Melanges offerts à Etienne Gilson. Etudes de Philosophie Medievale*, hors Serie. Toronto/Paris: 1959.

Knowles, M. David, O.S.B. *The Evolution of Medieval Thought*. New York: Alfred Knopf, 1964.

Knowles, M. David, O.S.B. *Saints and Scholars. Twenty-five Medieval Portraits*. Cambridge: Cambridge University Press, 1962.

Ladner, Gerhart B. "Aspects of Medieval Thought on Church and State," *Review of Politics*, IX (1947), 403-422.

Ladner, Gerhart B. *The Idea of Reform*. New York: Harper and Row, 1967.

Laehr, Gerhard. "Die Konstantinische Schenkung in der abendlandischen Literatur des ausgehenden Mittelalters," *Quellen und Forschungen aus italienischen Archiven und Bibliotheken*, XXIII (1931-1932), 120-181.

Laehr, Gerhard. *Die Konstantinische Schenkung in der Abenländischen Literatur des Mittelalters bis zur Mitte des 14. Jahrhunderts*. Berlin: 1926.

Lear, Floyd S. "The Literature on Public Law in Germanic Custom," *Rice Institute Pamphlet*, XXXVII (1950), 1-20.

LeBas, Charles Webb. *Life of Wiclif*. London: I. G. & F. Rivingston, 1832.

Lechler, Gotthard. *Johann von Wiclif und die Vorgeschichte der Reformation*. 2 vols. Leipzig: 1873.

Lechler, Gotthard. *John Wycliffe and His English Precursors*. Trans. Lorimer. London: Religious Tract Society, 1884.

Leff, Gordon. "The Apostolic Ideal in Later Medieval Ecclesiology," *Journal of Theological Studies*, N.S. XVIII (1967), 58-82.

Leff, Gordon. *Bradwardine and the Pelagians. A Study of His 'De Causa Dei' and Its Opponents*. Cambridge: Cambridge University Press, 1957.

Leff, Gordon. "The Changing Pattern of Thought in the Earlier Fourteenth Century," *John Rylands Library Bulletin*, XXXXIII (1961), 354-372.

Leff, Gordon. *Heresy in the Later Middle Ages*. 2 vols. New York: Barnes and Noble, 1967.

Leff, Gordon. *Medieval Thought: From St. Augustine to Ockham*. Baltimore: Penguin Books, 1958.

Leff, Gordon. *Paris and Oxford Universities in the Thirteenth and Fourteenth Centuries*. New York: John Wiley and Sons, 1968.

Lewis, Ewart. "Natural Law and Expediency," *Ethics*, L (1939-1940), 144-163.

Lewis, Ewart. "Organic Tendencies in Medieval Political Thought," *American Political Science Review*, XXXII (1938), 849-876.

Lewis, John. *History of the Life and Sufferings of the Reverend and Learned John Wiclif, D.D., together with a Collection of Papers and Records relating to said History*. Rev. ed. Oxford: The Clarendon Press, 1820.

Libri Feudorum in Authentica D. Iustiniani Imp. Avg. Novellarum Volumen. No editor. Lugduni: MDL.

Liebeschutz, Hans. "Chartres und Bologna, Naturbegriff und Staatsidee bei Johannes von Salisbury," *Archiv für Kulturgeschichte*, L (1968), 3-33.

Loserth, Johann. "Johann von Wiclif und Guilelmus Peraldus. Studien zur Geschichte der Entstehung von Wiclifs Summa Theologiae," *Sitzungsberichte der Kaiserlichen Akademie der Wissenschaften in Wien*, phil.-hist. Klasse, 180 (1917), 1-79.

Loserth, Johann. "Johann von Wiclif und Robert Grosseteste," *Sitzungsberichte der Kaiserlichen Akademie der Wissenschaften zu Wien*, phil.-hist. Klasse, 186 1918), 1-83.

Loserth, Johann. "Studien zur Kirchenpolitik Englands in 14. Jahrhundert II Teil. Die Genesis von Wiclifs Summa Theologiae und seine Lehre vom wahren und falschen Papsttum," *Sitzungsberichte der Kaiserlichen Akademie der Wissenschaften in Wien*, phil.-hist. Klasse, 156 (1908), 1-118.

Loserth, Johann. "Wiclifs Sendschreiben, Flugschriften und kleinere Werke kirchenpolitischen Inhalts," *Sitzungsberichte der Kaiserlichen Akademie der Wissenschaften in Wien*, phil.-hist. Klasse, 166 (1910), 1-96.

Lunt, William E. *Financial Relations of the Papacy with England to 1327*. Cambridge, Mass.: The Medieval Academy of America, 1939.

Maccarrone, Michele. *Vicarius Christi, storia del papale*. Romae: Facultas Theologica Pontificii Athenaei Lateranensis, 1957.

Maitland, F. M. *Selected Passages from the Works of Bracton and Azo*. Seldon Society, VII. London: 1895.

Manning, B. L. "Wyclif," *Cambridge Medieval History*, vol. VII, chapter 16. Cambridge: Cambridge University Press, 1932, 1958, 486-507, 900-907.

Marsilius of Padua. *The Defensor Pacis*. Trans. A. Gewirth. New York: Columbia University Press, 1956.

Matthew of Paris. *Chronica Maiora*. 6 vols. Ed. H. R. Luard. London: Rolls Series, H.M.S.O., 1876-1882.

McFarlane, K. B. *John Wycliffe and the Beginning of English Nonconformity*. New York: Macmillan Co., 1952.

McIlwain, C. H. *Constitutionalism Ancient and Modern*. Ithaca: 1947.

McKechnie, William Sharp. *Magna Carta: A Commentary on the Great Charter of King John with an Historical Introduction*. 2nd ed. Glasgow: J.

Miller, G. J. T. "The Position of the King in Bracton and Beaumanoir," *Speculum*, XXX (1956), 263-296.

Molnar, Amedeo. "Recent Literature on Wyclif's Theology," *Communio Viatorum*, VII (1964), 186-192.

Mommsen, T. E., and K. F. Morrison. *Imperial Lives and Letters of the Eleventh Century*. New York: Columbia University Press, 1962.

Morrison, K. F. *Tradition and Authority in the Western Church, 300-1140*. Princeton: Pinceton University Press, 1969.

New, Chester W. *History of the Alien Priories in England to the Confiscation of Henry V*. Chicago: University of Chicago Press, 1916.

Owst, G. R. *Literature and Pulpit in Medieval England*. Cambridge: Cambridge University Press, 1933.

Owst, G. R. *Preaching in Medieval England.* Cambridge: Cambridge University Press, 1926.

Pantin, W. A. *Documents Illustrating the Activities of the General and Provincial Chapters of the English Black Monks, 1215-1540.* 3 vols. London: Royal Historical Society (Camden 3rd Series, XLV, XLVII, LIV), 1931-1937.

Pantin, W. A. *The English Church in the Fourteenth Century.* Cambridge: Cambridge University Press, 1955.

Pauck, Wilhelm. *Harnack and Troeltsch.* New York: Oxford University Press, 1968.

Plucknett, T. F. T. *A Concise History of the Common Law.* 2nd ed. Rochester: Lawyers Cooperative Publishing Co., 1936.

Plucknett, T. F. T. *Legislation of Edward I.* Oxford: The Clarendon Press, 1949.

Pollock, Frederick, and Frederic William Maitland. *The History of English Law Before the Time of Edward I.* 2 vols. 2nd ed. Cambridge: Cambridge University Press, 1923.

Pollard, A. W. *Fifteenth-century Prose and Verse.* Westminster: A. Constable and Co., 1903.

Poole, Reginald Lane. *Illustrations of the History of Medieval Thought and Learning.* 2nd ed. London: S.P.C.K., 1920.

Poole, Reginald Lane. *Wycliffe and Movements for Reform.* London: Longmans, Green & Co., 1902.

Post, Gaines. *Studies in Medieval Legal Thought. Public Law and the State, 1100-1322.* Princeton: Princeton University Press, 1964.

Powicke, F. M. "England and Europe in the Thirteenth Century," in *Harvard Tercentenary Publications: Independence, Convergence and Borrowing.* Cambridge: 1937, pp. 142-661.

Powicke, F. M. "Reflections on the Medieval State," *Transactions Royal Historical Society,* XIX (1936), 130-148.

Powicke, F. M. *The Thirteenth Century.* Oxford: The Clarendon Press, 1953.

Registrum Johannis de Pontissara episcopi Wintoniensis. Ed. Cecil Deedes. Canterbury and York Society, XIX, XXX. London: Oxford University Press, 1915-1924.

Registrum Omnium brevium tam originalium quam iudicialium. No editor. London: 1531.

Richardson, H. G. "Heresy and the Lay Power," *English Historical Review,* LI (1936), 1-28.

Riesenberg, Peter. *Inalienability of Sovereignty in Medieval Political Thought.* New York: Columbia University Press, 1956.

Robson, J. A. *Wyclif and the Oxford Schools: the Relation of the 'Summa de Ente' to Scholastic Debates at Oxford in the Later Fourteenth Century.* Cambridge Studies in Medieval Life and Thought, new series, vol. VIII. Cambridge: Cambridge University Press, 1961.

Rotuli Parliamentorum ut et Petitiones et Placita. 7 vols. No date or place.

Rymer, Thomas (ed.). *Foedera, Conventiones, Littorse et cujuscunque generis Acta Publica inter Regis Angliae et alios quovis Imperatores, Reges Pontificies, Principes, vel Communitates.* 17 vols. Londini: A. & J. Churchill, 1704.

Schmidt, Martin. "John Wyclifs Kirchenbegriff. Der Christus humilis Augustins bei Wyclif," in *Gedenkschrift für D. Werner Elert.* Ed. Friedrich Hubner. Berlin: Lutherisches Verlagshaus, 1955, pp. 72-109.

Smalley, Beryl. "The Bible and Eternity: John Wyclif's Dilemma," *Journal of the Warburg and Courtaulo Institutes,* XXVII (1964), 73-89.

Smalley, Beryl. "Wyclif's Postilla on the Old Testament and His Principium," in *Oxford Studies presented to D. Callus, O.P.* Oxford: Oxford University Press, 1964, pp. 254-296.

Smith, A. L. *Church and State in the Middle Ages*. Oxford: Oxford University Press, 1913.

Spinka, Matthew. *Advocates of Reform from Wyclif to Erasmus*. The Library of Christian Classics, vol. XIV. Philadelphia: The Westminster Press, 1953.

Spinka, Matthew. *John Hus' Concept of the Church*. Princeton: Princeton University Press, 1966.

Stacey, John. "The Character of John Wyclif," *London Quarterly and Holborn Review*, CLXXXIV (1959), 356-359.

Stacy, John. *John Wyclif and Reform*. Philadelphia: 1964.

Statutes of the Realm. London: Record Commission, 1810.

Strayer, Joseph R. "Consent to Taxation under Phillip the Fair," in *Studies in Early French Taxation*. Ed. Joseph R. Strayer and C. H. Taylor. Cambridge, Mass.: 1939.

Strayer, Joseph R. "Defense of the Realm and Royal Power in France," in *Studi in Onore di Gino Luzzatto*. Milan: 1949, pp. 289-296.

Strayer, Joseph R. "The Laicization of French and English Society in the Thirteenth Century," in *Change in Medieval Society*. Ed. Sylvia L. Thrupp. New York: 1964, pp. 103-115.

Stubbs, William (ed.). *Select Charters and Other Illustrations of English Constitutional History from the Earliest Times to the Reign of Edward the First*. 9th ed. Oxford: The Clarendon Press, 1921.

Tatnall, Edith C. "Church and State According to John Wyclif." Unpublished Ph.D. dissertation, Department of History, University of Colorado, 1964.

Tatnall, Edith C. "John Wyclif and Ecclesia Anglicana," *The Journal of Ecclesiastical History*, XX (1969), 19-43.

Thompson, A. Hamilton. *The English Clergy and Their Organization in the Later Middle Ages*. Oxford: The Clarendon Press, 1947.

Thomson, S. Harrison. "The Philosophical Basis of Wyclif's Theology," *Journal of Religion*, XI (1931), 86-116.

Tierney, Brian. *The Crisis of Church and State, 1050-1300*. Englewood Cliffs: Prentice-Hall, Inc., 1964.

Tierney, Brian. *Foundations of the Conciliar Theory*. Cambridge: Cambridge University Press, 1955.

Tierney, Brian. *Medieval Poor Law*. Berkeley: University of California Press, 1959.

Ullmann, Walter. *The Growth of Papal Government in the Middle Ages*. London: Methuen and Co., 1955.

Ullmann, Walter. *A History of Political Thought: The Middle Ages*. Baltimore: Penguin Books, 1965.

Ullmann, Walter: *Principles of Government and Politics in the Middle Ages*. London: Methuen and Co., 1961.

Ullmann, Walter. *The Relevance of Medieval Ecclesiastical History*. Cambridge: Cambridge University Press, 1966.

Walsingham, Thomas. *Historia Anglicana*. 2 vols. Ed. Henry Thomas Riley. London: Rolls Series, H.M.S.O., 1863.

Wieruszowski, Helene. *Vom Imperium zum nationalen Königtum*. Historische Zeitschrift, Beiheft 30. Munich: 1933.

Wilks, Michiael. *The Problem of Sovereignty in the Later Middle Ages: The Papal Monarchy with Augustinus Triumphus and the Publicists*. Cambridge: Cambridge University Press, 1963.

Wood, Susan. *English Monasteries and Their Patrons in the Thirteenth Century*. London: Oxford University Press, 1955.

Wood-Legh, K. L. *Perpetual Chantries in Britain*. Cambridge: Cambridge University Press, 1965.

Wood-Legh, K. L. *Studies in Church Life in England under Edward III.* Cambridge: Cambridge University Press, 1934.

Workman, H. B. *John Wyclif: A Study of the English Medieval Church.* 2 vols. Oxford. The Clarendon Press, 1926.

Year Books, Edward I. Ed. A. J. Horwood. London: Rolls Series, H.M.S.O., 1863-1879.

Year Books, Edward III. Ed. A. J. Horwood and L. O. Pike. London: Rolls Series, H.M.S.O., 1883-1911.

INDEX